Structural Adjustment

Structural Adjustment

Retrospect and Prospect

Edited by
Daniel M. Schydlowsky

Westport, Connecticut
London

HC
59.7
S87365
1995

Library of Congress Cataloging-in-Publication Data

Structural adjustment : retrospect and prospect / edited by Daniel M.
  Schydlowsky.
    p. cm.
  Includes bibliographical references and index.
  ISBN 0-275-94433-6
    1. Structural adjustment (Economic policy)—Developing countries.
  I. Schydlowsky, Daniel M., 1940–
  HC59.7.S87365 1995
  339.5'09172'4—dc20   94-32920

British Library Cataloguing in Publication Data is available.

Library of Congress Catalog Card Number: 94–32920
ISBN: 0-275-94433-6

First published in 1995

Praeger Publishers, 88 Post Road West, Westport, CT 06881
An imprint of Greenwood Publishing Group, Inc.

Printed in the United States of America

The paper used in this book complies with the
Permanent Paper Standard issued by the National
Information Standards Organization (Z39.48-1984).

10 9 8 7 6 5 4 3 2 1

Contents

Contents

Preface

Structural adjustment has become the rubric under which policy has been prescribed for and implemented by the less developed countries (LDCs) in the last decade or more. Depending on what is meant or understood by the term, it has been held out to be the indispensable, unavoidable and right thing to do, or the bitter pill that has to be swallowed, even though it is painful, bad for the poor and destructive of development prospects.

In March of 1991 a collectivity of fifteen scholars, most of them economists, were brought together at The American University to review structural adjustment. Included were some of the early proponents of the policy, as well as a number of its critics. The purpose was to examine what had been learned about structural adjustment in the last decade, and what the implications might be for the future. The two days of meetings attracted an audience of several hundred, many of whom participated actively in the discussion. This volume includes most of the papers presented at this conference, thereby sharing a rich trove of thoughtful reflection by some of the profession's leading thinkers on a central topic of the current policy agenda of the developing world.

James H. Weaver leads off by reviewing what structural adjustment is. He walks us through the theoretical basis for structural adjustment, its relation to stabilization, the components of structural adjustment loans and the sequencing of reforms. He then reviews the studies examining whether structural adjustment loans have been successful in achieving their objectives and explores whether there are alternatives

viii   Preface

to orthodox structural adjustment, finally to conclude on a rather agnostic note.

Next follow two pieces reviewing the experience of the 1980s. Stanley
Fischer provides a generally approving view of the orthodox policy.
Countries had to adjust in some way in the 1980s, and better that they
do so sensibly. Moreover, stabilization and structural adjustment had
to be undertaken together, both for historical reasons and to make both
more effective. Fischer gives fascinating reasons why sooner is better
than later and why trade reform is so popular, especially with outsiders.
Moreover, he is careful to emphasize that reasonable intermediate targets, for example on inflation, may often be the desirable alternative.
He concludes with an optimistic view of prospects for the 1990s, centered on restarting growth.

Lance Taylor provides a differently nuanced perspective. He begins
by surveying the complexities of stabilization and adjustment, distinguishing among their varieties. He then discusses the role of the state in
theory and in practice, noting different extreme views of the role of government intervention and how these have evolved over time as well as
how they are supported or disputed by differing national experiences.
He concludes by discussing the policy sequencing that would occur under
a policy of structural adjustment which he labels "flexible gradualism."

We then turn to two essays on structural adjustment in Latin America.
John Williamson focuses on how the "Washington consensus" came to
be accepted policy in Latin America. He starts by listing the components
of the consensus, and notes what elements not initially included would
now be regarded as desirable elements. He then sketches the history of
policy reform in the region as well, and concludes that it has been
internally driven by a process of social learning, rather than imposed
from the outside.

Fernando Fajnzylber provides a fascinating counterpoint by focusing
on the "real side" of Latin America's economies, their features and their
requirements for growth. For Fajnzylber, growth and equity must go
together or neither will be achievable or maintainable. Moreover, to
achieve both, environmental sustainability is a requirement and is
embodied in "genuine" competitiveness. Improvement in human resources and in their application lie at the center of the process. Government action, largely empowering through general policies, but also
properly targeted, is essential to the achievement of a lasting and
sustainable improvement of Latin America's economic situation.

Next comes the turn of structural adjustment in sub-Saharan Africa,
again through two rather different views. Elliot Berg begins by refuting
the main criticisms that have been made of structural adjustment in
Africa: that the market-oriented prescription has been wrong, that these
programs have failed to produce growth, and that their costs have fallen

on the poor. He also reviews the deficiencies of empirical evaluations of structural adjustment in the region. Then he goes on to posit his "true dilemmas." These relate to aid money and political will, conditionality, distorted dialogue and ownership, and the linking of social dimensions to adjustment lending. He concludes with the advice to return to more traditional project lending and a narrower policy agenda.

George B.N. Ayittey takes a quite different tack. For him, structural adjustment policy has had some successes but has been deeply flawed. The fundamental problem lies in African governance: no amount of policy reform with the same individuals, ideology, and institutional system in place will make any difference. Political reform, respect for property rights and due process, civil liberties and a free press are all of the essence. Moreover, policy cannot disregard the existence of civil wars. Ayittey concludes by drawing the lessons from Eastern Europe and Russia that he considers central for Africa.

In turn, Norberto García and Jaime Mezzera discuss structural adjustment and the labor market in Latin America. They begin with a review of the progress of employment during thirty years, detailing the dynamic of the creation and growth of formal and informal employment in the area, concluding with the setbacks witnessed during the 1980s. They then discuss the consequences of structural adjustment for the 1990s, using a simulation model to present the likely developments in different types of countries on the basis of a basic and a rapid-growth scenario. In both cases, the share of informal employment in total employment remains a concern, showing a first stage of increase before a later one of decrease. Strong differences can be seen between different types of countries, depending on their rates of labor force growth and their relative progress in structural adjustment. They conclude noting that the degree of informality of Latin America's labor markets will most likely not decrease by the year 2000; however, the recent decline in real wages can be reversed, albeit with a wider dispersion of incomes. Labor market policies will, therefore, acquire enhanced importance.

The problems with implementation of structural adjustment are addressed next. Richard J. Moore tells us that recent evaluations at the World Bank highlight the importance of implementation, indicating that effective implementation can not be taken for granted. He proposes a strategic mapping of implementation, bringing together the reforms proposed and their objectives on the one hand, with the various political, administrative, stakeholder interest, organization and containability elements on the other. He concludes that implementation needs to focus on the policy process and not simply on a given institution or set of institutions.

The final part of this volume groups three papers taking a normative view of policy reform for the 1990s. Paul Streeten focuses on why human neglect continues. He claims that the determinants of the effective use of funds for social purposes can be grouped under five headings: institutions, skills and aptitudes, attitudes, levels of living, and policies. Whether each of these interacts with the others in a positive or negative way depends on a variety of elements, including political pressures, constituencies, obstacles and inhibitions. Neither a narrow self interest nor Platonic or Fabian benevolence properly explains behavior, and numerous contradictory examples exist. A more realistic view of normative political economy has room for common or shared interests between the rich and the poor, as well as bargains between them, interest conflicts within the ruling groups, empowerment of the poor, organization of "trustees for the poor" and "guardians of rationality," as well as international pressures and support. He enriches his discussion of these elements with numerous examples from different countries. He concludes that it is not inevitable that in the war on poverty, poverty should win.

Stephan Haggard addresses the-two way interrelation between democracy and economic growth. He approaches the topic by looking at both long-run and short-run elements affecting causality in each direction, citing theory and example as appropriate. Viewed over the long run, he finds an association between the level of economic development and democracy—however, no conclusive evidence that democracies have better economic performance. Poor economic conditions seem to have contributed to the recent wave of democratic transitions; however, crises tend to weaken whatever regime is in power. Moreover, domestic private sectors are not strong or principled supporters of democratic institutions. Finally, the transition to more market-oriented economies demands greater governmental capabilities, as well as forging new institutions.

The undersigned's essay concludes the volume. It argues for the need to reorient the analytical bases of the design of structural adjustment policy, by incorporating the long-lasting weaknesses in LDCs' price systems, which lead to equally long-lasting differences between efficiency and competitiveness. This inherent bias is said to be systematic, leading to a situation where efficiency is typically greater than competitiveness. As a result, market economies are prone to inappropriately shut down productive uses of existing capital, both physical and human. The result will be an unnecessary loss of income and wealth and the corresponding increase in the cost and delay in successful structural adjustment. A capacity utilizing structural adjustment policy for the 1990s is proposed.

                                            Daniel M. Schydlowsky

Part I
Introduction

What Is Structural Adjustment?

James H. Weaver

The purpose of this chapter is to explain the move to structural adjustment as the "orthodox" economic policy in developing countries in the 1980s and 1990s. There are eight parts. The first part defines structural adjustment, details the types of structural adjustment loans (SALs), and examines the rationale for the move to structural adjustment from the perspectives of the international financial institutions and of the governments of the less developed countries. The second presents the neoclassical economic theory underlying SALs. The third explains the process of stabilization that must precede structural adjustment. The fourth details the components of SALs. The fifth part analyzes the sequencing of reforms. The sixth examines the evaluations of structural adjustment. The seventh part asks whether there are alternatives to structural adjustment. The last part contains conclusions.

WHAT IS STRUCTURAL ADJUSTMENT?

The World Bank began making structural adjustment loans in the early 1980s. At that time, the rationale for these loans was to help less developed countries (LDCs) restructure their economies in order to cope with the changes taking place in the international economy—the second OPEC price shock, the world depression, high interest rates, low commodity prices, etc. Soon, however, the rationale for SALs and the scope of structural adjustment changed to focus on restructuring LDCs' economies to overcome unwise strategies and policies that had been pursued in the post–World War II period.

In the early 1980s the major thrust of the reforms came to rely almost exclusively on macroeconomic reforms to open the economy to the rest of the world by removing trade barriers, impediments to foreign investment, and to reverse the policies that had been established following import substitution industrialization. Later in the 1980s, the focus shifted to include microeconomic reforms involving restructuring the domestic economy as well.

A structural adjustment loan is a loan that provides quick disbursing foreign exchange to be used for virtually any purpose and which is conditioned upon an agreement about significant policy reform. The loans are of three primary types. Loans designed to change macroeconomic policy are generally referred to as Structural Adjustment Loans, or SALs. Loans which target policy reforms at the sectoral level are Sector Adjustment Loans, or SECALs. Loans that have an investment component as well as an adjustment component are known as hybrid loans.

The World Bank has been the most important agency providing adjustment loans. However, the International Monetary Fund (IMF) also moved into structural adjustment lending with the establishment of the Structural Adjustment Facility in 1986—followed by the Enhanced Structural Adjustment Facility in 1987—to provide additional support for low-income countries. Most bilateral aid agencies like the United States Agency for International Development also moved significant portions of their portfolios to policy-based assistance.

The Bank switch from project loans to SALs was justified by the argument that sound projects were not possible in an unsound policy environment. This link has been recently substantiated by a World Bank study that found a high degree of correlation between internal rates of return on projects and the policy environment in the country concerned.[1] From the perspective of the international financial institutions, a new instrument to influence developing countries' policies at the macro level was needed because existing loan instruments could only influence policies at the project and sector levels.

The reason LDCs accepted SALs is clear. SALs were virtually the only source of quick-disbursing foreign exchange available after the debt crisis of 1982, which followed Mexico's announcement of its inability to service its debt, and drastically reduced the flow of commercial loans. The international recession of the early 1980s led to sharply deteriorated terms of trade, higher interest rates on existing loans that had adjustable rates, and a very strong U.S. dollar, the currency in which developing countries had to repay debts and purchase major imports like oil. The price paid by developing countries to gain access to foreign exchange in this crisis situation was to agree to reform policies.

WHAT IS THE THEORETICAL BASIS FOR STRUCTURAL ADJUSTMENT LOANS?

A Return to Laissez-Faire, Free Trade

Clive Crook summarized the state of orthodox development economics in the 1980s in his widely acclaimed article in the *Economist*.[2] He argued that a laissez-faire, free trade strategy was the most likely strategy to bring about development and that successful developing countries, like Korea, which had followed interventionist policies would have done even better if they had followed a laissez-faire, free trade policy.

What does laissez-faire mean today? It means that government should *only* do those things which *only* governments can do and which are necessary for the successful operation of a market economy. Governments should provide those public goods that the private sector will not provide. These public goods include national defense, protection of persons and property, enforcement of contracts, making and enforcing the rules of the game, a sound system of money and credit, some public works, agricultural research, and the financing (although not necessarily provision) of public health and public education.

A remarkable convergence has taken place in the thinking of development practitioners concerning which policies are appropriate in developing countries. Theoreticians and policymakers from the left and the right agree that many strategies followed to date have generally led neither to rapid economic growth nor to equity.[3] The explanations for these failures focus largely on the domestic and international policies that governments have implemented.

The Problem Facing Developing Countries Today

We can consider three spheres in analyzing the problems faced by developing countries: the informal sector, the formal sector, and the rest of the world. Figure 1.1 reflects this view of the reality.

The informal sector includes those economic actors without access to foreign exchange or to subsidized credit from the government; and those who are not subject to governmental regulation or taxation. It includes subsistence and small-scale farmers, especially food crop producers; small-scale enterprises; urban squatters; smugglers; and petty traders.

The formal sector includes firms with access to foreign exchange and subsidized credit from the government; those which are taxed and regulated by the state. At the top of this sector we have the mercantilist state, which is intimately involved in the economy. It regulates input,

Informal Sector	Government Barriers to Entry Into Formal Sector	Formal Sector	Government Policies	Rest of the World
1. AGRICULTURE-RURAL AREAS Landless workers, subsistence farmers and near subsistence farmers Petty commodity producers--tools, beer, household goods, etc. Money lenders Midwives--traditional medicine Retailers--shops in homes 2. URBAN INDUSTRIAL SECTOR Petty commodity producers--household goods, clothing, etc. Retailers--street vendors Transport--unlicensed taxis Money lenders Urban squatters Black marketeers, smugglers Midwives--traditional medicine 3. CHARACTERISTICS Low income Small scale Labor intensive Little formal education Capital from moneylenders High interest costs	1. Licenses and permit requirements to operate a business--bureaucratic delays, red tape, corruption, bribes required. 2. Legal system makes it impossible for urban squatters to get title to homes and use as collateral for loans. 3. No access to formal sector credit or subsidized inputs, fertilizer, water, electricity. 4. Building codes make legal housing prohibitively expensive. 5. No access to foreign exchange to import inputs. 6. Low prices for agricultural products. 7. Unions closed to outsiders.	1. STATE SECTOR Professional, managerial class Military Civil servants State-owned enterprises State-owned banks Hospitals 2. INTELLECTUALS/ACADEMICS MEDIA 3. INDUSTRIAL SECTOR Import substituting industries Multinational corps Labor unions 4. AGRICULTURAL SECTOR Commercial farmers Export agriculture 5. CHARACTERISTICS High income Access to foreign exchange Access to import quotas, licenses Access to subsidized credit Access to urban hospitals and higher education subsidies Regulated and taxed by government Much income from rent seeking rather than production Capital intensive	1. Regulations to limit foreign ownership, to reserve certain industries to state and domestic ownership, to restrict profit repatriation. 2. Quotas and tariffs on imported goods to protect domestic firms. 3. Control and allocation of foreign exchange to favored firms. 4. Subsidized credit, low interest rates to favored firms. 5. Government subsidies to state-owned enterprises. 6. Tax holidays and loopholes for favored firms.	1. Multinational corporations 2. Multinational banks 3. Agro-industries 4. Exporters and importers 5. International aid agencies

Figure 1.1 Sectoral Segmentation in LDCs

producer and consumer prices (in Ghana, for example, some 6,000 items were subject to price controls); subsidizes credit and allocates import quotas to favored firms; allocates foreign exchange and access to foreign capital; sets wages and interest rates, and policies for the hiring and firing of workers; and has social insurance programs that may add as much as 30 percent to the wage bill.[4]

Below the mercantilist state, we have other actors including the military, the professional and managerial class, civil servants, the import substitution industries which are protected by tariffs and quotas, the parastatals, some multinational firms that are allowed to operate behind tariff walls, and the aristocracy of labor with jobs in large industrial firms.

Third, there is the rest of the world, in which the actors of interest are the multinational corporations, the international trading companies, multinational banks, and agro-industries.

A wall protects the formal sector from competition from the rest of the world. This wall is made of quotas and tariffs, overvalued exchange rates and exchange controls, investment codes that limit foreign investment to chosen sectors, or limit the repatriation of profits or the percentage of foreign ownership allowed in firms, and so on. Early structural adjustment loans were designed to break down this wall.

But a second wall has also been constructed by government to protect the formal sector from the competition of the informal sector through a host of regulations and barriers—requirements for licenses, permits, bribes etc.—that keep informal sector firms from becoming legitimate and competing with the formal sector and prevent their gaining access to capital.[5] By the middle of the 1980s, SALs and SECALs were being designed to break down this wall, as well.

Trade obviously takes place between the informal and formal sectors, and between the country and the rest of the world. But the walls are there nevertheless, and trade between these sectors is limited. The walls are kept in place by a patronage system which provides benefits to government supporters through payoffs to rent-seeking activity such as government allocation of foreign exchange, and the granting of import, export, or business licenses.

This analysis, though highly generalized, seems to accurately portray the situation in many developing countries today. Given that this situation exists, what is to be done? One answer is structural adjustment, a major focus of which is precisely to dismantle the barriers to competition from the rest of the world. A second major focus of structural adjustment is the breaking down of domestic walls to allow the informal sector to grow and compete openly with protected firms.

STABILIZATION AS A PREREQUISITE FOR
STRUCTURAL ADJUSTMENT

Stabilization is an attempt to bring a country's demand for foreign goods and services in line with their ability to pay for those goods and services. We measure a country's economic activity with the rest of the world by its balance of payments. Most LDCs run a deficit in their balance of payments, that is, they buy more goods and services from the rest of the world than they can afford. How, then, do they finance these deficits? They borrow from suppliers, commercial banks, and international financial organizations. They run up arrears, that is, they don't pay their bills, and let them mount up. But, eventually, suppliers will stop making credits available, and lenders will stop lending money. So, countries must achieve a balance between what they are earning abroad and what they are spending abroad. They must achieve a sustainable balance of payments. In order to do this, they must stabilize their economy. And this is where the IMF comes in.

The goal of the IMF is to help countries achieve a sustainable balance of payments without serious limitations on trade. The IMF tries to foster an open international trading system.

There are two techniques for resolving the problem of unsustainable balance of payments deficits. The first is called expenditure reduction. The second is called expenditure switching. Virtually all IMF agreements have an expenditure reducing component. Countries must reduce expenditures if they are going to bring their demand for foreign goods into balance with their ability to pay for these goods. If the country has a balance of payments deficit, expenditures are greater than income. The country is spending more than its income and it must reduce its spending.

The IMF looks to two ways to reduce spending. The first is to reduce the growth of money and credit. Limits are set on how much these amounts can grow. This will restrict business activity.

Second, limits are established on how much of the credit will go to the government. If no limits are established on government borrowing, government will borrow all the credit available and the private sector will be crowded out.

The problem with these policies is that a recession results. IMF programs are called austerity programs for a reason. Government spending is going to be reduced. Private spending is going to be reduced. People are going to lose their jobs. Incomes are going to fall. This is a painful process. And this is why countries are urged to do as much as they can with expenditure switching.

Expenditure switching means devoting more of a country's resources to producing goods for export, and to producing goods that compete with imports. If this happens, imports will fall, exports will rise, and the balance of payments deficit will be reduced. But how can we get people to switch their expenditures in this fashion?

The easiest way to bring about expenditure switching is to devalue the currency. Let's say the exchange rate of the Tanzanian shilling is Sh200 = $1. If we devalue to Sh400 = $1, what will be the effect on exports and imports? Imports that had cost $1, will now cost Tanzanians Sh400 instead of Sh200. The price of imports has just doubled. What will Tanzanians do? Import less. They will switch to domestically produced goods if such substitute goods are available. What about exporters? They previously got Sh200 for each $1 they earned for their exports. Now they will get Sh400 for each $1. What will they do? Export more. And that's exactly what we want to have happen. Imports go down. Exports go up.

Why are countries so reluctant to undertake devaluations, if they are so effective in switching expenditures? Primarily, there are two reasons. One, it is inflationary. Import prices go up, and this causes other prices to go up. However, if the central bank does not increase the money supply, the amount of inflation can be limited. Second, there is a prestige factor at work. Governments hate to devalue their currency. It implies a weak economy.

WHAT ARE THE COMPONENTS OF STRUCTURAL ADJUSTMENT LOANS?

There are seven elements in most structural adjustment programs. The first and most important is realistic real exchange rates.[6] Neoclassical economists disagree whether developing countries should use purely market-determined (floating) rates or fixed rates with provision for changing them when circumstances dictate change, but they all agree that foreign exchange rates should be as close to market-determined rates as possible.

The second-most important component is to open the economy to foreign competition.[7] This involves replacing quotas with tariffs, because import quotas give rise to corruption, bureaucracy, delays, etc. Once countries have switched to tariffs, there is a move to harmonize tariffs, to have the same tariff on all imports. Finally, the last stage is to gradually reduce tariffs to around 20 percent.

In addition to moving to tariffs and lowering them, countries are urged to open their economy to competition from the rest of the world with respect to foreign investment.[8] There is a great need for investment in LDCs today, and a shortage of capital to undertake it. This is particularly true in telecommunications, transportation, and energy. Many multinational firms would be willing to undertake investments in these sectors. But, in order to encourage them to come and invest, LDCs must revise investment codes to guarantee repatriation of profits, allow majority foreign ownership, set up one-step approval procedures, and introduce other steps to encourage investment.

A third component is to liberalize domestic trade and commerce[9] by removing price controls, reducing regulatory rigidities, eliminating legal monopolies, and by improving the economic functions of government so that private enterprise can flourish.[10] A very important element in this reform is to change the relative prices of capital and labor so that interest rates are relatively higher, and wages are relatively lower. In many LDCs, interest rates have been kept artificially low. This has led business to use capital rather than labor. Wages have sometimes been kept higher than market wages by government polices such as minimum wages and various social insurance schemes. This causes firms not to hire labor. Getting prices right for labor and capital is thought to lead to a great increase in the use of labor. Another element in liberalizing trade and commerce is to change the policies with respect to the requirement that government hire all college and high school graduates. This has been a fairly standard practice in many LDCs, and has resulted in bloated bureaucracies, inefficiencies, and corruption. Reducing the size of the civil service is a very difficult process and will necessarily involve some sort of transitional arrangement to help these graduates find alternative employment: start their own businesses, etc.

Reform of fiscal policy is called for to reduce the fiscal deficit and thus reduce inflationary pressures in the economy.[11] On the expenditure side, fiscal reform involves eliminating and/or reducing a wide range of subsidies on consumer goods, fertilizer, transportation, and fuel. On the revenue side, fiscal reform involves broadening the tax base, and reducing the tax rate. Decentralization of government to allow local governments to raise revenue and spend it for local infrastructure and services is encouraged as part of the fiscal reform effort. It has been found that local governments are far more effective in building and maintaining schools, farm-to-market roads, health clinics, and other local facilities than are central governments; and this infrastructure is absolutely necessary if agricultural transformation is to take place.

A fifth step, an important part of reducing the fiscal deficit, is the closing, privatization and/or reform of state-owned enterprises.[12] Accomplishing this has turned out to be extremely difficult, and the international financial institutions (IFIs) have lost their early single-minded enthusiasm for privatization as they have come up against the extraordinary difficulties associated with this process. Instead of trying to privatize, the IFIs have moved to remove the monopoly status of state-owned enterprises and allow private firms to compete with them. They have also introduced programs to reform these institutions including performance contracts for managers, bonuses for good performance, etc.

A sixth element of structural adjustment is reform of the financial sector.[13] The growth of money and credit should be limited so that inflationary pressures are reduced. Real interest rates should be market determined and mildly positive, and the practice of directing credit to particular sectors should be ended. Prudential regulation of financial institutions is necessary.

The final component is sectoral reform—of agriculture,[14] industry,[15] the urban sector, and the social sectors.[16]

SEQUENCING REFORMS

The Bank argues that a certain sequence must be followed in bringing about reforms.[17] The first step is stabilization. Unless the balance of payments deficit and the fiscal deficits are reduced to sustainable levels, efforts at domestic reform will fail. After stabilization, the next steps involve opening the economy to the rest of the world, removing legal and bureaucratic barriers to efficient markets, increasing factor mobility, allowing market prices to act as incentives, and establishing market-based and mildly positive interest rates. If these first steps are achieved, the Bank predicts an output response in two to three years. The third stage involves institution building to restore investment, restructure the financial system, restore growth, and stimulate domestic saving. The Bank predicts this will take from four to eight years.

The Bank contends that *new* governments which act boldly within months of coming to power are the most likely to successfully implement reforms, and that certain necessary steps must be taken to ensure that reforms are sustainable. First, governments must undertake a massive campaign to explain to the population that the dramatic policy changes are absolutely necessary. Second, it is necessary to organize the beneficiaries of the reforms because those who benefit are generally not organized while the potential losers are well organized, and know what they are likely to lose. Third, it is necessary to move quickly to make big changes in the areas of biggest distortion in the economy. There is little payoff for making small changes in big distortions or big changes in small distortions.[18]

HAVE SALs WORKED?

Three different methodologies have been used to assess the impact of structural adjustment loans. Some studies have compared performance before and after the loans. Others have compared the adjusting loan countries to a control group that did not receive SALs. A third approach is to simulate what would have happened in the absence of adjustment.

The "before and after" approach assumes that external factors remain the same over time, and the "control group" approach assumes that all differences between adjusting and nonadjusting countries are accounted for by the adjustment program. Therefore, the Bank, in *Report on Adjustment Lending II*[19] (RAL II), addresses these problems by simulating what would have happened if countries had not undertaken adjustment.

Those countries that received at least two SALs or three SALs or SECALs starting before 1985, were the focus of the study. These countries performed better than the other two groups with regard to three of four *indicators of policy* for the period 1985–88: a lower real effective exchange rate, lower fiscal deficit/GDP, and lower resource balance deficit/GDP. These countries performed far worse than the other two groups with regard to the fourth indicator, the rate of inflation.

These countries also performed better than the others vis-à-vis three of four *country performance indicators*: higher real GDP growth, higher savings/GDP, and higher exports/GDP. The group had, however, a lower rate of investment/GDP than the other groups.[20]

Two subsequent reports have presented contradictory results. A 1990 study found no significant effect (positive or negative) of Bank/Fund-supported adjustment programs on economic growth from 1982–86 for a sample of 93 countries.[21] A 1991 study of 75 countries during the period 1976–86 found that adjusting countries experienced more rapid economic growth, a less negative current account balance/GNP, and more rapid inflation than nonadjustors.[22]

The costs of adjustment for the poor have long been the most contentious aspect of this process. In the early 1980s, the Bank was confident that adjustment programs were not harmful to the poor. Even though adjustment programs were not designed to address poverty, equity, or distributional issues directly, the benefits of more efficient resource allocation would accrue to all. It was argued that the main beneficiaries of the large regulatory bureaucracies created under import substitution industrialization were the elites with connections to the people running the government, who handed out the quotas to buy foreign exchange and to import. Reducing these barriers would reduce the rent accruing to these privileged groups, and would allow the poor people in the informal sector to compete for credit, foreign exchange, etc. with the privileged firms.

Any negative effects on poorer people were thought to be "transitional," although proponents of "adjustment with a human face" contended that the costs of adjustment were unfairly borne by the poorest groups.[23]

The evidence in *RAL II* is mixed. Overall, the adjusting countries experienced an early decline in consumption which was reversed in the later period, virtually no change in nutritional status, but an increase in gross primary school enrollment ratios. However, the study shows that the 12 poorest intensely adjusting countries experienced declining levels of nutrition and declining school enrollments over time and also when compared with the larger group of all developing countries. However, they experienced a modest increase in per capita consumption after a sharp fall in the early 1980s.

The Bank correctly argues that correlation does not imply causality. It is difficult to separate the "effects" of adjustment from the effects of the world depression, long-term structural and human capital disinvestment, and unsustainable macroeconomic policies. Consequently, even the "losers" may be better off with reforms than without. For example, the Bank calculated that although poverty increased by 5 percent a year from 1980–84 in Côte d'Ivoire, an intensely adjusting country since 1981, it would have increased by 14 percent a year without SAL-supported agricultural price reforms.[24]

Second, "the poor" are not a homogeneous group, and the adjustment program affects different groups differently. The following short-term outcomes are common: a) increased unemployment among civil servants; b) reduced real income in the service sector, and increased real income in the tradable goods sector; and c) increased prices for food and other basic goods. Increased food prices hurt the urban poor and the rural landless, but help farmers as producer prices are allowed to rise. The poor may also be affected by price increases or cutbacks in government social spending. The poorest, however—particularly the landless rural poor—often have no access to government services, and will therefore not be much affected by cutbacks in these programs. If the poorest of the poor are beyond the reach of government spending cuts, then the opposite circumstance is also likely—marginal groups will not be positively affected by structural adjustment unless programs and resources are targeted to them.

Nonetheless, the distributional and equity effects associated with adjustment lending, even when arguably short-term, often damaged political support for adjustment—both domestically and in the international development community. Many countries' unwillingness to sustain reforms, and the persistence of long-term poverty, particularly in the low-income adjusting countries, resulted in a rethinking of the Bank's approach. The discussion about the importance of minimizing the social costs of adjustment has led to two new policies.

The first was a requirement that all adjustment loans include upfront, prior to presentation to the Bank's Board of Directors, an explicit analysis of the short-term impact of the program on the poor, and of measures proposed to deal with that impact.

The second was the development of a number of compensatory programs that attempt to replace general subsidies with programs targeted to severely affected groups. Bank-supported programs like the 1986 Emergency Social Fund (ESF) in Bolivia and the 1988 Ghana Programme of Action to Mitigate the Social Costs of Adjustment (PAMSCAD) have been designed to provide immediate assistance to directly affected groups.

ARE THERE ALTERNATIVES TO ORTHODOX STRUCTURAL ADJUSTMENT?

No one argues that developing countries do not need to adjust to the changes in the global economy that took place in the 1970s and 1980s. The point of dispute is how to adjust.

Some argue that orthodox programs are unnecessarily contractionary, and that an expansionary adjustment program is not only possible, but would be politically and economically less painful. Governments could subsidize exports produced in ISI factories and earn scarce foreign exchange, provide employment, income and increased government revenues. Others contend that we should simply write off existing capital, and focus on creating an environment that fosters new enterprises. In support of this view, Krueger points out that 80 percent of the national income in Korea came from new enterprises 10 years after Korea reformed its economy.[25]

Three countries in Latin America, Peru, Brazil, and Argentina, implemented heterodox adjustment policies in the 1980s. The countries vied with each other as to which would be the greatest failure. The people in those countries, especially the poor, have suffered terribly as a result of the rampant inflation, the drying up of investment, the cutbacks in government programs, and the lack of jobs.

CONCLUSIONS

The economic policies that will bring about successful development are still in dispute. The transition to a market economy is extraordinarily complicated.

Adjustment programs appear to have made a marginal contribution to more rapid economic growth in those countries undertaking adjustment, at least over the longer term. The initial state of the economy is an important determinant of adjustment performance. Adjusting countries had far higher debt levels than other countries, and these levels have increased in some cases. On the whole, countries that are very poor (usually African) and/or highly indebted (mostly Latin American) have performed less well than other groups of countries, although better than they were performing prior to adjustment.

As Table 1.1 reveals, economic growth rates of countries following widely different development strategies have been remarkably different. Clearly, the countries of East Asia performed remarkably well, and they have done it with extensive state intervention. China, for example, has experienced one of the most rapid rates of per capita economic growth of any developing country in history; no one would describe China as a laissez-faire/free trade regime. Korea is widely known for the highly interventionist role the government played in its development. The economies of South Asia which have not reformed or liberalized to any great extent also grew quite rapidly in the 1980s, adding further to our confusion.

It must give us pause when we see that the really successful economies, except for Hong Kong, followed policies quite contradictory to those being pushed by advocates of orthodox structural adjustment today.

The impact of adjustment on poverty is still a contentious issue. Most observers agree that, in the long run, the reforms contained in adjustment loans will benefit the poor. The early accusations that adjustment hit the poorer groups disproportionately hard have not generally been substantiated. However, there has been enough indication that the poor were suffering from the adjustment process in the short run to cause the Bank to take income distribution into account in designing SALs and to design compensatory programs for those who might lose in the short run.

The most searing critique of adjustment loans is that the status of the poor did not improve in the countries receiving adjustment loans. If development is primarily concerned with reducing poverty, structural adjustment must be judged a failure.

The left views SALs essentially as an instrument for bailing out the commercial banks. The World Bank and IMF lent to developing countries so that they would not default on their obligations to commercial banks in the developed countries and endanger the international banking system.

The right views SALs as attempts, not to reform countries' economies, but to preserve the regimes in sub-Saharan African and Latin American countries so that international stability could be maintained. The right argues that, without such assistance, corrupt regimes in developing countries would have fallen, and there would have been genuine capitalist revolutions in those countries because statism is largely discredited in the world and capitalism is the only viable option.

One must remain agnostic concerning the impact of structural adjustment. The evidence is not yet in to be able to judge the strategy's effect.

Table 1.1 Gross National Product and Growth Rate by Country

Country	GNP per capita 1990 Dollars	Average Annual Growth Rate (In percent) 1965-1990
Low Income Economies		
Mozambique	80	-
India	350	1.9
China	370	5.8
Kenya	370	1.9
Pakistan	380	2.5
Ghana	390	-1.4
Sri Lanka	470	2.9
Egypt	600	4.1
Lower-Middle Income Economies		
Bolivia	630	-0.7
Philippines	730	1.3
Morocco	950	2.3
Cameroon	960	3.0
Jamaica	1,500	-1.3
Turkey	1,630	2.6
Costa Rica	1,900	1.4
Botswana	2,040	8.4
Upper-Middle Income Economies		
Mexico	2,490	2.8
Brazil	2,680	3.3
Gabon	3,330	0.9
Korea	5,400	7.1
High Income Economies		
Hong Kong	11,490	6.2
United States	21,790	1.7
Germany	22,320	2.4
Japan	25,430	4.1
Switzerland	32,680	1.4

Source: World Bank, World Development Report, 1992, Table 1, pp. 218-219.

NOTES

1. D. Kaufmann, "The Forgotten Rationale for Policy Reform: The Productivity of Investment Projects," *World Bank mimeo*, Washington, DC, 1991.

2. Clive Crook, "A Survey of the Third World," *The Economist*, London, September 23, 1989.

3. For examples, from the left, see Alain de Janvry, *The Agrarian Question and Reformism in Latin America* (Baltimore: Johns Hopkins University Press, 1981); and, from the right, see Robert Bates, *Markets and States in Tropical Africa* (Berkeley: University of California Press, 1981), and Hernando de Soto, *The Other Path: The Invisible Revolution in the Third World* (New York: Harper & Row, 1989).

4. Bela Balassa, "The Interaction of Factor and Product Market Distortions in Developing Countries," in *World Development*, V. 16, No. 4, 1988, 449–463.

5. Hernando de Soto, *The Other Path: The Invisible Revolution in the Third World* (New York: Harper & Row, 1989).

6. World Bank, *World Development Report 1983* (Washington, DC: The World Bank, 1983).

7. World Bank, *World Development Report 1987* (Washington, DC: The World Bank, 1987).

8. *World Development Report 1987* (Washington, DC: The World Bank, 1987).

9. *World Development Report 1983* (Washington, DC: The World Bank, 1983).

10. *World Development Report 1988* (Washington, DC: The World Bank 1988).

11. Ibid.

12. Ibid.

13. *World Development Report 1989* (Washington, DC: The World Bank, 1989).

14. *World Development Report 1986* (Washington, DC: The World Bank, 1986).

15. *World Development Report 1987* (Washington, DC: The World Bank, 1987).

16. *World Development Report 1990* (Washington, DC: The World Bank, 1990).

17. Ibid.

18. "Adjustment Lending Policies for Sustainable Growth," World Bank Country Economics Department, PRS 14 (1990). This report is commonly referred to as *Report on Adjustment Lending II (RAL II)*.

19. Ibid., p. 15–16

21. Riccardo Faini, Jaime de Melo, Abdel Senhadji-Semlali and Julie Stanton, "Growth-Oriented Adjustment Programs: A Statistical Analysis," PRE Working Paper Series 426 *(June 1990)*.

22. Patrick Conway, "How Successful is World Bank Lending for Structural Adjustment?" PRE Working Paper Series 581 *(January 1991)*.

23. See for example, Giovanni Andrea Cornia, Richard Jolly, and Frances Stewart (ed.), *Adjustment with a Human Face*, Oxford: Clarendon Press, 1987.

24. *RAL II*, p 29, Box 3.1, World Bank, Washington, DC.

25. Anne Krueger is quoted in Michael Schrage, "Eastern Europe's Greatest Need: A New Generation of Entrepreneurs," Washington, DC, *Washington Post* March 29, 1991.

Part II
Structural Adjustment in the 1980s

2

Structural Adjustment Lessons from the 1980s

Stanley Fischer

The eighties are known in much of the developing world—in Latin America and in Africa—as the lost decade. They could also be known as the decade of structural adjustment. One of the key lessons learned from the eighties is that less of the decade was lost to countries that undertook structural adjustment early and decisively than for those that adjusted later or that, in some regrettable cases, still have not adjusted to the shocks of the early 1980s.

The etymology of the term structural adjustment appears to await scientific study. Structural adjustment lending was invented under that name in the World Bank in 1980 to deal with the second oil crisis.[1] That means that the concept of structural adjustment lending precedes the three massive shocks to the world economy in 1982 that set off the debt crisis, with which structural adjustment lending and structural adjustment are associated. Those shocks were the world recession, the accompanying rise in the real interest rate, and a very sharp decline in commodity prices. The conjunction of these shocks made it necessary for almost all developing countries to undertake two different types of structural adjustment.

The first component of structural adjustment is stabilization, or macroeconomic adjustment. The second component could be called structural transformation, or, if it were not for the resulting confusion, could be described as structural adjustment proper. Each component can happen without the other. For instance Brazil stabilized quite successfully, at least on the external side, between 1982 and 1985 without making any real changes in the structure of the economy. Other countries made important structural changes before stabilizing. Mexico is one example, and Argentina, which started privatization and tariff reform at the end of the last decade, is another.

Stabilization and structural transformation can be undertaken separately, and sometimes are. But there may be important reasons—for instance, massive losses by state-owned enterprises—that some structural changes have to be undertaken as part of stabilization. And there is certainly much evidence that structural changes are far less likely to succeed where macroeconomic stability has not been attained.

Why did countries have to undertake both components of structural adjustments in the eighties? The need for macroeconomic adjustment arose as a result of the massive decline in the volume of resource transfers from abroad. The size of the shocks varied across countries, but they were in many cases very large, in excess of 10 percent of GNP.[2] Heavily indebted countries suffered as a result of the debt crisis; the shocks hitting some commodity producers were even larger. There was no choice but to adjust *in some way* to the decline in the availability of foreign exchange. Some countries tried to adjust externally without also addressing domestic fiscal imbalances, and some succeeded for a while. But generally, external adjustment required simultaneous internal fiscal adjustment.

Many developing countries were under less immediate pressure to undertake the second component of structural adjustment, the changes in tariffs, domestic subsidies, regulations, fiscal reform, state enterprise reform, financial reform, and so on, that are now a familiar part of the adjustment process. There were two reasons to pursue these reforms. First, some of them caused macroeconomic problems. Second, and far more fundamental, many of these reforms were needed for the restoration of growth. It is true that many developing countries—especially some of those worst hit in the 1980s—were growing fast in the seventies—distortions and all. But that growth was based on large inflows of resources that were no longer available. When resources are hard to find, and when the pressure is on, it becomes necessary to run a more efficient economy.

STABILIZATION

The first lesson about stabilization learned from the 1980s is "the sooner the better." The countries that made reasonably rapid adjustments, like Korea and Chile, did better over that decade than the countries that failed to adjust, such as Brazil or Peru. This is not a call for instant and massive adjustment, for the size of the needed adjustment is not known until the permanence of shocks hitting the economy become clear, but it is a call for caution in borrowing to finance adverse external shocks, and for caution in interpreting favorable shocks as permanent. It is certainly a call for decisive adjustment when it becomes clear that adverse changes are likely to be long-lived. In the context of the debt crisis, the need for adjustment must have been clear by 1984.

A second stabilization lesson is that a country can try to adjust on the external side alone, but will rarely be successful. It can try to deal only with the balance of payments problem and leave internal macroeconomic difficulties to be sorted out later. Brazil seemed to have done this between 1982 and 1985. But the domestic macroeconomic difficulties— particularly fiscal problems—are likely to be at the heart of the external difficulties. In any case, when the budget deficit is unsustainable, and inflation is high, external achievements tend to dissipate fast.

Third, domestic stabilization typically requires a fiscal contraction and an attempt to bring the inflation rate down. No country has succeeded in bringing triple digit inflation down to single digit range in the post-1960 period without spending some time in the 15–30 percent inflation range.[3] Countries that have succeeded in getting to the 15–30 percent range, including Chile, Mexico and Israel, have succeeded in maintaining macroeconomic stability. Accordingly, that is a reasonable intermediate target for inflation.

Why emphasize fiscal contraction, when monetary tightening, too, helps reduce aggregate demand? Monetary-fiscal policy mix considerations come into play when the economy is operating in a low inflation zone, with a small budget deficit. With larger budget deficits, particularly in economies where the government has a limited capacity to borrow—internally because the financial markets are underdeveloped, and externally because external credit is not available—monetary policy cannot be conducted independently of fiscal policy. When the budget deficit is large, tight monetary policy is bound to be temporary, as high interest rates add to the budget deficit, and the dynamics of a rising debt drive domestic real interest rates up. Thus, fiscal tightening is almost always the key to stabilization. In addition, tight monetary policy tends to produce a strong currency, that is, an overvalued exchange rate, which is not generally consistent with the need to achieve sustainable external balance. Thus, fiscal contraction is typically necessary to attain both internal and external balance.

Almost every country that had to adjust in the 1980s was running too large a fiscal deficit even before 1982. The now heavily indebted countries were experiencing booms in the late 1970s, fueled by fiscal expansion—financed through borrowing or by government revenues from commodity booms—or export booms. In many countries, commodity prices feed directly into the budget. There is a common pattern of government receipts rising, leading to an expanding investment program, and then not declining when receipts fell. Côte d'Ivoire is an important example of this phenomenon.[4]

The euphoria that beset the now heavily indebted countries in the late 1970s was widely shared.[5] Many economists in the industrialized countries believed that the fund recycling and borrowing taking place at the end of the 1970s could continue. Supposedly flinty-eyed bankers must have thought so too. Without them, the debt crisis would not have been possible.

The importance of fiscal policy is hard to overemphasize. In the case of inflation and macroeconomic stability, the advice is "cherchez le deficit." The visitor to a country running a big balance of payments deficit and high inflation is often told that there is no deficit. The main task then is to find the deficit. If it is not in the central government accounts, it will be in the state-owned enterprise accounts. If not there, the central bank is likely to be running a large quasi-fiscal deficit, providing subsidized credit to farmers, or investors.

To emphasize the role of fiscal deficits is not to underestimate the difficulty of dealing with them. Stabilization is bound to be difficult politically, and will frequently cause short-term hardships. There may be deep-seated political reasons the deficit has arisen, and the government may not be strong enough to deal with its fiscal problems. While those difficulties are part of the justification for providing external support for stabilization, they do not reduce the need to adopt a coherent set of monetary and fiscal policies.

Lesson four was learned during the eighties, and was probably not well understood at the beginning of the adjustment process: targeted interventions are needed during the stabilization phase to assist those who will be hardest hit by policy changes. Frequently food subsidies are a very large part of the budget deficit, and the reduction of food subsidies is likely to affect the poor. Cuts in other social spending are also likely to affect the poor. Positive, targeted interventions, such as food stamps, or subsidized food available only in poorer areas, can protect the poor during adjustment. Such programs have been introduced in Bolivia, Chile, and Ghana, and have worked reasonably well.

It would be difficult—though less necessary—to undertake the measures needed for stabilization at the best of times. They are especially difficult when the country is not receiving funds from abroad, and has rather to be making transfers abroad. Significantly, several of the successful early adjusters, including Korea and Indonesia, were receiving positive net transfers at the time they stabilized. These inflows were coming from foreign direct investment, from the international agencies, and in some cases because the banks agreed to postpone debt service. Some of the later adjusters, including Mexico, stabilized under more difficult external conditions. Even so, they too were receiving large infusions of aid from the international lending agencies.

We have to recognize that it is difficult for any country, including this one, to make adjustments in the budget of the order of magnitude routinely demanded of the developing countries. To the extent their adjustments can be supported by the provision of aid, by agreements with the banks, and by agreements with official creditors to reduce the net outflow of resources, the more likely it is that the needed adjustments will be achieved rapidly.

The final lesson on stabilization is the same as the first—the sooner the better. The question about macroeconomic adjustment is not whether, but when and how. The 1980s were lost for Brazil, Argentina and Peru because they did not adjust. They will continue to experience disasters like those of the last few years until they do.

STRUCTURAL REFORMS

Structural reforms in the eighties—and in earlier decades too—started with trade. This is not only because trade is important, but also because impediments to trade are highly visible, especially to outsiders. Trade reform also permits the setting of quantitative targets, which make it possible to monitor progress and to condition aid.

A standard approach to trade reform developed during the decade. The process starts by removing and tariffizing nontariff barriers. Tariffs are then reduced, either proportionately, or in concertina fashion, with the highest coming down first, and moving toward uniformity. Some countries have even raised their lowest tariffs in order to produce greater uniformity. Tariffs should be reduced over a specified period of three to five years to a level somewhere in the range between 10–35 percent.

Why stop short of complete free trade? This is something the IMF generally gets right while other international agencies may not: tariffs are an efficient source of revenue in many developing countries which have very poor tax systems. Some countries have reduced tariffs too much, say to around 10 percent, to the point where they are unable to finance infrastructure investments needed to restore growth. The need for government tax revenues must be recognized in any adjustment program.

It is also important to develop a mechanism to give countries that undertake trade reforms credit in the GATT negotiations. It is, of course, in a country's own interests to reduce trade barriers, but since it is also in its interest for others to reduce their barriers, and since trade negotiations involve mutual "concessions," it is entirely understandable that countries may want to keep their concessions for an opportune moment.

There is an interesting question about trade reform, to which I believe we do not yet have a satisfactory answer. The question is why it is easier to maintain tariffs and export subsidies, as many countries do, than to get rid of tariffs and subsidies, and to operate with a devalued exchange rate. These alternatives are—aside from the capital account—analytically equivalent. They are clearly not politically equivalent.

It has been suggested that the difference is that the exchange rate approach requires greater fiscal discipline. That cannot be right, because, for a given external position, fiscal policy would have to be the same in these two cases. More plausibly, governments may prefer the commodity by commodity rent-seeking that takes place with tariffs and subsidies to the possibilities that arrive when the exchange rate is used to protect domestic producers.

To make the point clear, Poland has been operating with a severely undervalued exchange rate and very low tariffs. They could have tried to stabilize at the end of 1989 by going the other way, keeping tariffs high, putting on export subsidies, and devaluing less. Economists would tend to prefer the exchange rate method, but it is pursued less often than by using the direct intervention route.

The opening of the capital account is often thought of as the last stage of trade reform. It should rather be thought of as a macroeconomic reform: the opening of the capital account can complicate the task of maintaining macroeconomic stability in a situation where expectations are bound to be volatile. Some countries, such as Mexico, have to accept the openness of the capital account. Others, such as Indonesia, have made an open capital account work. Nonetheless, in general, the capital account should not be liberalized until a substantial measure of macroeconomic stability has been attained.

The desirability of liberalizing the capital account has often been argued on the grounds that it is extremely important to encourage foreign direct investment. Foreign direct investment is indeed very important, but it does not require a fully liberalized capital account. Rather, credible arrangements have to be made for the repatriation of profits, and for foreign exchange dealings by exporting and importing firms.

After trade reform—or better, at the same time—there is a need to clean up domestic distortions. Agricultural reform plays a special role. No country, except the Soviet Union, for some time has succeeded in growing fast while not encouraging agricultural development. Taxing agriculture heavily, subsidizing city dwellers, but not providing agricultural infrastructure is a sure way to delay development. Price reform in agriculture usually raises the incomes of rural dwellers at the expense of city dwellers, thereby reducing poverty. Aside from rural-urban distortions, there is typically extensive regulation of industry, which promotes productive inefficiency. Reducing and rationalizing the regulation of industry and labor markets is often an important part of structural adjustment.

Structural fiscal reforms lie at the heart of structural adjustment in many countries. In many countries, especially in Latin America, the first fiscal reform is to make people pay their taxes. The tradition of paying taxes is absent in many countries, but traditions can be changed by sending people to jail. Frequently, fiscal reform consists of getting people to pay as they are supposed to do. In other cases, administrative changes are needed to create the infrastructure of an efficient tax system. Tax reform is important not only for macroeconomic stability, but also because an inefficient tax system slows growth, and because some government spending is essential for growth.

Expenditure reforms, including reform of public enterprise spending, are the second component of fiscal reform. Just as in Eastern Europe, public enterprises have to be made to face hard budget constraints. As in Eastern Europe, some of these enterprises should be privatized. In every country, there are public enterprises that should not be in the public sector but should be privatized. But some will continue in the public sector, and they should run efficiently. That is possible.

The tendency has developed during the eighties to treat the financial sector in the way heavy industry used to be treated in the 1950s. The view is that the financial sector represents the commanding heights of the economy, and that its reform is the key to growth. The financial sectors of many countries do face severe bankruptcy problems, and they must be reformed. Their financial difficulties lead to inappropriate lending. Cleaning up bank balance sheets, and encouraging the development of a healthy banking system—as well as an adequate supervisory system—is very important for development. But going further, to develop a prematurely sophisticated financial sector, with bells and whistles, futures and option markets, and the full panoply of financial services, is counterproductive.

THE ROLE OF EXTERNAL AGENCIES

Structural adjustment and the external agencies—the World Bank, the IMF, and the regional development banks—are virtually synonymous in the developing countries. The IFIs—international financial institutions—played a key role in propagating structural adjustment in the 1980s. Many in the developing countries, and some in the industrialized countries, have been extremely critical of the IFIs' use of their financial muscle to impose reforms that countries were reluctant to make on their own.

The frequently put question is why countries need financing to undertake policies that are for their own benefit. This is not a very deep puzzle, because countries are not monolithic. For good reasons or ill, governments prefer not to impose hardships on their people. Frequently, the payoffs to structural reforms are somewhere off in the future, but the pain is immediate. That is enough reason for governments to prefer delay. External resources provided in support of adjustment reduce delay by helping reduce the pain.[6]

Beyond the financial aid, external agencies bring technical expertise. It is important that they use their expertise to assist countries to develop their own adjustment programs, and do not impose prepackaged programs. One of the key lessons learned from the eighties is that adjustment programs are more likely to succeed if they are "owned" by the country that implements them, rather than being seen as an imposition by the IFIs or donor governments. Governments have to sell programs to their people, and not say, as many governments do, that this is the program of the IMF or the World Bank—the implication being that the program is a charade that must be endured to get the money. Given the role of expectations, especially in determining the investment response to a program, such statements are likely to be self-fulfilling prophecies.

Those countries which have actually undertaken and pursued their own adjustment programs, such as Mexico, Chile, Korea, and Indonesia, have done better than countries where the government was pushed reluctantly into adjustment. That raises the question of what the international agencies are supposed to do when a country appears unprepared to implement and justify its own adjustment program. I believe they should wait awhile. Sometimes the international agencies have moved too soon, perhaps because the banks wanted to get paid. But it is important not to rush into adjustment lending before adjustment policies are implemented.

THE BENEFITS OF STRUCTURAL ADJUSTMENT

What benefits should flow from structural adjustment policies? To start with, there are static resource allocation improvements—welfare triangles. Economists customarily argue that triangles don't amount to much; it is, for instance, difficult to find any distortion in the literature that is convincingly estimated to have a flow welfare cost in excess of 2 percent of GNP. Triangles don't amount to much when distortions are small. But triangles can imply large welfare costs at the level of those distortions often seen in developing countries. The general theory of the "second best" prevents the simple addition of triangles to get total welfare costs of distortions. Nonetheless, I believe that getting rid of distortions in many developing countries is important, and will produce significant direct economic benefits. Further, countries that have removed impediments to the efficient allocation of resources are likely to be able to adjust better to the shocks that inevitably hit them.

The key issue though is whether—as asserted by advocates of structural adjustment programs—structural changes promote growth and, especially, sustainable growth. The most careful evaluation of the impact of adjustment programs on growth of which I am aware,[7] shows that countries that have had adjustment programs have typically grown faster for a few years as a result. This calculation adjusts for the amount of financial assistance that the country receives, since it is entirely possible that extra growth results from the extra financial aid, and has nothing to do with the adjustment programs. But that appears not to be the case.

The most interesting result that came out in the second World Bank report on adjustment lending[8] is that countries that received adjustment loans have grown faster than others, but with a greater decline in investment. That can be put in different terms: countries that have undertaken adjustment programs have tended to have larger declines in investment than others.

PROSPECTS FOR THE NINETIES

Looking toward the 1990s, the key issue for adjustment is whether countries will be able to move from slow- or no-growth adjustment programs to sustainable higher growth. For growth to resume, investment has to recover. But the restoration of investment does not come very easily. What can governments do to assist the process? There is strong evidence that the rate of investment is significantly affected by the stability of the macro economy—by stability of inflation, exchange rates, and output.[9] Structural adjustment programs are thus well directed to the restoration of investment.

There is clearly a lag between the stabilization of the economy and the return of investment. It seems to take two to three years before investment begins to respond significantly to improved macroeconomic stability and greater profitability prospects. This lag makes for political difficulties. But the evidence from countries like Chile, and now Mexico, should provide encouragement for others to persist in maintaining stability and avoiding the temptation to overstimulate the economy. Foreign direct investment too can contribute to the recovery of growth, so that measures to welcome foreign direct investment without providing exaggerated subsidies for it will also help restore growth.

There is considerable evidence of complementarity between infra-structure investment by the government and private investment.[10] Econometric evidence aside, there are many countries where the lack of, and need for, infrastructure investment is patently obvious. Government will need the funds to undertake public investments to promote growth.

What is likely to happen in the nineties? In Latin America, policies can be implemented and have already been implemented that will help the recovery of investment and growth. Most countries in Asia are growing rapidly at present, though India appears to be proceeding on its own track, making some of the macroeconomic mistakes that others have made, but a decade later.

Most countries in sub-Saharan Africa face adjustment problems that are far more serious and less susceptible to generalized macroeconomic stabilization plus distortion removal treatment than other countries. These countries face major institutional problems and have major human capital needs. The issue of governance, political accountability and responsibility, arises in many countries. Sustainable long-term growth will require also major improvements in agricultural productiv-ity. All these changes are very difficult and have to be brought about under far more difficult circumstances than these countries faced in the 1960s and 1970s.

These difficulties make adjustment more, rather than less, necessary. They also make it more important for the outside world to help. How-ever, countries that do not adjust because they are waiting for help are less likely to receive it than those that get on with the necessary adjust-ment policies. It is the countries that have pushed ahead, such as Mexico and Poland, that have been responsible for decisive breakthroughs in the debt situation.

The debt problem that so clouded the last decade is now showing signs of dissipating. The most recent moves in the debt crisis are very important and will have major long run impacts in Africa, in Latin America, and in Eastern Europe. The official sector has been becoming increasingly more generous in its dealings with the poorest countries and in the case of Poland, a middle-income country indebted to official bilateral creditors. Write-offs of African countries' bilateral debt are proceeding apace, and Africa, despite its heavy indebtedness, receives positive net transfers.

In Latin America, the Brady Plan provides an appropriate mechanism to help countries that are willing to adjust. Mexico has taken advantage of officially supported debt relief. Brazil can also take advantage of the Brady Plan at some point and, in any case, faces a much smaller debt problem than the other Latin American countries. Costa Rica has negotiated an excellent debt deal. Countries that are willing to adjust can deal with their debt problems.

The eighties were, for many countries, the lost decade, the decade of structural adjustment, the decade of the debt. The 1990s will see the debt problem significantly reduced, thereby making it easier for countries to undertake the adjustments they should, in any case, make as rapidly as possible, and will see more countries that have persisted with adjustment breaking through into renewed and sustainable growth.

NOTES

1. Program loans, which had been made from time to time in the two previous decades, are similar to structural adjustment loans.

2. See "Adjustment Lending Policies for Sustainable Growth," *Policy and Research Series Paper PRS 14*, Country Economics Department, World Bank Washington, DC (1990) for estimates of the interest rate and commodity price shocks that affected different developing countries.

3. Indonesia appears to be the only country that experienced triple-digit inflation in the 1960s and now has single-digit inflation.

4. This case is discussed in my paper, "Growth, Macroeconomics, and Development," *NBER Macroeconomics Annual*, 1991. Cambridge, MA: MIT Press.

5. Max Corden, "Macroeconomic Policy and Growth: Some Lessons of Experience," Proceedings of the World Bank *Annual Conference on Development Economics*, Washington, DC, 1990, pp. 59–84, summarizes the experiences of most of the larger countries.

6. One of the surprising findings of World Bank research reported in "Adjustment Lending Policies for Sustainable Growth," *op. cit.* is that countries that adjusted intensively suffered a smaller decline in consumption, *ceteris paribus*, than countries that adjusted less strongly.

7. See again "Adjustment Lending Policies for Sustainable Growth," *op cit.*

8. Report on Adjustment Lending II...

9. See for instance Luis Serven and Andres Solimano, "Private Investment and Macroeconomic Adjustment," World Bank Working Paper WPS339, Washington, DC, 1989.

10. See for example Robert Barro, "A Cross-Country Study of Growth, Saving, and Government," Cambridge, MA: NBER Working Paper 2855, 1989.

3

Policy Reform in the 1980s

Lance Taylor

The structural adjustment record in developing economies during the past decade is not heartening. Especially in sub-Saharan Africa and Latin America, output growth has not been much faster than population increase, and, in many cases, lagged significantly behind. Resource transfers toward the Third World continue to be negative in the $30 to 40 billion range, at the same time as realistic estimates suggest that a reversed sign (*positive* transfers of the same magnitude, or a swing of $60 to 80 billion) would be necessary to support a return to historical growth rates over the Third World. The particular magnitudes quoted come from studies sponsored by the World Institute of Development Economics Research (or WIDER) in Helsinki and are reported in Taylor (1991), but similar numbers come from other sources.

Under adverse external and fiscal circumstances stemming from low terms of trade and inadequate exports performance (in Africa) and from distributional and fiscal/foreign exchange limits due to the debt crisis (Latin America), it is not surprising that adjustment policy packages have not been very successful—you can't jump-start or drive a car which has only a trickle of foreign exchange gasoline. However, it is instructive to examine and explore the details of why well-intentioned policy packages fail.

STABILIZATION OR ADJUSTMENT

At the outset, we should draw a few terminological distinctions regarding the makeup of policy packages:

Stabilization vs. adjustment. Discussion of reform in developing countries tends to break down into two main topics: stabilization and adjustment. Stabilization is broadly speaking the province of the International Monetary Fund, which follows its well-known, short-term procedures. Adjustment is supposed to be a longer-term affair in which the economy is reconfigured to support sustained growth, and it is the domain of the World Bank. The transition from one process to the other is not necessarily easy. For example, Fund-type austerity does not exactly create the buoyant economic environment in which private investors will thrive, despite the Bank's best efforts at price reform and establishment of market-oriented rules of the game.

Shock treatments. Another distinction that commonly arises is between shock treatments and gradualism. Shock policies can be exclusively oriented toward stabilization, e.g. rapid imposition of austerity and/or a price freeze as anti-inflation moves. Alternatively, "global" shocks aim to attain stabilization and massive restructuring at one go. The Polish package of 1989–90 is the best-known recent attempt at global shock therapy.

Gradualism is less well defined, but hinges on the notion that both economic and political resistance can rapidly nullify policy shocks. Three examples help illustrate the gradualism line of thought:

1. After the initial maxidevaluations, monetary reforms, etc., in the February 1988 and the 1991 Nicaraguan and the January 1990 Polish packages, attempts were made to stabilize the wage and exchange rates in both real *and* nominal terms. Prices were not effectively restrained for weeks or months, however, leading to substantial real wage losses and exchange appreciation. A more gradual approach based on indexation of the nominal wage and exchange rates to price increases might have averted political strife without much extra inflationary cost. Indeed, experience in Nicaragua, Poland, and elsewhere strongly suggests that a maxidevaluation leading into a reform program is a clear signal that prices throughout the economy are going to rise. A sequence of minidevaluations in a crawling peg is a less blatant signal, and may achieve the same real depreciation with less overall inflation while, at the same time, making speculation against future large exchange rate changes a less attractive financial option.

2. The possibility of speculation and destabilizing financial flows also suggests caution in removing barriers to capital movements prior to liberalizing commodity trade (although, of course, some capital flight is always possible by overinvoicing imports, underinvoicing exports, etc.). The financial dislocations suffered by countries in South America's Southern Cone after they precipitously opened their capital markets in the late 1970s are often cited in this regard.

3. Even if one accepts the orthodox postulate that an undistorted trade regime is "optimal," it is still easy to set up fully neoclassical models in which a gradual transition from tariff-ridden to free trade makes sense. For example, if full capacity utilization and saving-determined investments are assumed, then the national capital stock at the end of a transition period will be higher if real consumption is held down by slowly falling tariffs in the first phases of the transition.

COMPLEXITIES OF STABILIZATION

Evidently, issues of both timing and content arise in stabilization or adjustment packages, but it is clear that stabilization has to come first—sustained growth is extremely unlikely in an economy with double- or triple-digit annual inflation rates, trade and fiscal gaps of the order of 10 percent of GDP or more, and open distributional conflict. But what sorts of problems do stabilization packages have to confront? Can appropriate packages feasibly be deployed by weak, understaffed governments in the Third World? It makes sense to address these questions briefly, drawing on case study material from WIDER as summarized in Taylor (1988) and other sources. The pressing issues are inflation and adjustment to external shocks, but we can also touch exchange rate adjustment, fiscal issues, and a few questions related to external balance.

Inflation itself may result as the economy seeks some sort of macroeconomic balance under foreign exchange restricted supply—both the inflation tax on money balances and forced saving resulting from inflation-induced income redistribution against low savers (real wages have fallen by more than 50 percent in every economy all over Africa and Latin America) are crude but effective means to limit demands to available supply. However, a price spiral is also likely to be exacerbated from the costs side by implicit or explicit contract indexation and the distributional conflicts involved in forced saving.

Broadly speaking, there are only four or five ways to break a cumulative inflation process:

1. Imports can be increased to ease local supply bottlenecks, at least for internationally traded goods.
2. Relative prices can be manipulated, e.g. the exchange rate can be appreciated in real terms, or the real wage reduced.
3. Incomes policies and other forms of market intervention can be deployed to muffle the most acutely conflicting social claims. The most obvious example is a "social pact" to reduce wage inflation while holding profit claims in line.

4. In a more extreme case, a price freeze plus contract deindexation—
   a heterodox shock in the jargon—can be attempted as a policy
   surprise.
5. Austerity can be applied, i.e. a cut in public sector borrowing
   coupled with monetary interventions involving increased interest
   rates and credit restraint.

Successful anti-inflation packages—which are relatively few and far
between—combine several such measures in either shock or
gradualistic form. Each economy's inflation process is unique, making
it difficult to generalize about which policies will be effective in any
case at hand. However, a few observations are worth making:

Austerity is likely to work better when "most" market transactions
occur in a regime of flexible prices, i.e. mark-up pricing and contract
indexation are not widespread. In practice, of course, the IMF both
preaches and practices austerity but often combines it with real wage
cuts, reductions in income support programs and subsidies, and so on.
All these measures reduce demand, so that the outcomes include reduced output and lower trade deficit (via import cuts) along with
slower inflation. The relative impacts of austerity and associated measures on inflation, output, and on the external deficit are of obvious
importance; experience, unfortunately, suggests that regressive distribution and output losses may come rapidly while inflation reduction
can be slow in an economy in which consciously organized social
classes have market power (a somewhat unpublicized aspect of the
Bolivian stabilization of the mid-1980s was its heavy-handed repression
of public sector wages and the tin-miner's union).

Combining austerity with other measures has been a recipe for success in other circumstances. Both Mexico and Israel, for example,
blended a modicum of demand restriction with heterodox shocks in
successful packages. However, both also included social pacts more or
less democratically ratified (less so in Mexico under the legendary labor
control of the PRI) and massive foreign exchange outlays (from external
support in Israel and from reserves built up over several years of
austerity in Mexico). These conditions are somewhat unusual, to say
the least, and also underline the difficulties of coordinating several
policies simultaneously in the anti-inflation fight.

Besides triggering inflation, external shocks are likely to cause output
losses and reduce capital formation:

1. By limiting imports, scarce foreign exchange squeezes either current output or capital formation, since in most developing economies production is dependent on intermediate imports while

foreign-made capital goods are an essential component in most investment projects.

2. At the same time, capital inflows are a source of saving, which must be replaced domestically if they are curtailed. As we have already observed, the required reduction in aggregate demand is often realized by accelerating inflation.

3. Finally, fewer funds will be flowing through the financial system, squeezing the supply of credit and thereby capital formation.

Several specific policy changes can be used to try to offset these problems, as well as a major one—devaluation. We begin with more targeted policy moves.

Fiscal restraint can ease credit markets, shifting the investment demand schedule upward while reducing monetarist-style inflationary pressure. But if investment goes up, then the foreign exchange limit will force current output to decline. Although it brings partial relief, austerity may prove politically difficult to pursue (perhaps less so in Asia than in Latin America or sub-Saharan Africa).

Higher public investment is likely to raise total capital formation, leading to faster inflation and reduced capacity utilization but also to sustained potential output growth. At least in the early 1980s, Brazil, South Korea, and Tanzania had some degree of success with this sort of policy.

Increased exports add to import capacity, raising output and reducing inflation while permitting some recovery of growth. The difficulty is that this option is really only available to semi-industrialized economies in which recession creates spare manufacturing capacity which can then be utilized to support sales abroad, e.g. Turkey, Korea, and Brazil. Exporters of primary products have no such possibilities unless one were to rely on options such as a vent for exporting surplus tea opening up as domestic consumption declines.

Tighter import quotas can be selectively applied to limit either immediate or capital goods imports, and perhaps induce a degree of import substitution. In diverse circumstances, Tanzania, Zimbabwe, Kenya, and Colombia utilized this option successfully in the 1980s.

Expansionary policy of increased public investment and fiscal dissaving lead to problems of the sort already discussed. For a time, they can raise capacity utilization and potential output growth, but at the cost of spiraling inflation. Peru's expansionism of the 1980s can be interpreted as a failed attempt to offset external restrictions by increased spending on the part of the state.

Policy coordination is never easy. Not many governments of developing (or developed!) countries are agile enough to deploy simultaneous fiscal restraint in current transactions, increased state capital formation, intelligent manipulation of quotas, and export incentives to offset all the ill effects of external shocks on capacity utilization, inflation, and growth.

Devaluation—often the IMF's prescription of choice for improving trade balance—has complicated, economy-wide effects. By increasing import costs, it may be inflationary and contractionary. However, if foreign exchange is severely constraining the system, the outcomes may go the other way: *any* net export response to depreciation generates scarce dollars. They can be used to reduce excess demand by allowing intermediate imports and production to rise, with a corresponding reduction in inflation. As recent Tanzanian and Ghanian experience suggests, capital inflows provided to support devaluation will make these outcomes more likely. A reasoned judgment about the likely effects of devaluation is essential to the design of stabilization programs. If any rule applies, it might be that small, open economies which are severely foreign exchange constrained are more likely to respond favorably to a devaluation/capital inflow package than are large, closed ones.

Issues also arise in coordinating devaluation with other policies. If depreciation is expansionary, for example, then it can be combined usefully with fiscal restraint. The exchange rate change improves the trade balance, while fiscal policy helps avoid an inflationary, excess demand situation. If devaluation is contractionary, on the other hand, combining it with austerity can lead to the sort of policy "overkill" for which the IMF is (un?)justly renowned.

Indeed, especially in an African context with many parastatals and marketing boards present, the exchange rate must not only be coordinated with tax and spending initiatives, but it is a tool of fiscal policy in and of itself. Exchange rate changes affect parastatal cash-flow positions which ultimately feed into either fiscal revenues or outflows, or to net credit creation by the banking system. Tracing these linkages can be very tricky.

A further question is whether devaluation will by itself markedly improve trade performance. A considered answer might well be in the negative. In general, getting rid of "bad" price distortions appears to be a necessary condition for (or at least is probably correlated with) greater "tradability" of domestic activities. But, as argued further below, price incentives are never sufficient. A real exchange rate with a reasonable, stable value is an invaluable stimulant to net exports. But it must be supplemented with directed trade promotion policies such as tax drawbacks, export subsidies, cheap credits, etc. as well as state interventions to improve infrastructure and the economic environment more generally.

Finally, how should the real exchange rate be held stable? As noted above, crawling peg policies which chain mini-devaluations to domestic inflation in order to keep the nominal exchange rate in line with the domestic price level have a fairly respectable track record in all corners of the developing world. The outcomes of exchange auctions have been more spotty, since they lead at times to speculative surges of consumer imports.

Besides the exchange rate itself, one also has to consider the implications for stabilization of commercial and capital market policy. As noted above, for example, import quotas have been intelligently deployed to offset external shocks; as argued below, they can also play a role in industrial policy. Changes in trade regimes can also bring substantial benefits, e.g. permitting "own-exchange" imports (no questions asked!) creates some problems with big imports of luxury goods, but can also effectively widen foreign exchange bottlenecks and perhaps reduce incentives for smuggling. Removing exchange controls in general, however, can prove to be an open invitation to capital flight. All such possibilities have to be weighed in terms of the history and institutions of the economy at hand.

Turning to fiscal questions, it bears emphasis that increasingly binding limits on public spending have been the rule in the 1980s. Both for governments now required to make large debt payments (largely, but not exclusively, grouped in Latin America) and those which have seen revenues from primary exports drop off (often but not exclusively, in Africa), the need to restrain both current and capital spending has become acute. At the same time, it has been increasingly recognized that public investment in both physical and human capital has strong complementarities with private capital formation (see below). How to take medium-run advantage of this "crowding-in" effect of public investment while maintaining fiscal responsibility is a major question for the next decade. In much of the Third World where it has never really been contemplated, tax reform may prove to be the only feasible solution to the fiscal constraint.

THE STATE AND ECONOMIC DEVELOPMENT

We now turn to "adjustment," or how to promote stable, nationally self-reliant, technically progressive, and relatively egalitarian economic development in the medium run. The role of the state in guiding development is a useful point from which to begin, since doubts about the ability of the public authorities to guide industrialization lie at the base of liberal policy recommendations emanating from the Bretton Woods Institutions.

As Shapiro and Taylor (1990) observe, there is an old debate in economics between opponents and partisans of market intervention, but, recently, its terms have shifted. The discussion is no longer about forms of market failure and whether a liberal environment can capture dynamic efficiencies. The claim of the "new neoclassical political economy" is much more radical: Although markets may be imperfect, any state intervention amplifies distortions and inhibits growth to such an extent that it just makes a bad situation worse.

The argument arrived at this turn in three stages. The first was occupied by the wave of development economists from around 1945 until the late 1960s, and the second and third respectively by "old" and "new" neoclassical critics. The main points stressed just after World War II by development scholars included the following:

1. Development is a disequilibrium process involving successive transitions from one configuration of steady growth or "circular flow" to another. A transition may be induced by technical innovation, and involves endogenous credit creation and inflationary macro adjustment (Schumpeter).
2. One can postulate conditions under which development will be more rapid, capital-intensive, and reliant upon a greater role of the state. In 19th-century Europe, for example, greater relative "backwardness" called forth more dramatic transitions (Gerschenkron).
3. Economies of scale are important. Coordinated investment across many sectors in a "Big Push" is required to give balanced output and demand expansion to take advantage of decreasing average costs economy-wide (Nurkse, Rosenstein-Rodan).
4. The investment must be planned, since pervasive market failures such as decreasing costs and imperfect tradability mean that price-driven, decentralized investment decisions will not be socially optimal (Scitovsky).
5. Modern analytical tools such as input-output models and social cost benefit analysis make public investment planning possible (Chenery).
6. On the other hand, planning tools are, at best, approximations, so that one should be on the look-out for inflationary balance of payments and other bottlenecks, and figure out how to break them in a process of perpetually unbalanced expansion (Hirschman).
7. Given the breakdown of the world trading system in the 1930s, export-led growth is a strategy option not worth detailed exploration (implicit consensus).

This 30-year-old literature was highly suggestive, but it had at least two major drawbacks. One was that while it was rich with diagnosis of development problems, it provided little concrete policy advice. Circular flow, relative backwardness, and balanced and unbalanced growth were intriguing metaphors but couldn't help being much more of academic than managerial interest.

The second problem is that the early development economists placed limitless faith in the capacity of the state to intervene in the economic system. Its inability to carry out its assigned development role(s) became apparent almost equally fast. The contrast with the teachings of liberal economics could not be more striking. Realistically or not, neoclassical economics at most requires that the state should be a "night watchman." The development economists needed the state to be much more active and effective, but they provided no reasons to expect why it could or should fulfill its tasks.

Around 1970, the first wave of critics concentrated on the "inefficiency" of state intervention as it had evolved. Using new analytical tools from trade theory, such as effective rates of protection and domestic resource costs, authors such as Little, Scitovsky, and Scott, Balassa, and Krueger showed that the incentive structures created by import-substituting industrial strategies (especially) were highly unequal for different economic actors. They further sought to correlate "distorted" policy regimes with poor economic performance; their mediocre success in this effort is described below. One of the neoclassical economists' problems, worth flagging now, is that when they applied computable general equilibrium models—their most advanced analytical tools—to estimate "welfare losses" from distortions, the outcomes were meager: 100 percent distortions might reduce GDP by one-half of one percent. Implicitly then, the first neoclassical critique was reduced to an assertion that eliminating distortions will lead the economy to jump to a noticeably more rapidly growing configuration of circular flow. We are back to economic poetry and metaphors.

Regardless of this difficulty, even when critics showed that many industries in developing countries had "negative value added" at world prices, they took the profession by storm. But they also transmitted a more powerful message. Read between the lines, these economists pointed to unfettered markets as the only viable alternative to an incentive mare's nest. The rapid growth rates of Taiwan and South Korea—at the time unrealistically postulated to have noninterventionist governments—were cited in support of the free market. Although they are not easy to substantiate, the notions that observed distortions inhibit growth and that rapid growers are noninterventionist now permeate the rhetoric and to an extent the actions of the World Bank.

In the 1980s, the debate took its second turn. Echoing P.T. Bauer, who questioned the efficacy of state intervention early on, recent authors postulate that "bureaucratic failure" is worse than "market failure." Figure 3.1 is a schematic representation of the latest neoclassical critique. The point it tries to emphasize is that the critics are not very

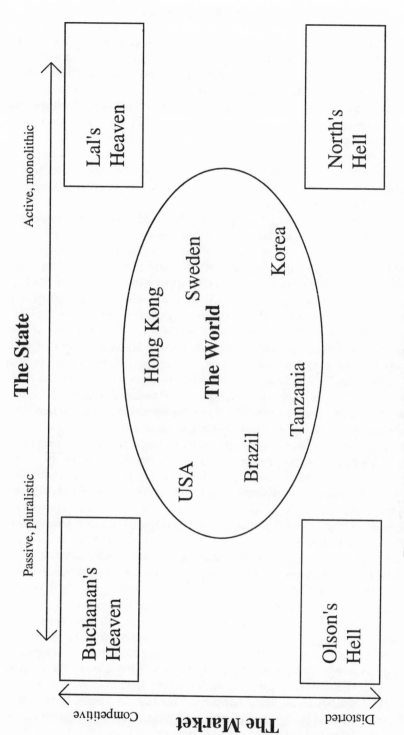

Figure 3.1 The New Neoclassical Political Economic Vision

relevant because their models push them into extreme positions with regard to the nature of both the market (highly distorted or truly competitive) and the state (very pluralistic and reacting passively to pressures, or monolithic and proactive).

For example, Mancur Olson argues that, because of bargaining costs and the presence of free riders, coalitions within the society form to protect their own interests. They seek to redistribute income toward themselves, instead of increasing efficiency in the national interest. A weak state cannot intervene, so the system tends toward a highly distorted market structure with the coalitions distributing the spoils: "Olson's Hell" in the diagram.

The public choice school, led by James Buchanan, elevates "rent-seeking" induced by government interventions—lobbying for state favors, paying a bribe to get an import quota or Pentagon contract, fixing a ticket for a traffic violation—to a deadly social ill. If real resources are devoted to pursuing rents or "directly unproductive profit-seeking" (DUP) activities in the jargon, the outcome can be a form of suboptimality resembling "Olson's Hell" for the society as a whole. Inventing DUP was a technical advance since deep wells of postulated corruption allowed numerical models to give satisfyingly large estimates of welfare losses from distortion. Moreover, the saving social graces may be a thoroughly night-watchmanly state supervising a competitive market—the latter condition guaranteed by international free trade. Under these conditions, DUP activity becomes unrewarding, and the invisible hand will guide society toward "Buchanan's Heaven."

A second form of bliss takes a more authoritarian cast. For Buchanan, the ideal state mimics the Cheshire Cat by vanishing to avoid being taken over by the special interests. Alternatively, the state can force the interests to vanish, or in Deepak Lal's words, "A courageous, ruthless, and perhaps undemocratic government is required to ride roughshod over these newly-created special interest groups." We ascend to another Heaven, although it is not clear why Lal's ruthless generals and bureaucrats will abstain from taking over the market also. The record of Third World authoritarian states in avoiding corruption and distortions is not encouraging in this regard.

Indeed a market distorted by the state for its own ends is a final extreme possibility in the diagram, one which can be associated with Douglass North, an economic historian (not to mention Paul Kennedy, another historian, who finds that their military-industrial complexes force great powers into decline). In a typical North example, a state may choose to raise revenue by creating monopolies, and then marshall political arguments in their support. The fate of Leninist centrally planned economic systems suggests that North is not wrong in pointing to potential damnation at the end of such a path.

The message of the diagram is that both the state and market, in principle, can arrive at extreme configurations which are easy to characterize. However, the Buchanan combination of a purely night watchman state and a completely undistorted market has never been observed in practice (certainly not in 18th-century Britain and contemporary Hong Kong, the two most widely cited putative examples). If it were ever created, a Lal equilibrium would probably not be stable and recent events suggest that even "North's Hell" is not forever, and the same is true for Olson's form of anarchy.

Indeed, as the central section of the picture illustrates, existing societies combine mixtures of state activism with market distortions: the country placements are arbitrary, but they are meant to illustrate stylized facts. Moreover, if it were possible to attach numerical coordinates to the points in the diagram where real countries lie, statistical analysis would almost certainly detect scant association between their positions and indicators of economic performance such as GDP growth rates (except for the likelihood of poor growth in countries with Hellishly distorted markets).

Beyond this hypothetical regression, a much more fundamental point is that the new neoclassical theory of the state is ahistorical and timeless. Abba Lerner once remarked that "economics has gained the title of queen of the social sciences by choosing solved political problems as its domain." He was certainly correct with regard to the theorists at the corner of our diagram. The last topic their models can address are the complex, dynamic interactions between state and market which have characterized economic development since it began two centuries ago. The best way to understand that reality is through historical case studies, as sketched in the following section.

STATE INTERVENTION IN PRACTICE

The historical record indeed suggests that, in at least some cases, governments have been able to walk the tightrope between being devoured by DUP activists and sheer ineffectiveness in promoting industrial development. We consider examples from South Korea, Brazil, Turkey, India, and Chile.

South Korea began postwar development with low-wage, labor-intensive industries, which helped provide the skills and foreign exchange to increase domestic technological capacity through licensing. Some scholars argue that Korea distorted relative prices in a deliberate attempt to get them "wrong," so as to shift resources to targeted sectors. Exporters were heavily subsidized through financial incentives and a protected market, which allowed them to sell domestically at inflated prices.

What distinguishes the Korean state is not its industrial policy per se but its power and willingness to discipline private firms, making prices less distorted in South Korea as compared to other countries. The state rewarded firms with low-cost financing in exchange for increasingly stringent export requirements. It had a broad array of instruments at its disposal, including control of the banking system and price controls to curb monopoly power. It also had the fiscal authority to tax the middle class, and the political leeway to keep social expenditures relatively low; both freed government funds for long-run investment. Despite a highly concentrated industrial structure involving large conglomerate firms or *chaebols* which were protected from outside competition, the nature of state policies generated intense competition which forced firms to become ever more productive.

The dominance of the *chaebols* may also have helped reduce the costs of rent-seeking activity. Given the *chaebols'* exclusive status, smaller, less-favored players were unlikely to compete. Their involvement in multiple activities reduced the costs associated with start-up and finding information about opponents. Their status as conglomerates also led to a "bundling of issues" which cut down transaction costs; bargaining was facilitated by the possibility of side-payments for related bargaining points. Furthermore, each *chaebol's* ability to move into almost any line of business generated competitive pressure to remain efficient. As a result, the social benefits of increased productivity outweighed the costs associated with government subsidies.

Korea's economic policies and institutions formed integrated, self-reinforcing packages. Different observers emphasize different aspects, but the lessons relevant to other LDCs are not so obvious. For example, although governments in many countries have relied on similar incentives and price distortions, the content of the institutional framework and the implementation of their policies have significantly varied. In Latin America, the state has been relatively weak. It has not had the disciplinary power or the fiscal authority of the Korean state. Therefore, subsidies have been provided without exacting performance criteria in return. States also faced pressures to spend on social programs and public sector wages, and faced repeated fiscal crises. Korea's class structure and other sociological and geopolitical factors exposed the state to fewer contradictory demands.

Brazil's experience with installing a domestic automobile industry in the 1950s and 1960s illustrates how such obstacles can be overcome. Under appropriate circumstances, even a relatively weak state may have the capacity to shape investment activity.

In the 1950s, Brazil was squarely in a second-best world. Foreign exchange was scarce, and its private and social costs were not closely aligned, so that Brazil could not afford the luxury of an unregulated transfer mechanism. The domestic economy was plagued with distortions. These conditions provided a strong motivation to promote import substituting industrialization, particularly in autos. On a global front, it confronted an oligopolized industrial structure in which economic rents would not be competed away. Accordingly, the country attempted to install domestic productive capacity and, thereby, save on the costs associated with imports. These costs included not only scarce foreign exchange but the rents paid to the importing firms and the positive production and technological externalities associated with the industry.

Given the nature of motor vehicles and the political economy of Brazil, domestic production was to be controlled by foreign rather than domestic capital, as is typically assumed in the literature on strategic trade. These foreign firms would also replicate oligopolistic behavior domestically. Therefore, the issue was not simply rent distribution between nations, but the internal distribution between the TNCs and the state.

Due to the state's limited resources and internal divisions, commercial policy was its primary instrument. The basic approach was to insulate the sector by closing the market to finished vehicles and guaranteeing its subsidized access to foreign exchange to import necessary components and pay off foreign financing. In exchange for these subsidies, firms had to meet an exceptionally ambitious domestic content schedule.

The Brazilian state successfully attracted foreign capital into the sector and met its planning targets. More importantly, the state's initial subsidies did not generate ongoing resource transfers to the sector. Rather, the state successfully taxed away an increasing share of the oligopolistic rents accruing to the industry. All of the forfeited revenue associated with the plan was ultimately recovered, and the sector became a significant source of revenue for a state with limited sources of fiscal income. The data reveal, therefore, a form of rent redistribution usually found between peripheral states and transnational firms exporting raw materials, with a growing share for the state through an increased tax bite. By the mid-1960s, significant idle capacity, intensified competition, increased demand sensitivity to price, and ultimately price controls, forced firms to pass along some of the declines in production costs to the consumer, and to absorb part of the tax bite themselves.

These results were not only due to sectoral policy per se, but to the nature of the Brazilian market and the macroeconomic environment, characteristics specific to motor vehicles, and strategies of the firms. Obviously, the size of the market made a domestic industry more viable; moreover, the initial inefficiency and required resource transfer resulting from low levels of production were more easily absorbed than they would have been in a smaller, weaker economy. Second, the repressed demand from the postwar years, and the fact that automobiles were a luxury good and relatively inelastic with respect to price, allowed firms to pass along their high costs to consumers. This also allowed the government to impose a high tax incidence on vehicles without diminishing total revenues. The same results would not have obtained had the policy involved an intermediate good rather than a consumer durable. The cost of a tax or inefficiency for an important manufacturing input would have had much broader economic ramifications.

An important aspect of Brazil's experience is that installation of the automobile industry was abetted by the relative consistency of the sectoral plan with macroeconomic policies. When these changes were not aligned—for example, when the industry could not fully meet its targets in the early 1960s due to an increasingly binding foreign exchange constraint—problems emerged. Moreover, the shakeout of the industry did not result simply from automatic price competition between firms, but rather from a macropolicy-induced crisis of the mid-1960s.

By the 1970s, the industry was a successful infant sector, as measured by improving export performance, and a declining cost curve. By 1979, the industry was producing over a million vehicles per year. Subsequent performance has been less buoyant, but that owes at least as much to Brazil's macroeconomic difficulties as to problems within the sector *per se.*

Turkey, our third example, entered very early into the process of import-substituting industrialization, beginning with an explicitly statist thrust under Atatürk in 1931. Waves of industrialization continued after World War II in ten-year cycles through the traditional "easy" to "hard" sectors to import substitutes as discussed in the next section, with the state typically managing the "commanding heights" through public enterprises, while the private sector concentrated on final goods. GDP growth fluctuated around a solid 6 percent average between 1950 and the late 1970s. There was well less than full employment, and at the close of each cycle the economy was constrained by saving, foreign, and fiscal gaps. Inefficiency, as measured by the standard methods, ran rampant: Turkey was a launching pad for many of the initial generalizations about rent-seeking and DUP.

Then in 1980, in connection with a relatively mild but regressive IMF stabilization program and ample capital inflow, Turkey broke from ISI and launched into state sponsored export growth. The success of this outward oriented development scheme was contingent on structural conditions specific to the Turkish economy. In fact, the export "miracle" rested upon the preexisting industrial base created by ISI, the regressive redistribution and other policies leading to contraction of domestic demand for manufactures, attempts at general prices reform, subsidies of up to one-third of export sales plus related incentives, and rapid growth in demand for the domestically produced products by culturally compatible buyers in the region (the Gulf and the Iran–Iraq War). Had any one of these factors been missing, the boom probably would not have occurred. Moreover, it was not accompanied by effective liberalization; export subsidies (and "fictional exports") proliferated, and Turkey's baroque quota and tariff structure was replaced by "funds" based on import levies arbitrarily manipulated by the bureaucracy.

How the Turkish experience works out remains to be seen. It has not generated export-led growth in the Korean sense, with foreign sales feeding back into latest technology capital formation and productivity growth, nor has investment been strong. But for decades industrialization has been state led with private producers serving as the troops, for a long period selling in a protected internal market with very low external trade shares (the export/GDP ratio was 5 percent in 1980) and then being pushed into the export option as markets materialized. A politically mature industrial bourgeoisie of the European type may now be emerging, but only as a consequence of a self-conscious etatist development project that began not long after World War I.

India also began post-independence industrialization under the aegis of the state, especially during the Second- and Third-Year Plans which were in force during a period of fairly rapid growth between 1950 and 1965 (the GDP growth rate was 4.2 percent, while manufacturing output grew at 7.8 percent). Then came a ten-year slowdown (GDP and manufacturing growth rates were 2.7 and 4.5 percent respectively), followed by recuperation to 5 percent growth on average between 1975 and 1989. What caused these fluctuations?

One key factor behind slow growth was a decline in public capital formation after 1965. As we will see below, public investment typically stimulates or "crowds in" private capital formation, and in India the overall effect was substantial. Gross capital formation peaked at 18 percent of GDP in 1966/67, and then declined to around 15 percent at the end of the 1960s. The investment/GDP ratio then recovered to 19 percent in the mid-1970s, and reached 22.5 percent in the 1980s. In one scholar's words, " . . . the revival mid-Seventies was to begin with an engineered revival. . ." with much of the engineering taking form of renewed public capital formation.

A second factor was a step in the direction of external opening associated with the devaluation of 1966 and orthodox stabilization progress early in the 1970s, followed by a step-and-a-half back toward stimulating domestic efficiency by other means. These included simply better management of the railroad system, but also moves toward promoting competition in industries such as cement and fertilizers. At the same time, the planning process was reestablished to set out " . . . a strategic concept of the direction in which the economy has to move, and the pace it must attain. . . ."

Finally, there was an ongoing dialogue between the state and (at least) large capital. Licensing requirements were removed to ease capital formation, and modest export subsidies were provided. The Indian state has never fully controlled the economy's commanding heights, but it has maintained an active economic presence since independence. Contrary to the claims of the both old and new neoclassical theory, India's accelerated growth for the past 15 years has *not* been accompanied by either extensive liberalization or a withdrawal of the state from the market. If anything, the trend has been toward more effective public guidance of the indigenous capitalist system.

Chile is an interesting final case, since its rapid GDP growth since the mid-1980s (about 7 percent annually) is often attributed to liberalization. At best, a half-truth is involved. The motors of growth have been an increased volume of copper exports from publicly backed mines, high copper prices in the second half of the decade, and expansion of fishery, forestry, and fruit exports from $191 million to $2,134 million between 1972 and 1988. Over five decades, the state—specifically CORFO or the production development corporation—has been behind the non-copper export push.

In forestry, as early as the 1940s, CORFO began to promote planting of Monterey pines, which reach maturity in only 10–20 years in the South of Chile. By the 1960s the agency was setting up pulp plants, which accounted for all the increase in exports during the 1970s. These plants plus state-promoted pine forestation supported steady export growth during the past decade. After reprivatization in the mid-1970s, the industry reached full capacity in the 1980s. Finally, in fruits, in the 1960s CORFO took on a series of problems in transport, cold storage, quality control, and packaging, which had prevented Chile from stepping into its "natural" role of selling off-season temperate zone products into the North American market. With these problems overcome, private grape, apple, and other producers leaped into exports in the 1980s.

The export push also relied on other factors: subsidies for pine plantations, soft credits for fruit growers, significant devaluation (real wage reduction, in other language), elimination of export red tape, relaxation of labor legislation, provision of ownership guarantees, etc. Obviously, the state was behind these "liberal" initiatives which were designed to support private sector activity. Indeed, Chile's "miracle" is very much a public/private sector joint affair.

POLICY SEQUENCING

We can close the discussion by considering policies that can underlie economic adjustment under "flexible gradualism." The obvious question is how to pursue policy sequencing, which is a contentious issue. Drawing on various country experiences, however, some suggestions about a reasonable order of changes can be made.

Stabilization first. As already observed, it is difficult to see how long-term growth is possible if the economy is severely destabilized in its own historical terms; i.e., if inflation is running significantly faster than previous levels, imports are severely foreign exchange–constrained, trade and fiscal deficits amount to more than (say) ten percent of GNP, etc. Moreover, if prices are "badly" distorted—to the tune of tens or hundreds of percent of exchange appreciation, highly negative real interest rates, extreme micro or sectoral price distortions according to effective rates of protection (ERP) or domestic resource cost of foreign exchange (DRC) criteria, etc.—then sustained growth in a market context is unlikely. However, as noted above, growth is also improbable if the economy is subject to permanent fiscal and monetary austerity, while all "success cases" to date suggest that getting prices roughly right is, at best, a necessary but far from a sufficient condition for sustained economic expansion.

A social contract. Stabilization and adjustment have to be socially and economically feasible. Raising agricultural producer prices, for example, means that urban incomes will decline in the short run unless farmers spend a lot of their extra revenue on urban produced goods, and there is excess capacity in that sector. This example suggests that both the political power of different social groups and the economic linkages among them will determine the fate of reform attempts based on changing relative prices. Stabilizing an inflation by austerity and real income reduction also raises obvious political problems. Packages will almost certainly fail unless they have social support. For example, the relatively successful adjustments in Chile and Mexico as opposed to deadlock in Argentina and Brazil can be attributed to rather more successful social arrangements (partly due to repression) in the former countries.

Setting up a plan system. If managing capitalism in the local context is the goal, the examples discussed in the last section show that the state has to take steps toward achieving competence in that endeavor. Extending planning beyond a rolling policy framework paper toward serious analysis of public investment projects, and providing incentives and guidance for the private sector are steps that should be taken early on. Illiberal interventions such as export subsidies, licensing production in industries subject to economies of scale, and use of seed money should be considered, so long as they make production in the desired lines amply profitable for the private sector. Finally, potential complementarities between public and private capital formation should be explored. Both new infrastructure and even state production of key inputs (utilities, transport, some commodities) can stimulate the private sector. In economies which now have a large state presence, however, the real issue may involve slimming down, and not pushing state economic activity too far.

Financial restructuring. Developing countries attempting reform from a previously socialist system (e.g. Nicaragua, Cuba, and many African nations) will often have a banking system geared exclusively toward issuing liabilities to collect the inflation tax while extending unrecoverable credits to keep state enterprises afloat. The normal banking function of guiding money flows from where they are available to where they are needed is completely ignored. Such a financial structure has to be broken down, and replaced with a traditional central/commercial bank system, with several commercial banks competing to gain deposits and place loans in a market framework. In most developing countries, commercial banks share short-term markets with informal suppliers of credit, and may have to be supplemented with state development banks oriented toward long-term lending. But they play a key financial role, and, if a viable banking system does not exist, it certainly has to be invented. In a longer period, other financial entities such as pension funds, building societies, or even a stock market should be encouraged or strengthened in economies where they already exist. Financial deepening or the evolution of nonmonetary intermediaries is a necessary concomitant of long-term growth.

Fiscal restructuring. Historically, major flows of saving in now developed economies have come from diverse sources: the public sector in Scandinavia, corporations in the U.S., and households in Japan. Given their relatively large state apparatuses, generation of sustained net, public sector saving flows to finance both public and private investment may be a natural route for developing countries to take. Many, however, are now fiscally constrained. Countries with major external debt burdens, for example, direct potential saving flows aboard while aid recipients often use the domestic counterpart to their import support to cover recurrent fiscal deficits. Breaking out of such traps via both expenditure control (while maintaining the competence of the state) and tax reform should also come early in restructuring programs. Fiscal viability is also a necessary condition for financial sector reform. At the same time, as argued above, the public sector should maintain a limited but critical investment program.

Internally vs. externally oriented reform. On the whole, the Bretton Woods agencies advocate externally oriented reform, e.g. the removal of import quota regimes, tariff reduction, and decontrol of at least the current external account. However, a case for internally oriented packages can also be made. Agroexports are unlikely to rise in Tanzania, for example, unless the cooperatives are reorganized and the transport system improved, regardless of what happens to the exchange rate and producer prices. In a much larger economy, recent Indian experience, as described above, suggests that stimulation and intelligent regulation of internal competition is far more effective than trade liberalization as a means to spur industrial efficiency. Initial conditions, such as the extent of trade intervention and boundary conditions such as the country's size, obviously matter, but it is hard to see how a big push toward external liberalization will bear much fruit when the price system is not drastically out of line with the rest of the world's. Internally directed reform efforts may prove far more productive. Finally, as noted above, there is no reason why the external capital account should be liberalized before the current account; indeed, for effective regulation of internal financial markets, there is a great deal to be said in favor of capital controls.

State enterprise reform. One main difference between even the most socialistically oriented developing economies and Eastern Europe is that in the former group much economic activity remains in private hands. At the same time, a case can be made that in markets for food, fertilizer, agroexports, etc., public enterprises can be effective. The implication is that some developing country parastatals should be restructured, others privatized, and others simply closed down, all in connection with restructuring the assets of the banking system. In this area, especially, intelligent planning and flexible gradualism make sense, although when the rules change for any given firm, its management should clearly be given the message.

A critical path. These reflections suggest a standard critical path of reform, which can be modified to fit particular cases. It goes through the following stages:

1. A prior decision to guide the economy toward managed capitalism, with the government enjoying enough political support to undertake a degree of austerity and pursue the wealth and income redistributions that are implicit in wide-reaching reform.
2. A stabilization package supported by a social contract, leading to a stable inflation, sustainable fiscal and trade deficits, and a price system without extreme distortions.
3. Reorientation of the state's mentality and activity toward regulation rather than management of production; design of directed interventions and a public investment program in line with articulated agricultural and industrial strategies.

4. Steps should be taken to assure an early supply response in key sectors, for example exports. This will typically require action on several fronts, such as price reform, infrastructure investment, establishment of marketing channels, provision of credit, and so on.
5. If necessary, there should be a financial reform beginning with the banks, aimed at creating effective intermediation.
6. Steps toward fiscal reform and the generation of a sustained flow of public saving, perhaps supplemented by foreign aid.
7. A degree of trade liberalization and removal of distortions, but no wholesale opening of the external current and (especially) the capital accounts. Policies aimed at stimulating internal competition and efficient acquisition of new technology should be vigorously pursued.
8. Rationalization and some privatization of state enterprises; liquidation of the worst public firms.
9. Gradual elaboration of an industrial/trade strategy based on selective interventions in a broadly open system; further development of financial intermediation; better communication between public and private sector regarding economic goals and crucial areas for public intervention.

Speed of transition. Once stabilization is attained, deliberate speed in reform is a sensible rule. Widespread privatization cannot happen in a day. It may also make sense to phase in price reforms in terms of providing effective protection to viable import substituting and exporting sectors, while holding down unproductive consumption (assuming that the thirst for "incentive imports" is not too intense). At least some positive benefits from restructuring for the public and productive enterprises should be forthcoming in a fairly short period, perhaps from infusions of foreign assistance, but, more durably, from a visible supply response in critical producing and income-generating sectors.

Credibility. At least four considerations are important here: the statement of a target model, graceful correction of mistakes, avoidance of indecision and unnecessary policy reversals, and staying away from policy announcements that open sure options for speculative gains.

The target model should be effectively enunciated, and expressed in state actions and legislation in line with local norms. Under mixed capitalism, the private sector is more economically important than the state, and should be brought into the reform process from the start.

Errors will surely be made in designing and implementing reforms—stabilization is not easy, and the task of creating a new economic system is far more complex. The main point is that missteps should be recognized and rectified as soon as possible; if promises cannot be honored, explanations are in order, and recompense may have to be paid. Again, since the private sector is essential to reform, it makes no sense to turn entrepreneurs or enterprises into scapegoats for the government's mistakes.

Policy changes caused by prior bad decisions or changed circumstances should be properly explained and, perhaps, (given contingencies) even anticipated. Relating them to the target model is an essential public relations task, while locking oneself into a policy which has failed just to preserve face can be a fatal mistake.

Preannouncement of policy stances can also be an error. If a consumer price increase is proclaimed for tomorrow, there will certainly be a run on the market today, with possibly devastating effects on stocks. If the nominal exchange rate is firmly stated to be frozen while inflation marches on unchecked, there is a clear incentive for capital flight in anticipation of the "corrective" maxidevaluation that will ultimately come.

The bottom line is that perceived uncertainty, indecision about the goals of reform, lashing out at the private sector when it is supposed to be the agent of change, and creation of one-way speculative options can all derail the restructuring train. On the other hand, reformers may gain credibility if they recognize their own errors and changed circumstances, and act accordingly forthwith.

REFERENCES

Shapiro, Helen, and Lance Taylor. "The State and Industrial Strategy," *World Development*, Vol. 18, 1990: pp. 861–878.

Taylor, Lance. *Varieties of Stabilization Experience*, Oxford: Clarendon Press, 1988.

———. *Foreign Resource Flows and Developing Growth*, Helsinki: WIDER, 1991.

Part III
Structural Adjustment in Latin America

4

Policy Reform in Latin America in the 1980s

John Williamson

Most of the elements of what is today understood by the term "policy reform" were already a subject of debate in Latin America in 1980, but, at that time, they were at best controversial and, in most cases, a minority viewpoint. They jelled into a new conventional wisdom only late in the decade. Chapter 4 starts by sketching the content of this new conventional wisdom. It proceeds to discuss where and to what extent it had been implemented by the end of 1989. In the final section I speculate on the reasons for the remarkable change in policy attitudes that occurred in the second half of the decade.

CONTENT

When I first addressed this subject (Williamson 1989, reproduced as Chapter 2 in Williamson, ed., 1990), I suggested a 10-point taxonomy of the policy reforms being urged on Latin America by "Washington," meaning primarily the World Bank, the IMF, and the U.S. government. I labeled this the "Washington consensus," but I have subsequently come to regret the term, partly because it suggests wider agreement than actually exists, but mainly because it seems to have been interpreted by some as a prejudgment of the question discussed in the final section of this chapter: namely, from what source the change in policy attitudes originated. So far as substance is concerned, however, I still think that my original effort captured most of what policy reform has been about, so I summarize my taxonomy here.

Fiscal Discipline. Budget deficits, properly measured to include provincial governments, state enterprises, and the central bank, should be small enough to be financed without recourse to the inflation tax. This, typically, implies a primary surplus (i.e., before adding debt service to expenditure) of several percent of GDP, and an operational deficit (i.e., the deficit disregarding that part of the interest bill that simply compensates for inflation) of no more than about 2 percent of GDP.

Public Expenditure Priorities. Policy reform consists in redirecting expenditure from politically sensitive areas which typically receive more resources than their economic return can justify, like administration, defense, indiscriminate subsidies, and white elephants, toward neglected fields with high economic returns and the potential to improve income distribution, like primary health and education, and infrastructure.

Tax Reform involves broadening the tax base and cutting marginal tax rates. The aim is to sharpen incentives and improve horizontal equity without lowering realized progressivity. Improved tax administration is an important aspect of broadening the base in the Latin American context. Taxing interest earned on assets held abroad ("flight capital") should be another high priority for broadening the tax base in the coming decade.

Financial Liberalization. The ultimate objective is market-determined interest rates, but experience has shown that, under conditions of a chronic lack of confidence, market-determined rates can be so high as to threaten the financial solvency of productive enterprises and of government. Under that circumstance a sensible interim objective is the abolition of preferential interest rates for privileged borrowers and the achievement of a moderately positive real interest rate.

Exchange Rates. Countries need a unified (at least for trade transactions) exchange rate set at a level sufficiently competitive to induce a rapid growth in nontraditional exports, and effectively managed so as to assure exporters that this competitiveness will be maintained in the future.

Trade Liberalization. Quantitative trade restrictions should be rapidly replaced by tariffs, and these should be progressively reduced until a uniform low tariff in the range of 10 percent or, at most, around 20 percent is achieved. There is, however, some disagreement about the speed with which tariffs should be phased out (with recommendations falling in a band between 3 and 10 years), and about whether it is advisable to slow down the process of liberalization when macroeconomic conditions (recession and payments deficit) are adverse.

Foreign Direct Investment. Barriers impeding the entry of foreign firms should be abolished; foreign and domestic firms should be allowed to compete on equal terms.

Privatization. State enterprises should be privatized.

Deregulation. Governments should abolish regulations that impede the entry of new firms or restrict competition, and ensure that all regulations are justified by such criteria as safety, environmental protection, or prudential supervision of financial institutions.

Property Rights. The legal system should provide secure property rights without excessive costs, and make these available to the informal sector.

I compared my own taxonomy outlined above with the list of policy reforms presented by Stanley Fischer in the paper included in this volume. He mentioned no less than eight of the ten reforms on my list. The two that he passed by were elimination of barriers to foreign direct investment, and property rights (which has always been the Cinderella of the list; only in the East European context has the World Bank given priority to this subject).

Fischer also included three topics that were not among my ten. The first was agriculture; but that is a topic of primary importance to Africa rather than to Latin America. The second was targeted interventions to help the poor. When I invented my taxonomy I debated whether I could conscientiously include that among Washington's policy priorities, and decided, to my regret, that the Reagan assault on concern for distributive objectives had still not been reversed. But attitudes have been changing, and I am delighted to accept Fischer's assurance that this objective again commands acceptance. Fischer's third addition was administrative reform of state enterprises, including hardening of their budget constraints. I suspect that this is again a topic inspired primarily by concerns regarding Africa, but there is ample scope for it to be applied in Latin America as well, in those cases where state enterprises cannot be privatized. On the whole, I am reassured by this comparison that my taxonomy provided a reasonable summary of what mainstream Washington had been seeking.

THE COURSE OF POLICY REFORM

The program of policy reform sketched above, which may be summarized as macroeconomic prudence, microeconomic liberalization,[1] and outward orientation, is very different to the easy acquiescence in budget deficits and foreign borrowing, the reliance on state enterprises, the import substitution and dependency theory that still flourished in Latin America in 1980.[2] Where and when did the changes start?

The first major break with the *ancien régime* consisted of the Southern Cone liberalization programs of the late 1970s. Argentina, Chile, and Uruguay all liberalized trade, the financial system, and the capital account (though Chile was more restrained in the latter regard), and launched stabilization programs that aimed to end inflation by relying on international arbitrage and a preprogrammed deceleration in the rate of depreciation of the currency. These programs all ended in fiasco even before the debt crisis broke, which implies that their failure must be explained by features of the design of the reform programs. Four failures of design/implementation have been pinpointed in subsequent analysis (among others, Ardito Barletta et al. 1983, and Corbo and de Melo 1987):

1. It is now generally agreed that the capital account is the last thing that should be liberalized. Failure to heed this advice in an era when funds were readily available on the international capital market led to overvalued currencies, erosion of the productive capacity of the tradable goods sector, and excessive buildup in foreign debt (much of which was used to finance capital flight).
2. Argentina (though not Chile) failed to establish fiscal discipline.
3. Financial deregulation was not accompanied by a strengthening of prudential supervision.
4. Arbitrage proved to be an insufficiently powerful mechanism to stop inflation in Chile until the currency had become unsustainably overvalued, given the existence of backward-looking wage indexation.

The next major round of policy changes in the region occurred in response to the outbreak of the debt crisis in August 1982. The initial policy reactions did include some changes that are consistent with the program of policy reform sketched above, notably currency devaluation and fiscal retrenchment, but they also included measures that went in exactly the opposite direction, such as an intensification of import restrictions and nationalization of the banks in Mexico in late 1982. The macroeconomic reactions look more like the standard response to a balance of payments crisis than the beginning of a shift to a new policy model. Indeed, at that time, everyone hoped that creditworthiness would be restored quickly, whereupon the banks would begin to lend again, and growth could resume. All this was expected to occur without the need for any fundamental change in the policy regime.

The realization that growth was not going to resume on the basis of the old model, and hence that major changes were in order, began to dawn in the middle of the decade. The program of radical liberalization that accompanied the stabilization of the Bolivian hyperinflation by the incoming Paz Estenssoro administration in August 1985 was the first dramatic case of policy reform, as that term is now used. But, in fact, already in 1984 the Chilean government had shifted from crisis management to a new program of structural adjustment based explicitly on a commitment to export-led growth. It was also in 1985 that Mexico initiated the radical program of import liberalization that has transformed its economy from one of the most autarkic in the world to one sufficiently open to contemplate a free trade arrangement with the United States. (It was also in that year that the then U.S. Secretary of the Treasury, James Baker, called for a supply-side strategy for the resumption of growth in debtor countries, in his speech to the IMF-World Bank Annual Meetings in Seoul.)

Bolivia, Chile, and Mexico, plus Costa Rica and perhaps Uruguay among the small countries, are the ones in which policy reform was adopted sufficiently early and comprehensively to justify hoping that results might already be visible. Those results are, in fact, still rather mixed. Chile is a clear success story by almost any criterion save that of the Bundesbank (inflation has never got down even to single digits). Costa Rica has also had a reasonable growth rate (though one that started from a base that had fallen back severely during the crisis) combined with inflation that is low by the standards of the region, and a vigorous growth of nontraditional exports. Mexico has also re-established positive per capita growth, though it remains much below that registered during the precrisis boom. But both Bolivia and Uruguay can claim to have done no more than stop the rot. Clearly, the evidence does not justify a claim that even determined policy reform can be guaranteed to work quickly. Those initiating policy reform had better understand that this is a remedy whose promise is long-term. Unrealistic hopes for quick success that induce constant policy shifts could jeopardize the prospects of any success at all.

A new wave of policy reform came at the end of the decade, following electoral success by candidates who formerly had a populist reputation: Carlos Andres Pérez in Venezuela and Carlos Menem in Argentina. The process continued after the turn of the decade in Brazil, Peru, and Colombia (a country whose macroeconomic policy was never in need of much policy reform, as demonstrated, inter alia, by its relatively prompt response to the discovery that it could not ride out the difficulties of the early 1980s, but whose microeconomic policies remained "mercantilist"). Policy reform has become a new conventional wisdom.

My 1990 study attempted to summarize how much policy reform had been undertaken by the turn of the decade in 10 countries and in 9 of the 10 areas listed above. (The tenth topic, property rights, did not elicit enough answers from the authors of the country studies to justify inclusion in the table.) Table 4.1, which is reproduced from the 1990 study and has not been updated, displays the judgments that I made, based primarily on the country studies prepared for the conference. I concluded that the record showed quite an impressive effort to institute policy reform.

REASONS FOR POLICY REFORM

The question that remains is why Latin America has made this remarkably widespread and relatively rapid change in its policy stance. Two possible explanations have been suggested by Miles Kahler (in Joan Nelson, 1990, p. 33): (1) that a resurgent orthodoxy was imposed on a cowed but unconverted South; and (2) that it represented a case of social learning.

I find the first explanation quite unconvincing. First, if I have represented correctly the content of current policy reforms, it differs in important respects from any old orthodoxy that I can recall. Consider the divergences (listed above) from the Chicago-inspired Southern Cone programs of the late 1970s. Or ask which exponents of orthodoxy have worried about redirecting public expenditure priorities, rather than cutting public expenditure in the easiest way possible, or about tax reform or deregulation. If we allow Stanley Fischer to add targeted interventions to help the poor to the list of policy reforms, the agenda looks even less orthodox. Second, the Institute's 1989 conference (reported in Williamson 1990) suggested that much of the (Latin American part of the) South had indeed been converted, and I would even say that it is easy to identify individual economists whose views have evolved in that direction over the period.[3] Third, the history of international relations is not noted for instances of countries that have done things that they conceived to be against their national interests because they were overawed by a fear of international disapproval; the Iraqi defiance of UN sanctions prior to its military defeat is more typical.

The alternative explanation, that this is a case of "social learning," suggests that the main impetus behind policy reform has been provided by the power of example. Some countries have succeeded in developing in the period since the Second World War—Spain, and the East Asian NICs, for example. Now Southeast Asia and Chile (and little Mauritius) are following the same path. Their policies have differed in a number of respects, but all of them come closer to macroeconomic prudence, reliance on markets and outward orientation than to the prevalent Latin American model of a decade ago. Intellectuals and policymakers see what works, and eventually they draw the right conclusions.

My use of the term "Washington consensus" to describe the agenda of policy reforms that currently constitute the conventional wisdom apparently had the unfortunate effect of suggesting to some that I perceived Washington to have figured out what Latin American countries should do, leaving them with the role of doing as they were told. It was not my intention to give that impression. In fact, I regard both Washington and Latin America as having been part of a worldwide intellectual trend, to which both have contributed (with the most influential Latin American contributions having come from Hernando de Soto's Instituto Libertad y Democracia in Lima). I even have the impression, based on his chapter in this book, that Lance Taylor is catching up with the trend!

REFERENCES

Ardito Barletta, Nicolas, Mario Blejer and Luis Landau, eds. *Economic Liberalization and Stabilization Policies in Argentina, Chile, and Uruguay* (Washington: World Bank), 1983.

Corbo, Vittorio, "Development Strategies and Policies in   Latin America: A Historical Perspective," mimeo, World Bank, 1991.

Corbo, Vittorio, and Jaime de Melo, "Lessons from the   Southern Cone Policy Reforms," *World Bank Research Observer*, vol. 2, no. 2, 1987.

Nelson, Joan M., ed., *Economic Crisis and Policy Choice* (Princeton: Princeton University Press), 1990.

Williamson, John, "What Washington Means by Policy Reform," reproduced as Chapter 2 in Williamson (1990), 1989.

———, ed., *Latin American Adjustment: How Much Has Happened?* (Washington: Institute for International Economics), 1990.

NOTES

1. In view of Lance Taylor's position (see chapter 3 in this book), it is worth emphasizing that liberalization is about strengthening markets rather than weakening the state. It is quite true that this process involves state withdrawal from a number of activities, but, in many cases, liberalization involves a change in the form of state action rather than the arrival of laissez-faire. For example, financial liberalization involves getting the state out of the business of deciding who should receive credit; but it is now widely recognized that financial liberalization demands a strengthening of prudential supervision if the risk of financial crises is to be contained. A state too weak to supervise the financial system properly will jeopardize the functioning of the market. Unfortunately, no one has yet invented a neat way to summarize the change in the role of the state that is needed to support a market economy.

2. For a good discussion of the evolution of development strategy in Latin America, see Corbo (1991).

3. Incidentally, I count myself among their number, which may help to answer the question I have sometimes been asked as to whether my taxonomy was supposed to be an account of what others advocated or a description of what I would recommend. It was in fact intended to be the former. I do sympathize with all the items on the program, but my own manifesto would have come out somewhat differently, with an explicit emphasis on redirecting public expenditures to benefit the poor (including Fischer's targeted interventions), reforming tax systems to internalize environmental externalities, land reform, and a major priority to the extension of birth control.

5

Changing Production Patterns with Social Equity and Environmental Sustainability

Fernando Fajnzylber

INTRODUCTION

The primary focus of my remarks in this chapter will be the document originally entitled *Changing Production Patterns with Social Equity*, in which ECLAC presented its development proposal for the 1990s to the governments of Latin America.[1] The original and complete document is readily available elsewhere, but here I will draw your attention to some facets which I feel are particularly relevant to this book.

First, I will refer to the questions which ECLAC's proposal attempted to answer and to the method used for formulating its questions, since this may be just as important as the answers it proposes. In the second part, which concerns the central points that I would like to discuss, I will attempt to focus on the particular aspects of those answers that are most directly related to the subject of environmental sustainability. In the third and final part, I will outline the principal messages of the entire document, as well as those areas which might be thought of as "pending": i.e., subject areas which have not yet been fully explored and in which we are now working. Environmental sustainability is one of those subject areas. Although environmental sustainability is one of the proposal's objectives, and figures as an integral part of the line of reasoning developed in the document and as the subject of many of the examples cited therein, ECLAC is still just beginning to address this issue.

QUESTIONS AND METHODOLOGY

The proposal attempted to answer three main questions. The first question is: Can Latin America perpetuate its previous development pattern? If the answer to this question is "no," as ECLAC indeed contends that it is, then the second question is: In what direction should Latin America reorient its development? Once that has been determined, then the third question is: How is this to be done? What policies and institutions are needed in order to promote this change in Latin American development?

Given the scope of these questions, I feel it is important to discuss the method that was used to formulate ECLAC's proposal. Five different types of analyses were undertaken in order to answer the questions set out above.

First, we analyzed the baseline situation, i.e., what occurred in Latin America during the closing years of the 1980s, which were a decade of "painful lessons" for the region. Second, we examined the international context. No proposal concerning the present development of Latin America can fail to incorporate, and to internalize, the international framework for that development effort. Third, we undertook a comparative study of the history of the Latin American development process and the development of other countries which were also late-comers to the industrialization process. In other words, we conducted a long-term comparative study for the purpose of identifying those factors which are specific to this region. Fourth, we looked at the actual situation and attempted to pinpoint examples, illustrations and sets of circumstances which indicated the direction in which events were moving. Finally, throughout the period during which the proposal was being formulated, we engaged in an ongoing dialogue with some of the leading actors in the development process of Latin America at the public, private and academic levels.

I mention these methodological details in order to highlight a fundamental difference between this proposal and other development proposals which may at times be highly attractive precisely because of their simplicity. ECLAC's proposal is not so simple, and its essential points will probably not be so easy to grasp. Why? Because it has been built on the basis of a real-world situation, and a proposal which is based on the real world is necessarily more complex than a proposal derived from a simple theoretical model which is alluring precisely because, during times of turmoil such as those we are now living through in the region, simplicity has an especially strong appeal.

This proposal was not derived from a simple theoretical model, a model whose comparison with the real situation was used as a means of identifying the differences between the two, whereupon its authors say: "Now all we have to do is eliminate everything in the real situation that doesn't fit the model."

The point of departure for this proposal was, as I have previously indicated, the immediate situation, the downstream situation, the external context, very real events in sectors, agents and enterprises of the region and, finally, the perceptions of some of the agents whose behavior and views have an impact on development. I should add that specialists with a variety of different backgrounds, orientations and attitudes took part in that undertaking. Thus, it constituted an attempt to arrive at a sensible and feasible proposal based on internal and external realities as well as on the aspirations of the region.

ON CONTENT

Here, I will concentrate on two main aspects of those questions: (1) Why can we not continue as before? and (2) What is the proposal's line of reasoning as regards the direction of change?

All the governments around the globe, in all the continents, whatever their geographic position, geopolitical situation, and cultural context, appear to share two major objectives, regardless of the different ways in which we may interpret their meaning: growth and social equity. The first step in exploring this subject is to see what has been done in Latin America as regards the achievement of these two objectives.[2]

Figure 5.1 provides a clear picture, spanning quite a long period of time, of how we have been doing in terms of growth and social equity; we are not going to discuss the current situation or particular cases in this connection because what interests us here are those factors which are specific to Latin America. This matrix, in which the countries' placement corresponds to their performance in terms of growth and social equity, reveals the following: some countries, such as Brazil, Mexico, Colombia and a number of others, have been particularly successful in achieving growth, while some other countries, such as Argentina and Uruguay, have had notable success in promoting social equity. (The time period we are considering for these purposes is 1965–1985, because this permits it to use indicators that can be compared with those of other areas of the world.) A third group of countries has not met with success in terms of either growth or social equity; in other words, they have not distinguished themselves by being particularly dynamic or equitable. But the most important thing which this figure shows us is that no country in Latin America has managed to combine growth with social equity.

Since we are a rent-seeking and self-complacent continent, for quite some time we thought this was a normal state of affairs, that there was a tradeoff between growth and social equity. Thus, we thought that

Equity: <u>40% Lowest Income</u> (1)
          10% Highest Income

	< 0.4		≥ 0.4
< 2.4	Bolivia Chile Costa Rica El Salvador Guatemala	Haiti Honduras Nicaragua Peru Venezuela	Argentina Uruguay
	GDP: 21.0 (2) Population: 22.1 (2)		GDP: 13.0 (2) Population: 8.7 (2)
≥ 2.4	Brazil Colombia Dominican Republic Ecuador Mexico	Panama Paraguay	
	GDP: 66.0 (2) Population: 69.2 (2)		

GDP per Capita Growth Rate

(1) The Equity measure of 0.4 is half the equity measure for industrialized countries.
(2) Percentage of countries in Figure (all of Latin America).

Source: Joint ECLAC/UNIDO Industry and Technology Division.

Figure 5.1 Latin America: Growth-Equity Matrix

those countries which had done well in terms of growth might later on have more success in promoting social equity, and vice versa. But then we began to realize that this "empty box" situation, in which no one managed to couple growth with social equity, did not apply to the whole world.

Using the same indicators, the same time period and the same sources of information in all cases, we discovered that there are countries in other parts of the developing world which, like those of Latin America, have had some measure of success as regards either growth or social equity (but not both) or which have not made any major advances in either of the two. But the most important thing we learned was that 73 percent of the economic activity of developing countries in other parts of the world—once again, according to the same indicators and parameters and during the same period of time—is accounted for by countries which have indeed managed to combine growth with social equity. In other words, something is wrong in Latin America. This inability to reconcile growth with social equity is not an inherent characteristic of newly industrialized countries. In all the countries shown in the "box" which, in the case of Latin America, is "empty," industrialization is just as recent a phenomenon as it is in the region (see Figure 5.2).

The next question is: What differentiates this continent, which has not managed to reconcile growth with social equity, from these other countries, which have differing geographic situations, differing cultures, differing political systems and differing supplies of natural resources? This is a crucial question because in answering it we will be identifying those factors which are specific to Latin America; until we know them, we will not be able to determine what types of proposals will be functional in the specific context created by those factors.

We do not have sufficient space here for a detailed discussion of the significance of these questions. However, we do have an important clue about what sets this continent apart from other developing regions.

What does Table 5.1 show us? It shows us the following: that our greatest contribution to mankind takes the form of population. Latin America contains 8 percent of the population of this planet. If we begin to look at what this population does, we see that its GDP represents 6 percent of the world total, its industrial output is 6 percent, its production of machinery and equipment . . . and so on, down to our contribution to scientific literature, which accounts for 1 percent of the world total. In other words, one particular trait of this continent, which is not uncommon in rent-seeking societies, is that we add little intellectual value to what we do, to our people, or to our resources. Moreover, our foothold in the international market is a precarious one. We will return to this last point later on, but, for now, we can sum up the foregoing as follows: one of the characteristic traits of Latin America that is brought out by comparison with other regions—which were also late-comers to the industrialization process but have nonetheless reconciled growth with social equity—is its limited capacity for adding intellectual value to its resources and its people and, as a consequence, its precarious international position.

Based on these so readily discernible factors, which are no more than the point of departure for our thoughts on this subject, we can begin to ask ourselves how we should go about seeking solutions for

Equity: <u>40% Lowest Income</u> (2)
          10% Highest Income

	< 0.4	≥ 0.4
< 2.4	Cote d'Ivoire Kenya Philippines Zambia GDP: 3.5 (3) Population: 3.8 (3)	Bangladesh India GDP: 17.1 (3) Population: 35.1 (3)
≥ 2.4	Malaysia Mauritius Turkey GDP: 6.4 (3) Population: 2.7 (3)	China Portugal Egypt Republic of Hong Kong Korea Hungary Spain Indonesia Sri Lanka Israel Thailand Yugoslavia GDP: 73.0 (3) Population: 58.4 (3)

GDP per Capita Growth Rate

(1) These countries represent 80.2% of the population and 79.5% of GDP of the total developing countries excluding Latin America.

(2) The Equity measure of 0.4 is half the equity measure for industrialized countries.

(3) Percentage of countries in Figure.

Source: Joint ECLAC/UNIDO Industry and Technology Division.

Figure 5.2 Other Developing Countries: Growth-Equity Matrix (1)

this problem. At the very outset, we know that they are not going to be trivial solutions, because our problems are not trivial. Trivial solutions may be very attractive by virtue of their simplicity, but in all probability they will not be effective, because the situation underlying the percentage figures constitutes a problem with far-reaching implications. Moreover, it is a problem which has an impact in terms of the very different way in which Latin America approaches the subject of environmental sustainability.

Table 5.1 Latin America's Participation in World Total
Circa 1985

Category	Percent of World Total
Population	8.3
Gross Domestic Product	6.0
Manufacturing Product	6.0
Capital Goods	3.2
Engineers and Scientists in Research and Development	2.5
Research and Development Resources	1.3
Manufactured Exports (1)	1.8
Scientific Authorship	1.3

(1) Manufactured exports: SITC, Sections 5-8, excluding Division 68.

Source: Joint ECLAC/UNIDO Industry and Technology Division. Calculations based on official figures.

Now we are prepared to turn back to the first question: Can Latin America continue as before? The answer, based on what has been said, is "no, it cannot." The model worked so long as the region realized a large profit from its natural resources, had access to external credit, and had the possibility of running a fiscal deficit which allowed it to postpone internal decision-making. However, these three inertial forces—which enabled Latin America to perpetuate an uncreative development pattern that rendered it incapable of combining growth with social equity—have been depleted. Thus, there is no other alternative, regardless of how the events of the past are assessed. This pattern of development cannot be prolonged further because neither the world nor our societies are willing to do so.

Let us now move on to the second question. Since the answer to question one is negative, in what direction should we steer our development? Which course of development should we now consider? To answer this question we must take a closer look at the rationale that underlies what ECLAC is proposing.[3]

Here we have a very simplified outline, as is necessary in this type of presentation, of the main postulates and cause-and-effect relationships set forth in the proposal. Social equity and growth are the primary objectives. Competitiveness can contribute to growth. It can also contribute to social equity, but it is clearly not enough in itself to resolve the problem of equity. That is why we need redistributive policies as well (see Figure 5.3).

There are two kinds of competitiveness. First, there is the type which disregards environmental sustainability and technical progress. This is what we call "spurious competitiveness," because it is based on the depredation of natural resources and declining wages. Second, there is "genuine competitiveness," which differs from the former precisely in that it incorporates technical change and safeguards environmental sustainability.

In today's world, environmental sustainability is a competitive factor, although at times it may not be expressly thought of in those terms. Yet there can be no environmental sustainability without technical progress. In the case of Latin America, technical progress is furthered by the opening of the economy when this process is undertaken on a rational basis; i.e., when agents realize that the absorption of technical progress is necessary for their survival.

Growth is clearly conducive to technical progress. We might say that, in very general terms, this provides a simplified outline of the proposal's rationale. Three of the central elements of this proposal set it apart from other development proposals: the relationships among technical progress, sustainability and competitiveness.[4]

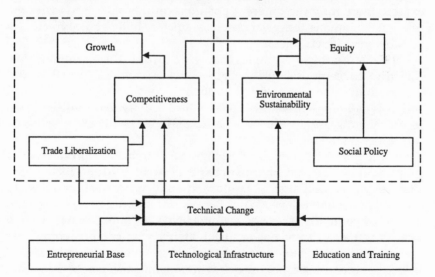

Figure 5.3 Causal Relations

The diagram shown in Figure 5.3 also highlights the contrasts between our approach to the issue and some of the other ways in which it has been addressed. Before citing some relevant examples, there are two extreme cases which, clearly, do not correspond to the ideas that I present here.

The thesis known as the "deep ecology" approach stresses three of the terms which appear in Figure 5.3: *sustainability, social equity* and *social policy*. The other thesis, which represents a strictly economistic approach to the issue, primarily emphasizes *openness, competitiveness* and *growth*.

These two propositions appear to be incompatible, since they seem to suggest that it is necessary to choose between sustainability and competitiveness, and between social equity and growth. In fact, they definitely do become incompatible if the potential contribution of technical progress is not taken into account.

The extent to which these proposals disregard the element of technical progress determines the extent of incompatibility between sustainability and competitiveness, and between growth and social equity. But what I wish to demonstrate here is precisely that their incompatibility disappears when we incorporate this dimension, which is not solely a physical/technological issue but also an institutional, organizational and educational question, a question of changing certain attitudes that are characteristic of societies which are not overly concerned with the future, with technical progress, risk and innovation.

Thus, what I would like to underscore by means of the following examples—on the understanding that the purpose of this chapter is to explore more fully the different positions on this subject—is why the relationship among technical progress, sustainability and competitiveness is such a crucial factor.

Let us look at three examples that will illustrate these relationships. The first concerns the relationship between technical progress and sustainability; the second refers to the relationship between technical progress and competitiveness; and the third deals with the link between technical progress, on the one hand, and competitiveness and sustainability on the other.

Finland's forestry industry (see Figure 5.4) trebled its production of pulp and quadrupled its output of paper between 1970 and 1988. At the same time, its discharge of liquid and solid wastes was reduced to one-fifth its previous level. Why? Because Finland, a country subject to conditions similar to those of the other Nordic countries, has made a determined effort to reconcile sustainability with competitiveness by adding intellectual value and technical progress to its natural resource base. The second example is also drawn from the same part of the world. The Nordic countries have, although to a lesser extent than Latin

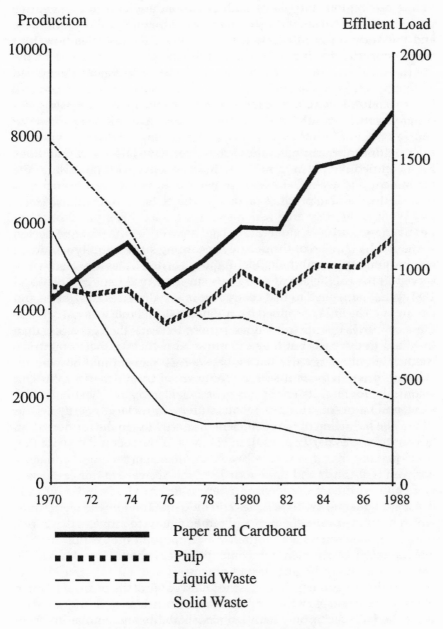

Production   Effluent Load

— Paper and Cardboard

▪▪▪▪▪▪▪▪▪ Pulp

– – – – – Liquid Waste

——— Solid Waste

Source: <u>Trends in the Finnish Forest Industry</u>. 1990.

Figure 5.4 Finland: Forest Industry Production and Effluent Load,
1970–1988 (In thousands of tons)

America, a relatively generous endowment of natural resources, but unlike our region, they have built the foundations of a competitive position in the world market on the basis of that natural resource base and the addition of intellectual value. Table 5.2 illustrates how four small countries having a very small share (about 1 percent) in the international market for capital goods have nonetheless developed certain product lines in which they have achieved excellence. Denmark has specialized in cold storage equipment and food processing machinery, and Finland, Norway and Sweden have followed a similar course of action in other areas. Thus, by adding intellectual value to their natural resource base, these countries have laid the foundations for a competitive position not only in those resources, but also in the equipment and technical expertise needed to tap those resources, to process them and to produce related products. Now for the third example. What is the only area which synthesizes technical progress, competitiveness and sustainability? The answer is the energy sector, without which much of the debate concerning sustainability would, in our judgment, be unintelligible. Figure 5.5 illustrates the trends observed in the coefficient of energy use in the world between 1970 and 1987. What happened to that coefficient in the United States, Japan and Germany? The index dropped from 150 to 100, and this was not because these countries did not grow during those 18 years; they grew less than they had in the past, but they did grow. Nonetheless, these countries' coefficients of energy use fell by between 40 percent and 50 percent. What occurred in the rent-seeking continent of Latin America? Without technical progress, its energy use coefficient remained virtually constant, and Latin America, as a whole, suffers from a large energy deficit. Why? The reduction of the coefficient of energy use in the former group of countries was partly a result of changes in the sectoral distribution of energy use, but it was chiefly a consequence of technical progress. Between two-thirds and three-fourths of the decrease in this coefficient is accounted for by the incorporation of technical advances into the design of housing, motor vehicles and industries and by the regulations which prompt entrepreneurial and public agents to move in that direction. Competitiveness was certainly an important motivation for that technological effort. Genuine competitiveness cannot be attained by wasting and despoiling natural resources.

These three examples illustrate the "hard core" of the proposal, which seeks to reconcile growth with social equity and, in so doing, to overcome the false dichotomy between sustainability and competitiveness on the basis of the absorption of technical progress.

Bearing in mind all that has been said above, let us now try to understand just what sets this region apart from other developing regions in terms of its international position.

Table 5.2 Northern Europe's Specialization in Engineering Products,
by Country and Category
1987

Country	Category	Percent of World Total
Denmark	Refrigerating equipment, non-domestic	4.30
	Transmission apparatus, radio or television	3.50
	Food processing machinery	3.40
	All Engineering Products	**.74**
Finland	Paper and pulp machinery	9.70
	Ships and boats	3.00
	Mechanical handling of equipment and parts	2.80
	All Engineering Products	**.67**
Norway	Ships and boats	8.70
	Agricultural machinery	1.20
	Paper and pulp machinery	1.00
	All Engineering Products	**.45**
Sweden	Electrical apparatus for telephone and telegraph	7.50
	Paper and pulp machinery	6.71
	Motor vehicles for transport of goods	6.10
	All Engineering Products	**2.38**

Source: Joint ECLAC/UNIDO Industry and Technology
Division, based on data from United Nations, Bulletin of
Statistics on World Trade in Engineering Products,
1987. U.N. Publication, Sales No. E/F/R/89.II.E.5.

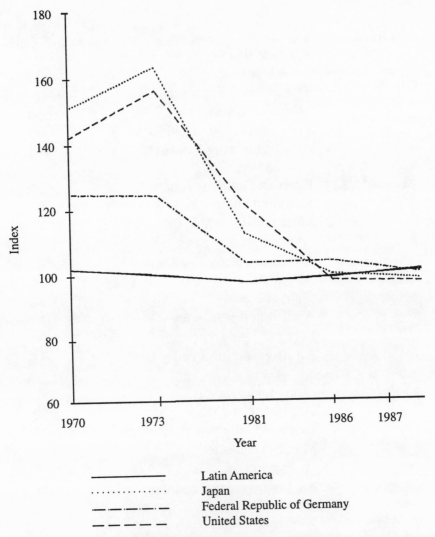

Source: Joint ECLAC/UNIDO Industry and Technology Division, based
on data from OECD and OLADE.

Figure 5.5 Energy Intensity Latin America and OECD Countries
(Base Year 1985 = 100)

Latin America is a continent which is richly endowed with natural resources (see Table 5.3). Of the 10 largest enterprises in each of the Latin American countries (which account for over 30 percent of the GDP of the medium-sized countries and for approximately 15 percent of that of the large countries), those that deal with natural resources generated nearly 80 percent of total sales in the medium-sized countries and approximately 60 percent of total sales in Brazil and Mexico, the two largest countries.

In other words, it would be a striking departure from reality, to say the least, to talk about the development of Latin America without referring to its natural resource base. Let us see how this situation is reflected in the region's position in the economy; to do so, we must first analyze what has happened in terms of the imports of the developed countries and particularly those of the large and dynamic OECD market, although it is obviously not the only important import market. Figure 5.6 shows how the pattern of what developed countries import from all over the world has changed during the past 10 years; it bears out what we would have expected: as a proportion of total OECD imports, natural resources declined from 14 percent to 10 percent, energy imports fell from 20 percent to 10 percent, that natural resource–based manufactures grew at almost the same pace as total growth, thereby decreasing slightly; and over the past decade the type of imports which showed real growth were manufactures not based on natural resources, which climbed from 50 percent to 65 percent.

When exports from Latin America are compared to that pattern, our initial reaction would be to say that Latin America was following international market trends quite closely: the proportion of natural resources and fuels in total exports declined slightly and that of non-natural resource based manufactures rose slightly. Unfortunately, this pattern is the result of the changes that have occurred in only two countries: Brazil and Mexico. The export pattern of the rest of Latin America has remained virtually unchanged over the past 12 years.

Figures 5.7 and 5.8 show Latin America as a supplier of natural resources to the developed countries. However, Latin America supplies barely 10 percent of the nonfuel natural resources imported by the developed countries. What is surprising and, to some extent, a new development is that the seven largest developed countries themselves (the so-called "G7"), supply over 30 percent of the natural resources imported by the developed countries as a whole; if the Mediterranean, Scandinavian and Eastern European countries are added to the picture, what we will see is that Latin America's natural resource exports amount to little more than a "drop in the bucket" as compared to the natural resources that the countries of the "North" themselves export to the OECD.

Table 5.3 Sectoral Composition of Sales of the Ten Leading Enterprises and Overall Percentage of Gross Domestic Product

1989

(In percent)

Sector	Argentina	Brazil	Chile	Colombia	Mexico	Peru	Venezuela	All Latin America
Natural Resources (1)	5.4	13.0	59.6	0.0	0.0	44.8	14.3	13.0
Petroleum	57.6	39.3	24.8	50.8	56.3	36.5	71.5	65.9
Manufacturing								
Transport Equipment	5.4	7.2	...	6.0	26.5	...	...	...
Capital Goods	0.0	11.3	...	0.0	0.0	...	...	...
Non-Resource Based	5.4	18.5	0.0	6.0	26.5	0.0	1.6	11.3
Resource Based	12.4	14.6	7.9	21.2	3.5	5.1	4.5	4.9
Other Sectors	19.2	14.6	3.7	22.0	13.7	13.6	8.1	4.9
All Sales	100.0	100.0	100.0	100.0	100.0	100.0	100.0	100.0
All Sales as Percent of GDP	31.4	14.6	38.2	14.9	14.7	20.9	29.5	10.7

(1) Petroleum excluded.

Source: Joint ECLAC/UNIDO Industry and Technology Division.

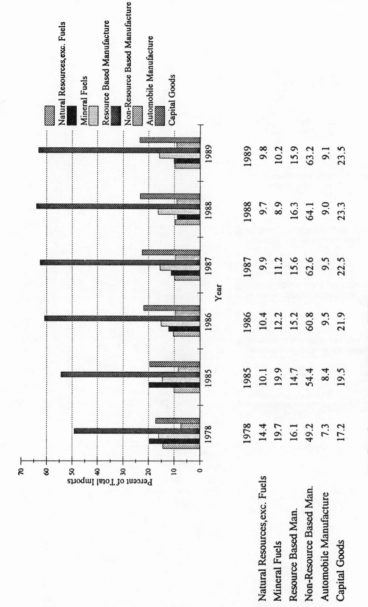

	1978	1985	1986	1987	1988	1989
Natural Resources,exc. Fuels	14.4	10.1	10.4	9.9	9.7	9.8
Mineral Fuels	19.7	19.9	12.2	11.2	8.9	10.2
Resource Based Man.	16.1	14.7	15.2	15.6	16.3	15.9
Non-Resource Based Man.	49.2	54.4	60.8	62.6	64.1	63.2
Automobile Manufacture	7.3	8.4	9.5	9.5	9.0	9.1
Capital Goods	17.2	19.5	21.9	22.5	23.3	23.5

(1) East Germany excluded from OECD.

Source: ECLAC Division of Industry and Technology.

Figure 5.6 OECD Imports from Latin America (1)

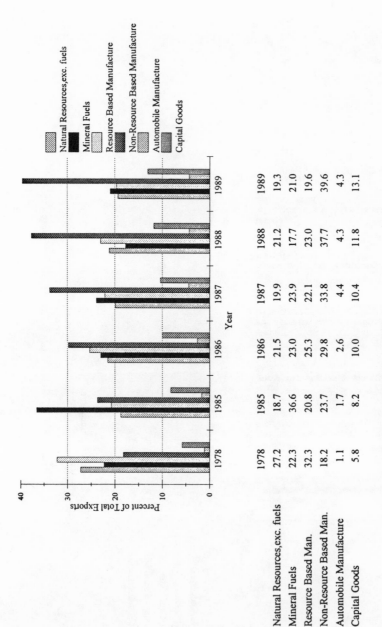

	1978	1985	1986	1987	1988	1989
Natural Resources,exc. fuels	27.2	18.7	21.5	19.9	21.2	19.3
Mineral Fuels	22.3	36.6	23.0	23.9	17.7	21.0
Resource Based Man.	32.3	20.8	25.3	22.1	23.0	19.6
Non-Resource Based Man.	18.2	23.7	29.8	33.8	37.7	39.6
Automobile Manufacture	1.1	1.7	2.6	4.4	4.3	4.3
Capital Goods	5.8	8.2	10.0	10.4	11.8	13.1

(1) East Germany excluded from OECD.

Source: Joint ECLAC/UNIDO Industry and Technology Division.

Figure 5.7 Latin American Exports to OECD (1)

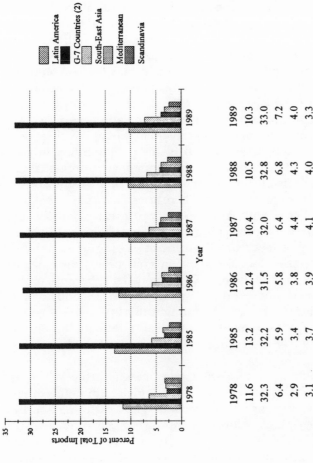

	1978	1985	1986	1987	1988	1989
Latin America	11.6	13.2	12.4	10.4	10.5	10.3
G-7 Countries (2)	32.3	32.2	31.5	32.0	32.8	33.0
South-East Asia	6.4	5.9	5.8	6.4	6.8	7.2
Mediterranean	2.9	3.4	3.8	4.4	4.3	4.0
Scandinavia	3.1	3.7	3.9	4.1	4.0	3.3
Eastern Europe	3.3	2.4	2.5	2.6	2.7	2.4

(1) Excludes mineral fuels.
(2) East Germany excluded from OECD.
Source: ECLAC Division of Industry and Technology.

Figure 5.8 OECD Natural Resource Imports (1)

From the standpoint of development options, the foregoing has two implications in terms of environmental sustainability. The first relates to the fact that the technological pattern associated with natural resources has already been set by those developed countries that supply natural resources to other developed countries. Canada alone produces a surplus of natural resources and natural resource based manufactures equivalent to that of the whole of Latin America, to say nothing of the United States, Australia, New Zealand, England, Norway, Denmark, etc. It should therefore be stressed once again that the technological pattern as regards natural resources has already been established by the countries that supply the vast market of the developed world.

Consequently, environmental sustainability in Latin America should not be seen only as an environmental problem in the capital cities or an issue that sparks a reaction on the part of the people living in areas where the environment has seriously deteriorated; environmental sustainability is a requirement for the maintenance of a position in the international market in coming years. There are already sufficient indications in areas such as mining, fruit production, forestry products and fishing that environmental protection will become an increasingly important factor in the next few years. If we do not take the necessary steps now, we are going to seem foolishly naive in a few years time when we complain that our exports are being unfairly penalized, because protectionist barriers will certainly be erected against exports that do not meet environmental standards. It might be thought this is not an overriding reason for promoting environmental sustainability, but we should realize that it could very well affect the living standards of this continent's population.

Consequently, when we think about environmental sustainability we should also consider this facet of the issue which, although perhaps prosaic, has other implications. The technological pattern associated with natural resources in developed countries has generated a wealth of flourishing industrial activities relating to environmental sustainability over the past 10 years. In the developed countries today, 3 percent of the production sector's total investment is in environmental protection, and annual current expenditure on environmental protection in the developed countries accounts for between 1 percent and 2 percent of gross output.

In Latin America it is estimated that at the present time about US$2 billion are invested in environmental equipment and facilities; this is between one-fifth and one-tenth of what we would be spending on this item if the Latin American countries were allocating the same proportion of their resources to environmental equipment and facilities as the developed countries do. During the next decade it is estimated that, bearing in mind all the relevant internal and external considerations, the demand for environmental equipment and services, including research and basic technology, will grow by about 10 percent per year.

ON LESSONS AND PENDING ISSUES

In this part of the chapter, I will try to sum up the main messages of ECLAC's proposal and the issues that are still pending. The first message concerns the region's own efforts and responsibilities which cannot be transferred or delegated to others. Our success or failure in meeting the historic challenge now facing us will depend on our own efforts and decisions. In the future, this continent cannot afford to delegate the intellectual, economic or political responsibility for its problems to outsiders. Consequently, the first message is that we must assume responsibility for confronting these challenges ourselves. Responsibility for the woeful lack of social equity and the senseless plunder of our natural resources cannot be shifted onto other countries; the basic responsibility is ours. It may be easier, perhaps more pleasing or attractive, to delegate responsibility than to assume it, but I doubt that, at this point, anyone in this region is seriously prepared to believe that the solution to our problems will come from elsewhere, and no one outside the region thinks so either. The first message is therefore that of the centrality of our assumption of responsibility.

The second message is that the main tasks are the achievement of social equity and competitiveness; not just any type of competitiveness; not spurious competitiveness based on the plundering of natural resources and declining wages, but rather genuine competitiveness, which is based on the absorption and dissemination of technical progress. This type of competitiveness is directly related to environmental sustainability. No one who is concerned solely with social equity and who disregards the element of competitiveness can—in a world whose growing transparency is bringing about a convergence of aspirations— maintain a vision of social equity without competitiveness for very long. History has also demonstrated conclusively that no one who is solely concerned with competitiveness, especially if it is a spurious form thereof, and disregards considerations of social equity, can sustain that vision for long. The reason for this is one worth exploring in some depth; competitiveness is a systemic phenomenon, and competitiveness is a systematic phenomenon.

In today's world, individual business enterprises do not compete; systems of production compete, and their underlying educational research, financial transport and communications systems play a crucial role in this regard. Therefore, countries whose social fabric (including its educational dimension) are deteriorating also suffer from an erosion of their competitiveness. The United States is perhaps the most notable example. In that country, people have now come to the conclusion that one of the factors responsible for the decline in its competitiveness is its strained, substandard educational base, which obviously jeopardizes the ability of the country's production system to compete on international markets.

The third message is that although many different steps must be taken to promote competitiveness and social equity, there is one factor to which it is impossible even to aspire, within the realm of reality, for the achievement of competitiveness and social equity, and that factor is human resources. Latin America has no possibility of reproducing the courses of action which have fostered competitiveness and social equity in other regions unless it seriously addresses this issue and makes human resources a central element of its development effort. There are many and very different acts of circumstance in Latin America, and the relationship between education and growth, or education and social equity, is neither trivial nor linear; there are many complications, but one thing that is clear is that the quality and coverage of the Latin American educational system—primary, secondary and higher education as well as vocational training—are absolutely incompatible with our oft-mentioned aspirations to competitiveness and social equity.

In the fourth message the ECLAC document asserts that the type of State needed to promote the implementation of its proposal—based on the inseparable elements of internal effort, social equity, genuine competitiveness, human resources and the dissemination of technical progress—is different from the type of state that promoted development over the past five decades. This latter type of state took on the primary responsibility for production either directly, through public enterprises, or indirectly, by encouraging the establishment and expansion of large private enterprises.

Table 5.8, concerning the leading enterprises in the region, leaves no doubt that it was the state which assumed the central responsibility for the direct or indirect promotion of the growth of the production base. However, the state overlooked two vital factors that probably should have been an integral part of that effort: social equity and genuine competitiveness (and hence environmental sustainability).

The type of state that will be capable of implementing the ECLAC proposal is a state that delegates responsibilities in the area of production to an entrepreneurial base possessing all the skills relevant to the particular situation in each country and one that assumes the prime responsibility for promoting social equity, genuine competitiveness and environmental sustainability.

Finally, the fifth message points out that external cooperation can undoubtedly help to achieve many of the objectives set forth in the proposal. The external debt is now clearly a serious problem that must be solved, and ECLAC's proposal asserts the need to secure external support in order to help bring about changes in production patterns coupled with social equity rather than, as has occurred in the past, to postpone such changes instead of promoting them. The type of external support which is needed will help carry forward changes that will require the region to assume its inescapable responsibilities rather than helping the region to defer those changes.

In a nutshell, the proposal's five main messages are: regional efforts; social equity coupled with genuine competitiveness; education combined with the dissemination of technical progress; a new role for the state; and external cooperation to accomplish these tasks rather than postpone them.

Finally, what are the pending issues that have not been dealt with in sufficient depth by this proposal? There are undoubtedly many such issues. This document is only one phase of a process of reflection in which persons from within and outside the institution are participating. We are currently working to rectify, at least partially, those shortcomings in three main areas: detailed policies for the promotion of social equity; an educational strategy for bringing about changes in production patterns; and environmental sustainability coupled with changes in production patterns and social equity.

NOTES

1. ECLAC. *Changing Production Patterns with Social Equity*, LC/G.1601/Ses 23/4, Santiago, Chile, March 1990.
2. Fernando Fajnzylber. *Unavoidable Industrial Restructuring in Latin America*, Duke University Press, Durham and London, 1990.
3. IBD–OECD Development Centre, International Forum on Latin American Perspective. F. Fajnzylber, *Technical Progress, Competitiveness and Institutional Change*, Paris, November 1991.
4. ECLAC. Sustainable Development: Changing Production Patterns, Social Equity and the Environment, LC/G.1648 (Conf. 80/2) Rev. 1, Santiago, Chile, February 1991.

Part IV
Structural Adjustment in Sub-Saharan Africa

6

African Adjustment Programs

False Attacks and True Dilemmas

Elliot Berg

Sub-Saharan Africa differs in many ways from Latin America and from most other parts of the developing world. It is the least developed region—almost half of its 50-odd states are in the United Nation's category of "least developed." It is also the most vulnerable region—the least industrialized, the most dependent on commodity exports, the least successful exporter and domestic saver, the most dependent on official development assistance for foreign exchange, budget support and investment. And it is the primary arena of formal, externally sponsored structural adjustment or policy reform programs. By 1990 some two-thirds of the states in the region had received policy-based loans from the World Bank and 31 had received adjustment loans under the IMF Structural Adjustment Facility.

The appropriateness and efficacy of these programs has been the subject of heated debate—probably more so in Africa than the other developing regions. For example, the analytic or intellectual foundations of the market-oriented reforms that are at the center of these adjustment efforts have been "officially" attacked by the UN Economic Commission for Africa (UNECA), something which has not to my knowledge happened in Asia or Latin America. The ghost of Raúl Prebisch may no longer roam in Santiago, but it is alive in Addis Ababa.

Three sets of criticisms have been most persistent: first, that the prescription is wrong—market-oriented policies have been pushed too far and too fast; second, that these programs have failed to produce growth; and third, that their costs have fallen heavily on the poor.

Assessment of these attacks on market-oriented adjustment is the subject of the first part of the chapter. I will try to show that the criticisms are not well-founded because better strategies for adjustment and growth do not exist; the growth record does not permit the conclusion that the "orthodox" adjustment programs have failed; and there is precious little evidence to support the charge that the adjustment programs of the 1980s have hurt Africa's poor.

While the mainstream attacks on market-oriented policy reforms are wrong, it does not follow that all is well with adjustment policies and processes in Africa. In fact, experience in the past decade has revealed some fundamental problems, mostly in the *process* of reform. I call these true dilemmas, and single out three for discussion in the second part of the chapter. First, heavy aid inflows and especially highly fungible policy-based money, are tending to erode political will and the commitment to reform. Second, policy money is believed to require lots of explicit conditionality, but this impedes true dialogue and severely inhibits local "ownership." Third, the introduction into reform programs of "social dimensions" has weakened the intellectual foundations of the program and also probably reduces the prospects of successful reform. These dilemmas or contradictions seem important enough to force a rethinking of present approaches, in particular the reliance on policy-based lending as the main reform vehicle.

The issues that are raised here are so many and so complex that detailed discussion of each is clearly out of the question in this short chapter. The analysis that follows sets out only the outlines of the arguments, but it attempts nonetheless to capture the essential issues and key points.

THE POLICY PRESCRIPTIONS ARE WRONG

From their first appearance on African policy agendas in the early 1980s, market-oriented reform programs were widely attacked as unsuitable for Africa. The attack had many themes, most of them familiar from the structuralist literature of earlier decades.

Markets are Highly Imperfect

Factor markets, especially for land and capital, are very thin. Entrepreneurs are scarce. Infrastructure is poor, information flows slowly. These economies exhibit great structural rigidities; they respond slowly or not at all to changes in relative prices.

In these circumstances, most of the market-oriented reform policies are inappropriate. The argument has been set out forcefully in the 1989 United Nations Economic Commission for Africa report *African Alter-*

native Framework to Structural Adjustment Programmes for Socio-Economic Recovery and Transformation:

Underlying the current adjustment programs is the well-known argument, based on classical economic theory, that output, employment, and prices (including wages, interest rates, and the exchange rates) are best determined by the free play of market forces, and that prices are the most effective instruments for the efficient allocation of resources.

In the African situation (however) the simple truth is that many countries have moved toward free markets without being in a position to take full advantage of available market opportunities because of low capacity to adjust their production structures. The consequences of these structural rigidities are evident in many areas, but most notably the limited capacities of African farmers to respond to price incentives without assured supplies of relevant production inputs, and in the failure of domestic production to respond to new opportunities in export and domestic markets, following a currency devaluation, because of a myriad of technical and supply difficulties; and, in the slow response of savings to high interest rates. These rigidities imply that the main burden of adjustment has been borne by drastic reductions in domestic expenditures with serious economic and social consequences that have tended in many cases to retard rather than promote the process of structural transformation.

Liberalization is a Flawed Option

Liberalization of foreign trade regimes, another pillar of World Bank/IMF–sponsored structural adjustment programs, is similarly viewed as a flawed option. Genuine liberalization of imports might devastate much of African industry. And, more important, export-led growth is not viable for African economies, which are primary product exporters. Price prospects for raw materials are poor. Low price and income elasticities make output expansion self-defeating, except for minor producers. If all the poor countries that produce beverages or fibers or oilseeds were to expand output, the argument goes, resulting falls in prices might mean lower export earnings rather than higher. There's no way, the critics say, that expansion of primary product exports can generate an acceptable rate of growth of output in exporting countries.

Privatization

Privatization is attacked as another erroneous element in standard adjustment packages; it has been pushed in a doctrinaire fashion. However, it's not ownership that counts but competition, and, in African circumstances, small markets rule out much of that. Local capitalists are too few and too small to buy and run many of the larger state enterprises, and they are more interested in protection and special privileges than in competition anyway. Where foreigners are allowed to buy, fears of recolonization are kindled.

To fully assess these arguments would require more space than I have here. I will focus on a few main points.

Imperfect alternatives. We are dealing always with imperfect alternatives—with flawed models, not ideal types. Greater reliance on a weak, small private sector has to be weighed against continuing dominance of a heavily bureaucratized, ill-paid public sector. Strategies other than one based on export expansion have to be considered in the light of past experience with import substitution and state-led growth, and the limited alternative uses of climate, land, and labor. More specifically, the alternatives to orthodoxy, for example those set out in the UNECA report, are extremely unconvincing—a vague mélange of food self-sufficiency, minimum guaranteed prices for food crops, multiple exchange rates, centralized allocation of credit and subsidized interest rates, tolerance of budget deficits and guaranteed, industrial import substitution on a regional basis.

Removal of structural deficiencies. The existence of "structural" deficiencies should lead to efforts to remove them, not to continuation of failed policies of the past. If markets function poorly, their operations should be improved; they should be made more transparent and competitive, for example, but not returned to control by state monopolies/monopsonies. Moreover, the validity of any strategy depends on how effectively it erodes structural constraints to development. Encouragement of private provision of "public" services, for example, is the most obvious way to stimulate the growth of an entrepreneurial class. Entrepreneurship is rarely hatched inside public sector organizations.

Agriculture. In agriculture, prices do matter and can be powerful engines of transformation. Certainly, it would be better if higher prices were accompanied by good credit systems, research and extension, etc. But, in fact, in the bulk of sub-Saharan Africa it is not feasible. New technology, truly usable at farm level, is sparse. Credit and extension systems are usually paralyzed for want of money and organizational capacity. Input-supply arrangements are similarly crippled. In such circumstances price policy may be the only feasible instrument available to spur agricultural growth. And in all cases, even where it is not sufficient, good price incentives are necessary.

Despite the prevailing pessimism about agricultural supply response, there do exist African examples of how policy changes (better prices, liberalized marketing systems, freedom of organization of production, improved land tenure laws) can have large impacts on output, and induce structural changes in agriculture. The most spectacular example is probably that of Mauritania. Spurred by a 1983 change in land tenure law which gave greater access to private landholding along the lower Senegal River, and by good prices for paddy, a group of new farmers emerged, many of them traders, businessmen and civil servants without previous farming experience. These new farmers have constructed generally rudimentary irrigation canals, bought small diesel pumps, and brought in hired labor. Production began in 1984. By 1986 16,000 ha. were brought under cultivation, three times more than the 15-year-old efforts of the state-controlled irrigated rice sector. Paddy production rose from about 20,000 tons in 1986 to 70-80,000 in 1988—six times the average output of the early 1980s.

Similar policy-induced changes have occurred in Madagascar. A 1983–85 rice market liberalization program led to freer marketing and higher producer prices. Farmers responded by improving their irrigation facilities, buying more inputs (tractors and fertilizers), reallocating land (with smallholders renting to larger, more efficient growers), draining old, neglected fields, and making new plantings of upland rice. The impact on production was masked for several years by bad data, and by bad rains in 1988. But recent trends are clearer: paddy production has increased more than at any time in the past twenty years.

Many other examples of agricultural responsiveness to policy reforms can be cited: the growth of maize and sesame production in Somalia after liberalization there in the early 1980s; the rise in cocoa production in Ghana after that country's 1983 reforms; and the tripling of maize production in the North Shaba province of Zaire in the mid-1980s, among others. There is a paradox here. Pessimism predominates in the econometric studies of supply elasticities. But anecdotal and case study evidence shows much more responsiveness to the policy environment.₄

Trade regime liberalization and exports. The attack on trade regime liberalization is exaggerated and fails to define viable alternatives. Nowhere in Africa have adjustment programs entailed massive removal of tariff or other forms of protection. What Bank/Fund-sponsored programs generally seek is lower and more even levels of protection. In reality, very few countries are ready to dismantle tariff and other barriers, or to completely liberalize import regimes, and few have been asked to do so.

On the export promotion side, export pessimism has been exaggerated. Meat, citrus, fish, some fibers, and rubber are among commodities with higher income elasticity of demand or with environmental advantages that make their prospects reasonably good. Except for cocoa, African producers occupy minor shares in world markets and, given reasonable assumptions about elasticities, can therefore increase export earnings by expanding output. And in any case, what are the alternatives for primary exporters? If individual countries or subregions do not continue to fight for export markets by increasing production and productivity they will lose market share to competitors, as they did between 1960 and 1980, when African exporters of beverages, fiber and minerals saw their market shares fall by a third to a half.

In terms of viable alternatives, the "inward-looking" alternatives to an export-based growth strategy are hardly appealing—slower output growth, lower income, greater constraints on imports, a reduction in the "training effect" that comes from competition in export markets, less exposure to new ideas and opportunities and, hence, reduced potential for discovery of new economic options.

Where regional economic integration presents promise, it should be more actively pursued; unification of small national markets into larger regional ones can be a potential source of new growth. Opportunities undoubtedly exist in new, more carefully studied, import substitution. But none of this need be incompatible with better performance in export production and marketing, which under any likely scenario is sure to be—at least for a generation—the principal engine of development in most African countries.

Privatization. Finally, privatization of state assets, the main target of anti–free-market critics, does indeed have its limits. The gains from the sale of state assets, though almost always positive, are not likely to be large unless prudently executed and accompanied by other changes— for example, the creation of a more competitive market structure. Moreover, many obstacles have become evident, and these suggest that asset sales will have a relatively limited scope, especially in the poorest countries. Privatization approaches can be improved by greater transparency in negotiation, and by greater willingness to allow nonviable enterprises to die.

Most important, privatization is likely to have greater impact in areas other than privatization of property, notably privatization of management via leasing of state assets, arranging various types of management contracts, and, above all, bringing in private service providers by deregulation (allowing free entry), and by utilization of the many techniques available to privatize service delivery—contracting out, franchises, voucher systems, etc. These are feasible and still neglected ways to mobilize private energies and resources, and to nurture entrepreneurship at the same time.

HAVE AFRICAN ADJUSTMENT PROGRAMS FAILED?

The UN Economic Commission for Africa has been a major participant in debate on this issue, as on the validity of the orthodox approach to policy reform. In its report on alternative adjustment strategies the

UNECA[1] writers say: "poverty in Africa has worsened in the 1980s. The average annual growth rate of per capita income in 1980–1986 was either stagnant or negative in most of the countries implementing adjustment and stabilization programs. In a few cases where improved per capita income was recorded, it was largely at the expense of higher external debt and the deterioration of social services. By 1988, average real incomes in Africa, south of the Sahara, are ... no more than 80 percent of their levels in the 1970s."

The UNECA paper cites in support of its analysis the findings of the World Bank study *Report on Structural Adjustment Lending*, 1988 (commonly known as RAL I); the sub-Saharan countries studied in that report experienced a fall in GDP growth to 1.8 percent *after* adoption of adjustment programs, compared to 2.8 percent growth prior to adoption. Also, investment ratios fell and budget deficits rose after implementation of adjustment programs.

The RAL II study,[2] however, while noting slow growth in African countries, concluded that the adjustment programs worldwide seem to have had positive impacts in terms of growth. The thirty countries with adjustment programs did better than those without adjustment loans. The study found also that middle-income adjusters did better than low-income, and twelve "adjustment–lending–intensive" countries did best of all. They noted, however, that all countries did relatively poorly in the 1980s, that sustainability was not assured, and that subSaharan Africa experienced especially slow growth.

A later World Bank report, *Adjustment and Growth in Africa in the 1980s* (1989), came out with a more positive assessment. It says that there have been signs since the mid-1980s of faster growth, and that this is evidence that adjustment programs are working. Economic performance in nineteen African countries with "strong reform programs" is better than in other countries of the region. These conclusions have been strongly attacked by the UNECA, among others. The UNECA, defining country classifications differently, concludes that African "adjusting" countries have done worse than any other group of countries in terms of GDP growth and some other indicators.

Evaluation of the effectiveness of policy reform programs is extremely difficult. If the main criterion is growth in per capita income, then two fundamental and well-known truths make evaluation difficult. First, good policies are only one factor in explaining growth; the best policy reforms may not help much in the short and medium term if export markets collapse or if drought hits. Second, evaluation must take into account the "counterfactual" or "without-adjustment" scenario, which is difficult to do.

Other, somewhat less obvious factors impede evaluation of success or failure in policy reform. There are many countries at issue, within each of which the speed and nature of reform varies. Countries that are star performers in one year fall off track two years later. The intensity of reforms varies; in one country, trade liberalization may involve a minor overall tariff reduction with small effects, while in another there may be a truly significant opening up to external competition. Another consideration is that where severe distortions prevailed before "adjustment," most of the economy may already have adjusted informally, via ubiquitous parallel markets; the effects of a formal reform program will thus be much diluted.

Most important, reforms are only partially implemented in most instances. A decree may announce full liberalization of grain marketing, but multiple market restrictions may remain—movement controls, licensing requirements, etc. A tariff reduction may be frustrated by informal increases in administrative controls of imports. A devaluation may occur, but fear of capital flight and other factors may lead to persistence of export-constraining administrative requirements on exporters. In these conditions of fragmentary implementation the reform program has not been tested, so evaluation is inappropriate.

In many cases, finally, it is too soon to judge. In sub-Saharan Africa, for example, it was not until 1985 or so that effective reform programs predominated; in 1984, for example, real effective exchange rates had *appreciated* in more African countries than they had depreciated, and real producer prices showed little improvement over 1980. Effective reform in much of the region got under way only in 1985—too recently for serious evaluation of impacts.

In my view, these approaches to assessment of the "success" of structural adjustment inevitably yield contestable and fragile results. Problems of choice of time period, country classification, and weighting are monumental. The World Bank's RAL I for example, defined "adjusting" groups to include any country that had received an adjustment loan by 1984. The Bank's 1989 report (*Adjustment and Growth in Africa in the 1980s*) defined reforming countries as those with an acceptable program in place in 1986–1987. So the *Adjustment Lending* report includes Sierra Leone, Sudan, Zambia, and Zimbabwe among the "adjusters," and excludes from this category eight African countries that had programs in 1986-1987 but not by 1984: Burundi, Central African Republic, Gambia, Guinea, Madagascar, Mauritania, Niger, and Zaire. It's no wonder that conclusions about outcomes differ.

Results are also sensitive to treatment of outliers. If Mauritius is excluded from the list of strong reformers (on the arguable grounds that its policies have never been severely distorted), and Liberia from nonreformers (because its growth rate was far below all others in that category) the unweighted average GDP growth rate of nonreformers is substantially higher than of adjusting countries—about a third higher in 1986 and 50 percent higher in 1987. Such sensitivity certainly raises questions about the robustness of any general statement about the impact of policy reform on growth in Africa.

Despite these weaknesses, the World Bank estimates of the impact of policy reform are probably more meaningful than those of the UNECA. The UNECA classification, which puts in the "adjusting" category any country that adopted any Bank/Fund program since 1963, is not reasonable, given that so many programs quickly go off track.

The existing set of cross-country comparisons, then, provide few credible or firm answers to the question of whether adjustment programs in Africa have "failed" or "succeeded." Additional analyses along these lines may be more enlightening. But to know whether or not adjustment is working in sub-Saharan Africa, much more needs to be known about the intensity of reform and about the realities of implementation. More needs to be known about the softer criteria of structural change, such as the reduction of institutional barriers to faster growth, and the extent of social learning. Has the process of defining adjustment programs generated new insights into the obstacles to growth, and new ideas about overcoming them? Has local "ownership" increased, or minds been changed about what is good and what is bad policy? Are policymaking processes and institutions stronger? For insight into these kinds of issues more and better case studies are needed.

IMPACT ON THE POOR

This has become perhaps the most discussed aspect of adjustment policy. It provides an unusually interesting example of the use of ideas as weapons of social policy. Beginning in 1984 and 1985, even before many adjustment programs had been adopted, and certainly before many impacts could be observed, the criticism was put forward that their "social costs" were falling most heavily on the lower ends of the income and asset distribution. Combined with world recession, adjustment was said to be the source of declining standards of nutrition, health and education. According to a 1984 UNICEF publication, "the present crisis . . . has severely aggravated the situation of several social groups . . . (since) child welfare indicators . . . are unambiguous in pointing to a deterioration in child status. . . ." "In most countries one observes . . . a serious deterioration in indicators of nutrition, health status and school achievements."[3] And in 1985 UNICEF spokesman Richard Jolly made similar assertions:

As it operates at the moment, adjustment policy transmits and usually multiplies the impact on the poor and vulnerable. The result, as shown in many countries, is rising malnutrition in the short run, and, in the long run, reinforcement of a style of development which will primarily rely on accelerated growth and trickle down, if it works at all, to reduce malnutrition in the future.[4]

Evidence presented to support these and similar assertions was extremely sparse. As a reviewer of the 1984 UNICEF pamphlet pointed out, the remarkable fact is that these studies provided so little evidence of deterioration in children's status in the countries reviewed; to the contrary, the available data show continuing improvement in nutrition, mortality and school attendance.[5] Another observer puts it this way: "a set of studies that seem to lead to the conclusion of little, or at least unproven, systematic impact of recession and economic adjustment on health and nutrition, is summarized as finding that adjustment policy usually multiplies negative recessionary impact on the poor and vulnerable."[6]

The idea that the "social costs" of adjustment are heavy, and are borne mostly by the poor, has gained widespread acceptance, despite its extremely thin empirical foundations. At an important meeting in Khartoum in 1988, World Bank representatives pleaded guilty to neglect of these social costs in the framing of adjustment programs. The extraordinary growth of concern with social dimensions of adjustment since 1987 is at least in part a reaction to the accusation of earlier neglect.

Recent research, however, is confirming earlier doubts that the social impacts of market-oriented policy changes have been generally negative. The World Bank's Second Report on Adjustment Lending analyzes recent data on average living standards, which is almost surely indicative of changes in the status of the poor. The report concludes that short-run indicators of living conditions have not deteriorated in adjusting countries, and long-run indicators have continued to improve. Adjustment lending programs increased the growth of per capita consumption between 1985 and 1988. For all country groups, nutrition improves after 1983, immunization data show increased coverage, and mortality data show continued progress. For a small sample of countries (12, none of them African) the incidence of poverty did not systematically increase in adjusting countries; it fell in the 1980s as often as it rose in these countries. In 10 of 12 intensive adjustment countries in Africa, nutrition improved between 1983–84 and 1986, though it worsened in 8 of 12 between 1980 and 1983–84. In about half of the 22 African countries analyzed, nutritional status seems to have worsened between 1980 and 1986; adjusting and nonadjusting countries performed about the same on this indicator.[7]

A number of recent papers point out that public expenditures in general and social sector expenditures in particular have not suffered in the 1980s in sub-Saharan Africa.

- IMF data on trends in real government expenditures in a sample of 22 African countries show a more or less steady increase in the 1980s, and a level in 1986–87 about a third higher than in 1980. Real per capita public expenditures also grew in most years and in 1986–87 averaged 10 percent higher than in 1980.[8]
- Hicks and Kubisch, looking at data for 32 developing countries in the 1970s, concluded that social expenditures were the most protected category of public spending. Pinstrup-Anderson et al. found similar results for Africa for 1979–84. Sahn found that health and education expenditures in Africa have been highly elastic with respect to total government expenditures and to GDP (near or more than unity between 1985 and 1987); their elasticity has increased since 1974. A study of education and health spending between 1980 and 1987 in 20 African countries shows that health and education budget shares grew slightly or remained steady over the years 1980–1987.[9]

Little of the available data, then, support the view that adjustment programs have had generally negative impacts on living conditions or indicators of health and education status. This is not direct evidence that the poor have not been hurt by some adjustment situations, but it certainly casts doubt on broad assertions, such as in the UNICEF *Report on the State of the World's Children 1990*, that adjustment programs have raised infant mortality rates and resulted in slashed social sector budgets.

In fact, with very few exceptions, the best available data indicate that infant and child mortality rates in Africa continued to decline in the 1980s, that health and education spending grew in real per capita terms, or at least didn't fall much, and that indicators of educational access and achievement such as enrollment rates and literacy show no general deterioration.

TRUE DILEMMAS

Aid Money and Political Will

It has always been understood that aid money, in general, and policy-based lending, in particular, is a two-edged sword. It can cushion the negative impacts of a reform program and thereby facilitate its adoption. But it can also hold back reform by reducing economic pressures to change bad policies. Policy money is especially prone to these re-form-retarding effects, since it is more fungible than other aid.

This should be a big problem in Africa because aid is so important there. In the 1980s the region received an annual average of $22 per capita in ODA, four times as much as other poor areas; aid is 5 percent of GDP on average (six times more than elsewhere), and it provides a third of all domestic investment (10 times more than other developing regions) and a quarter of imports, or five times the average elsewhere. Moreover, these are averages. For many countries the pie of aid is much greater. In some years in the past decade, for example, aid has been more than 10 percent of GDP for 20 countries and for perhaps a dozen countries it has approached 20 percent, with aid providing as much as domestically raised revenues and as much foreign exchange as exports of goods and services.

A growing share of this aid is in the form of policy-based lending. The use of conditionality is supposed to avoid or reduce its possible nega-tive consequences. But the *effective* use of conditionality—i.e., the im-position of sanctions for nonperformance—has been constrained by other considerations, notably the pressure on donors and lenders to keep spending to avoid financial crises and/or economic collapse in aided countries.

Judging from the official evaluations, such as the World Bank's two reports on adjustment lending (RAL I, 1988 and RAL II, 1990), the threat has not materialized. RAL II notes with some satisfaction that compli-ance with conditionalities has been reasonably good everywhere and is getting better; two-thirds of the conditions in loan agreements (which are regarded as key conditions) were fully implemented at final tranche release, and 84 percent at least substantially implemented. For policy loans to sub-Saharan Africa the rates were somewhat lower—60 percent of key conditions were fully implemented and 80 percent substantially implemented. This report, like RAL I, signals no serious difficulties with compliance or with the process of policy lending, either in Africa or elsewhere.

This picture of good and improving compliance with conditionality is not altogether in accord with micro level information—casual obser-vation, case studies, anecdotes and opinions of informed people. If you ask World Bank or Fund or bilateral aid agency staff to list the African countries they think are strong implementers of policy reforms you will rarely be given more than six or seven examples. Some of these, more-over, are countries whose economies were never seriously distorted to begin with (Botswana, Swaziland, Mauritius, for example). Others will be contested; Ghana, for example, which is usually on everybody's list, has its detractors, who say the reforms there have been restricted mainly to stabilization measures, and that not much else has been done since 1984.

Case study information is still rare. But a recently completed study of adjustment in Senegal—also a highly rated country in most rankings of policy reformers—gives a different picture of the implementation process and of the consequences of conditionality. The country has had four Structural Adjustment Loans, several IMF Structural Adjustment Facilities and Expanded Structural Adjustment Facilities and significant bilateral policy loans. Yet almost none of the country's structural constraints have been addressed. Issues of exchange rate overvaluation and competitiveness are more formidable now than ten years ago. The stated goal of a slimmed-down and more efficient public sector has not been achieved. Civil service employment has grown, not shrunk; the reduction of employment in agricultural parastatals was slower between 1985 and 1989 than between 1979 and 1984 when there was no adjustment program. The reform program in agricultural policy was not implemented; real agricultural prices were lower in most years in the 1980s than they were in the 1970s and the announced policy of raising consumer rice prices to stimulate local cereals production was not implemented. An industrial and trade policy reform was implemented partially in 1986, but was then significantly modified in 1989.

The point here is to underline the argument that implementation of reform programs in Africa has been substantially less effective than is suggested by the cheerful assessment in RAL II and other official documents. In fact, even the numbers in RAL II are not quite as impressive as these documents indicate. RAL I noted, for example, that tranche release was held up in three out of four adjustment loans, and some 40 percent of policy conditions were not implemented. RAL II states that in sub-Saharan Africa 45 percent of conditions were not fully implemented; for loan agreement conditions, the nonimplementation figure was 40 percent. When we take into account the fact that many of the hardest, most significant reforms are likely to be in the unimplemented category, and the fact that there is undoubtedly much surface or cosmetic compliance, the proportion of conditions that are not implemented can easily be interpreted as showing very poor implementation. This would be consistent with the microlevel observations.

It is also consistent with a priori expectations. In most African countries there coexist three circumstances designed to induce slow and partial implementation of reforms. The first is the external sponsorship and heavy explicit conditionality of almost all reform programs in the region. This has meant that there is little sense of local "ownership" of the policy reform programs. The second is the existence of relatively large aid inflows—large as a major share of GDP, public expenditures, foreign exchange earnings, total investment. These have reduced "normal" pressures for reform—for example, by assuring minimal levels of imports, making resources available to maintain public employment levels and wage bills and the continuation of subsidies to state enterprises or for other purposes. Third is a no-sanctions environment. Donors and lenders have been unwilling, except in a few cases, to stop aid disbursements in the face of poor reform performance. The result has been the creation of a generalized soft budget constraint.

Out of this combination of factors has come an erosion of political will and commitment. Lack of these motivations is widely cited as a source of failure in reform efforts. This is not necessarily wrong. But it is not by itself very helpful. The charge of lack of political will can for example be levied against any government that sacrifices some efficiency objectives for other goals. More important, commitment to reform is not an all or nothing quality; some of it exists among the national leadership in all countries. The interesting question is what is it that determines the strength of political will to reform, or determines the intensity of commitment?

One useful way to think about this question is to put it in a cost-benefit context. Few governments are anxious to undertake reforms that are politically risky and potentially disruptive socially, especially when doubts prevail about the suitability or efficacy of the reforms in question. So, in making reform decisions, the authorities estimate expected benefits—their certainty, size, timing and incidence. On the other side, they estimate two kinds of costs—the expected social disruptions and political risks if reforms are introduced, and avoidance costs—the costs of avoiding reform actions. In present-day Africa the avoidance cost is a loss of donor esteem and less aid.

If no sanctions (in terms of reduced aid flows) are likely to follow nonperformance on conditionality, avoidance costs (less aid) are reduced and the cost-benefit calculus made by the political authorities moves in favor of noncompliance. I believe that this is what happened in many, perhaps most African countries in the 1980s. The relatively heavy inflows of foreign aid, coupled with the low credibility of donor conditionality, created a soft budget constraint that encouraged slow, partial and often cosmetic reform actions.

Conditionality, Distorted Dialogue and Ownership

The growth of adjustment and other policy-based lending in the 1980s has been accompanied by a proliferation of explicit conditionality. RAL II reports an average of 44 conditions or actions per policy loan in SSA. The elaboration of conditions and the supervision of their implementation has become the essence of the reform process; it is during these activities that most policy dialogue occurs, and success or failure is judged mainly by implementation records.

The main rationale for conditioning policy loans is well known: without it, the aid inflows can be used to finance basic disequilibria and postpone real adjustment. As noted above, serious questions can be raised about the extent to which conditionality has in fact been implemented and hence been effective in meeting its objective.

Conditionality introduces profound distortions into the reform process. First of all, it is not conducive to genuine dialogue and the changing of minds, but encourages game playing instead. Both parties—recipient government officials and staff of the lending agencies—want disbursement to proceed. On the government side this means a frequent willingness to sign agreements without looking too closely at the fine print. Where basic disagreements exist, pressures to close financing gaps often lead the parties to search for words of art that will permit both sides to agree, and move the loan agreement forward. Once the agreement is effective, both parties have an interest in keeping it on track. Except in cases of flagrant, repetitive and unrepentant violation of conditionality, disbursement proceeds.

This means that the main players become absorbed in system maintenance, as it were, and diverted from the true goals of policy dialogue—the joint analysis of policy and institutional problems and the joint discovery of ways to solve them. This requires open and unhurried exchanges of views in a noncontentious setting. This kind of policy dialogue has been very rare.

More commonly, it works like this. A loan agreement condition specifies that so many state enterprises have to be privatized by a given date. During the elaboration of the adjustment loan, the reservations of the local authorities on the privatization component are not debated, nor is the feasibility of the timetable questioned. In fact, government commitment to the privatizations is very weak, and the institutional capacity to implement the program extremely thin. So nothing is done by the target date, and the privatization action is a condition of tranche release. As the deadline approaches, and under much prodding from the World Bank, government meets the condition at the last minute by simply putting an ad in the newspaper announcing that the enterprises are up for sale.

In fact, the enterprises were not ready for sale, nor had a decision been made even to privatize all of them; two of the main enterprises mentioned were, in fact, shortly thereafter removed from the list, and actual privatizations occurred much later, or not at all. But the announcement in the press allowed the Bank to decide that the condition for tranche release had been met.

More significant kinds of distortions are introduced into the substance of reform by the conditionality-laden environment. One of the ways this can happen is as an unintended consequence of the choice of performance criteria. For example, a common reform area is in public expenditure management. New public investment programming systems are often part of adjustment programs, as part of an effort to improve the quality of public investment.

One of the conditionalities imposed in one such program called for a formal evaluation of 80 percent of the projects in the first year of the rolling public investment program. Annual monitoring of this condition involved investigation of the project files by World Bank staff to see whether such evaluations had been done.

Given this signal, planning agency staff in the recipient country proceeded to concentrate on formal evaluations of the projects in the Public Investment Program. But this quickly became a highly mechanical operation, with staff merely taking such numbers as were provided by the spending agency on costs, demand estimates, and technical coefficients, and calculating an internal rate of return. Field visits to project sites were practically nonexistent, questioning of input and output data was rare, poor projects continued to pass through the system.

The result was a step forward in a formal sense, but no significant improvement in project screening capacity and the quality of investment. In this case, the search for measurable criteria that would allow monitoring of reforms led to imposition of conditionality that slowed institutional capacity growth.

The final negative consequence of conditionality is more in the nature of a basic contradiction. Everybody says that the key to sustainable policy reform is local ownership; despite the externally sponsored nature of almost all African reform programs, local authorities have to feel that the program is theirs. But the growth of a real sense of ownership is not compatible with the heavy explicit conditionality that characterizes these programs.

The issue is not the same for stabilization and for structural reform measures. Nobody expects borrowing countries to feel ownership of a Fund program, any more than I feel ownership of financial conditions a Bank imposes on me when I want to open up a line of credit. But when it comes to making durable changes in basic policies and institutions— shifting relative prices, reallocating priorities within the school system, strengthening budgeting arrangements or deregulating markets, ownership would certainly seem to be a precondition. In fact, the most fundamental and most commonly cited objection to externally sponsored policy reform lies here—that durable reforms cannot usually be imposed from outside.

The Linking of Social Dimensions to Adjustment Lending

The third dilemma arises from the preoccupation with the social dimension of adjustment, which has grown enormously in recent years, and has brought much new spending on severance pay arrangements for public employees, urban employment creation projects, and general poverty-focused projects.

As noted earlier, the preoccupation with social dimensions had much of its origin in unproven assertions that policy reforms introduced in adjustment programs had hurt the poor. There is, in fact, extremely little evidence that in Africa the condition of the poor has worsened more in so-called adjusting countries than in other countries, or that social sector spending of importance to the poor has been particularly affected by formal adjustment programs. In Africa as elsewhere, moreover, indicators of education and health status continued to improve almost everywhere in the 1980s.

The linking of social costs or dimensions with structural adjustment programs has had an important negative intangible effect. Apparent acceptance by the World Bank of the idea that adjustment policies have imposed social costs on the poor, as symbolized by mea culpas in various public fora, and by the mounting of its large Social Development Assistance project, has contributed to the undermining of the moral and intellectual foundations of market-oriented reforms. The European Economic Community, through its European Development Fund, contributes in a similar way; some of its staff have described their role as being the "social firemen of adjustment."

Current doctrine has it that concern with social dimensions and with poverty, more broadly, is fully compatible with structural adjustment. This is said to be so in two senses: first, that labor-intensive growth, expanded health and education opportunities and focus on small farmers are central to long-term adjustment; and second, that protecting the poor from social costs of policy change will facilitate the political acceptability of change and assure its sustainability.

This is certainly true to some extent. But it is hard to accept the proposition that there are no trade-offs between social- and poverty-focused programs and the efficacy of adjustment policies.

- Aid money going to "social cushioning" and poverty-focused projects in general normally means some reduction in other aid spending, such as infrastructure financing or policy loans, which may be more conducive to longer-term growth. Certainly an urban employment project involving patching up of city streets can't rank high in its contribution to future growth, nor can the many civil servant departure or severance pay schemes financed as part of social dimensions of adjustment programs.

- •Cushioning schemes can have several negative long-term consequences. The first is to retard the maturing of political leadership. In a number of countries, it has become common for the authorities to say they can't take difficult steps without donor assistance. In some cases, shrinkage of government payrolls and/or liquidation of budget-draining state enterprises is delayed until donors finance the legal severance payments. Since these are, in fact, often financed this way, the strategy works, and the necessity for choice is avoided. Second, cushioning with external aid can reduce general acceptability of reforms. When governments are truly up against the wall, and the till is really empty, it is easier to convince wage earners, civil servants, and farmers of the need for sacrifice than when escape from sacrifice is always possible if a willing aid donor can be found.
- •The local political class may not agree with donors about the priority or terms of trade-off between poverty-focused aid and other kinds of programs. If so, or if there is no domestic political consensus about it, then the donor community may have to impose new and especially intrusive forms of conditionality. Among other consequences, resolution of the ownership problem would become more difficult.

Some of the implications of these concerns over the process or environment of structural adjustment are clear: less conditionality; a shift away from policy-based lending to more traditional lending instruments, or at least to hybrids with light policy content; more concern about the possible tradeoffs between social dimensions and growth and reform; and a gradual cutting back of volumes of aid in those sub-Saharan Africa countries that are especially heavily aided.

NOTES

1. United Nations Economic Commission for Africa. *African Alternative Framework to Structural Adjustment Programmes for Socio-Economic Recovery and Transformation*, Addis Ababa: United Nations, 1989.

2. "Adjustment Lending Policies for Sustainable Growth," World Bank Country Economics Department, PRS 14, Washington, DC. 1990.

3. Cornia, G.A. in Richard Jolly and Giovanni A. Cornia, *The Impact of World Recession on Children*. Oxford, England, Pergamon Press, 1984.

4. Jolly, R. "Adjustment with a Human Face," UNICEF pamphlet, 1985.

5. Preston, Samuel H. "Review of Richard Jolly and Giovanni Andrea Cornia, editors, *The Impact of World Recession on Children*, in *Journal of Development Economics*, May 1986.

6. Behrman, J. "The Impact of Economic Adjustment Programs," in *Health, Nutrition and Economic Crises: Approaches to Policy in the Third World*, Auburn House, 1988.

7. World Bank. *Adjustment Lending Policies for Sustainable Growth*, Sept. 1990, Ch. 3.

8. Ferroni, M. and R. Kanbur, "Poverty Conscious Restructuring of Public Expenditure," in Chibber, Ajay and Stanley Fischer, *The Analytics of Economic Reform in Sub-Saharan Africa*, World Bank, 1991. Another review of public expenditure data in the 1980s concludes that for most African countries expenditures rose or at least stayed steady, "despite the proliferation of IMF and World Bank loans that often carry with them conditions involving budgetary austerity. . . . " Sahn, D. "Fiscal and Exchange Rate Reforms in Africa: Considering the Impact on the Poor," Cornell University, Food and Nutrition Program, March, 1990.

9. Citations in Ferroni and Kanbur, 1991.

7

Why Structural Adjustment Failed in Africa

George B.N. Ayittey

We [should] send three sacks of angry bees to the governor and the president. And some ants which bite. Maybe they [will] eat the government and solve our problems.

Amina Ramadou, a peasant housewife in Zaire.

Africans are angry, particularly at the increasing pauperization of their people. Once a region with bountiful stores of optimism and hope, the African continent now teeters perilously on the brink of economic disintegration, political chaos, institutional and social decay. In 1990, Africa's income per capita declined for the twelfth consecutive year despite receiving more than $100 billion in cash and various forms of aid over the last decade. Agricultural growth has been dismal, with output growing at less than 1.5 percent per year since 1970. Industrial output across Africa has also been declining with some regions experiencing *deindustrialization*.

In sub-Saharan Africa (or black Africa), the crisis is particularly trenchant. Black Africa, with a population of 450 million, has a GDP similar to that of Belgium with a population of only 10 million. So severe has been the economic deterioration in black Africa that this region now has the dubious distinction of being home to 24 of the world's 34 poorest nations (World Development Report, 1991; p. 204). The decline has been calamitous even in Nigeria which could not translate its oil bonanza into sustainable economic prosperity (World Bank, 1989).

Of all the regions of the Third World, black Africa has registered the weakest economic performance, as Table 7.1 indicates.

Table 7.1   Growth of Real GDP per Capita by Region, 1965–2000
(Average Annual Percentage Change)

Region	Population, 1989, in millions	1965 -1973	1973 -1980	1980 -1989	Projection 1990s
Industrial Countries	773	3.7	2.3	2.3	1.8-2.5
Developing Countries	4053	3.9	2.5	1.6	2.2-2.9
Sub-Saharan Africa	480	2.1	0.4	-1.2	0.3-0.5
East Asia	1552	5.3	4.9	6.2	4.2-5.3
South Asia	1131	1.2	1.7	3.0	2.1-2.6
Europe, Middle East, and North Africa	433	5.8	1.9	0.4	1.4-1.8
Latin America and Caribbean	421	3.8	2.5	-0.4	1.3-2.0

Source: World Bank, World Development Report, 1991, p. 3.

The economic statistics paint a grim picture, even without taking into account ecological degradation, institutional decay, a growing refugee problem and appalling human suffering. About one in four children dies before the age of five in Burkina Faso, Ethiopia and Mali. Malnourishment accounts for 40 percent of infant mortality in Zambia.

Every year, the United Nations Development Program annually ranks countries, not by their wealth, but by the quality of life for the average citizen, using ratings known as the human development index. This year, 1992, nine of the ten worst countries are in Africa. Guinea is the worst, followed by Sierra Leone, Afghanistan, Burkina Faso, Niger, Mali, The Gambia, Djibouti, Guinea-Bissau and then Somalia.

As Claude Ake, the Nigerian scholar, put it, "Most African regimes have been so alienated and so violently repressive that their citizens see *the state* and its development agents as enemies to be evaded, cheated and defeated if possible, but never as partners" (*Africa Forum*, Vol. 1, No. 2, 1991; p. 14). To solve Zaire's economic crisis, Amina Ramadou, a peasant housewife, suggested: "We send three sacks of angry bees to the governor and the president. And some ants which bite. Maybe they eat the government and solve our problems" (*The Wall Street Journal*, Sept 26, 1991; p. A14). The message is getting through. Citing "the credibility gap between the people and the leadership built up through years of mismanagement," Mr. Mohammed Boudiaf, the head of Algeria's High Executive Council (HEC), lamented: "A large segment of the population has, I am afraid, lost confidence in the capacity of the leadership to provide jobs, housing, health care, and its ability to combat corruption" (*Financial Times*, June 17, 1992; p. 4).

Back in May 1986 African leaders collectively made a stunning admission before the United Nations' Special Session on Africa: past government policies were misguided, and had contributed in no small measure to Africa's economic crisis. This admission was all the more astonishing, coming from leaders with a mordant predisposition to lay the causes of Africa's economic woes at someone else's doorsteps. Finally, came the refreshing concession from these leaders that they themselves played a role in Africa's precipitous economic decline.

Subsequently, many African countries agreed to Structural Adjustment Programs (SAPs) under the auspices of the World Bank and the IMF. Under a typical SAP agreement, an African country would undertake to restructure its economy away from *dirigisme* (state-directed development), placing more emphasis on free market forces and private sector development in return for loans to ease balance of payment, debt servicing and budgetary difficulties. Measures undertaken by the recipient country include devaluing the local currency, selling off unprofitable state enterprises, reducing the size of the overly distended state sector, removing subsidies, dismantling price controls and curtailing the pervasive hegemony of the state in the economy. By 1989, 37 African countries had signed SAP agreements.

There was remarkable progress in some sectors and countries after the adoption of SAPs. Ghana, for example, registered an impressive 6 percent average rate of growth of GNP since the inception of the program in 1983 through 1990. Sectoral performances have been equally astounding. For example, the Ashanti Goldfields Corporation (AGC), which accounts for 20 percent of Ghana's foreign exchange earnings, increased its output from 272,000 ounces in 1987 to 355,700 ounces by the end of 1989. (*West Africa*, Feb 5-11, 1990; p. 190). Despite excessive rainfall and flooding, maize production rose by 19 percent between 1988 and 1989, enabling a surplus to be exported, while yam and sorghum increased by 7 and 8 percent respectively.

In some areas, privatization of state-owned enterprises in Africa has worked remarkably well to turn things around. Premier Breweries Ltd, an Anambra state-owned concern in Nigeria, is an excellent example, going from a monthly loss of 3.1 million *naira* in 1987/88 to a profit of N10 million in 1989.

Despite these successes, however, the overall record of what Nigerians ingeniously dubbed "Stomach Pain Adjustment" across Africa has been disappointing. In fact, the World Bank's own March 1990 internal report lamented: "Adjustment lending appeared to have been relatively less successful in the highly-indebted countries and *Sub-*

Saharan Africa" (p. 21). Only Ghana and Tanzania, out of the 37 adjusting African countries, were deemed "successful performers" by the World Bank.

WHAT WENT WRONG?

The World Bank (1989) admitted that: "Responsibility for Africa's economic crisis is shared. Donor agencies and foreign advisers have been heavily involved in past development efforts along with the African governments themselves. Governments and donors alike must be prepared to change their thinking fundamentally in order to revive Africa's fortunes. However, Africa's future can only be decided by Africans. External agencies can play at most a supportive role (p. 2)"

The rest of this paper will be devoted to the examination of mistakes on the part of the donors, in particular the World Bank's design of Structural Adjustment, and those on the part of African governments. It is hoped that this discussion will help shed some light on why Africa's economic crisis remains intractable and why the various reform measures came to grief.

Flaws in SAP

Structural Adjustment, as designed by the World Bank, was beset with various internal flaws. First, SAP, in most cases in Africa, amounted to reorganizing a bankrupt company and placing it, together with a massive infusion of new capital, in the hands of the same incompetent managers who ruined it in the first place. Worse, there was often no input by Africans, the very people who would be most affected by World Bank decisions. Wrote Wayne Ellwood:

> "Time and time again local communities are ignored.... The Bank needs its own *glasnost* so that informed public debate can take place," says Probe International's Pat Adams. "Decision-making," she adds, "should be returned to the people who have to live with the physical consequences of the decisions . . ." (*New Internationalist*, Dec 1990; p. 6).

The World Bank employs the services of hordes of expatriate management consultants. Less than 0.1 percent are Africans.

> "Over 100,000 expatriate advisers working in Africa are paid $4 billion out of donor funds each year," a World Bank chief of mission in East Africa, Mr. Stephen O'Brien, said recently. Mr. O'Brien termed the scenario a scandal. . . . The World Bank official also said that almost 40 percent of the

annual net aid flow to Africa is currently spent on technical assistance. *African Mirror*, Feb/March, 1992; p. 34.

Characterizing this as the "great consultancy rip-off," *South* (Feb. 1990) had earlier noted that "there is increasing concern [World Bank] advice is often overpriced, poorly researched and irrelevant" (p. 42).

Second, SAPs assume that development takes place in a vacuum, and that the senseless civil wars, environmental degradation, infrastructural deterioration, and a generalized state of violence and terror in Africa have no effects on economic development. In Mozambique, for example, the 12-year-old civil war has cost at least $8 billion and an estimated 900,000 civilian lives. Over a third of its population have been displaced. Yet, Western donors and institutions seek to "restructure" Mozambican and Angolan economies, mindless of the raging civil wars. But the most ludicrous "restructuring programs" are in Sudan and Somalia, where the World Bank seeks to restructure economies that do not exist—devastated, as they were, by civil wars.

Third, economic reform without concomitant political reform is meaningless since economic reform under dictatorships is generally not sustainable. Black Africa is characterized by dictatorships or weak authoritarian regimes which maintain their authority through personalistic patron-client relations.[1] These relationships are prone to sudden and erratic changes, producing political instability. It is no wonder that its record of economic reform has been spotty.

African governments restructure not to save their economies but their regimes. Further, restructuring proceeds in cycles: aborted when the crisis abates, and reinstated upon reemergence (Sudan, Equatorial Guinea, Zaire, Liberia). Even during restructuring, measures are often implemented perfunctorily without the conviction and the dedication needed to carry them through (Ayittey, 1989). In many cases, public confidence in the program was shattered by government dishonesty and tomfoolery.

Disregard for private property rights by modern African government has been the norm. Looting and arbitrary seizures of property by undisciplined soldiers have become increasingly rampant in much of Africa, and make a mockery of new foreign investment laws. Yet, for some strange reason, development experts, aid agencies and multilateral institutions assume that such lawlessness and banditry by African governments has no effects whatsoever on economic development.

At the African Business Round Table in Cairo (March 1, 1990), Babacar Ndiaye, president of the African Development Bank, warned:

In order to improve the flow of foreign investment into Africa, he urged African governments to focus more on areas such as ownership law, settling of disputes, exchange controls, incentives and political stability (*West Africa*, March 12–18, 1990; p. 423).

A few others may be added: transparency in government, tax policies, infrastructural rehabilitation and support as well as peace (ending those civil wars). But even so, the emphasis on foreign investment is misplaced.

The most effective way of attracting foreign investment is by attracting *domestic* investment! If Africans themselves would not invest in their own countries, why would foreigners? Even the same government officials who plead for more foreign investment themselves have too little faith in their own African economies to invest their ill-gotten wealth there. They choose Switzerland.

Nor is domestic investment spurred by the imposition of stifling regulations, excessive taxes, contradictory policy reversals and arbitrary seizures of commercial property. Even in Africa's supposedly "primitive and backward" system, there was hardly such nonsense.

On precolonial African law and custom, Frances Kendall and Leon Louw (1987) observed that: "There were no powers of arbitrary expropriation, and land and huts could be expropriated only under extreme conditions after a full public hearing" (p. 18).

This view is corroborated by Koyama (1980):

> In Xhosa law, as in other African legal systems, livestock in general, and cattle in particular, are the main objects of *private ownership* . . . In the old days, the method of protection of ownership as well as possession, was a *rei vindicatio* at the chief's court, but nowadays the *mandament van spolie* and the interdict are also employed but in the magistrates' courts . . . *In practice, therefore, the rights of the individual were never nullified* (p. 69).

Those tribal societies may be backward. But at least they understood that without the rule of law and private property rights protection, economic progress was impossible. There was a chief's court to adjudicate property disputes. Anyone could attend such court hearings. Nor could the chief himself whimsically seize someone else's cattle. The council of elders served as a check. But "educated" African leaders understand no such rule of law and private property rights.

The disrespect for property rights, policy acrobatics, and lack of commitment to reform have bedeviled the success of SAP in many African countries. Nigeria's Technical Committee on Privatisation and Commerce (TCPC) was established in 1988, with a mandate to privatize 127 state enterprises. Two years later, only 17 had been privatized. In 1985, Tanzania was offering ideological asylum to 460 state enterprises—the largest collection of such "refugee" enterprises on the continent. Two years later, only 3 had been privatized in spite of the Structural Adjustment agreement signed with the IMF. Blacknost has proven to be no *Afrostroika*. In fact, by 1988, the Nigerian newspaper, *National Concord*, had written an obituary on structural adjustment midway through its country's program, claiming its operation has, in some very critical respects, been flawed (June 30, 1988). Furthermore, it seemed that, where adopted, structural adjustment rather served to impede the democratization process by bailing out failed dictatorships. Writing in *New African* (Nov. 1988; p. 47), Stephen Duah stated with elegant simplicity: "If Western governments and the IMF would stop giving loans to dictators in (Africa), they would not survive to terrorize their nations, let alone extend their acts into the international arena."

The Pathology of Problem Solving in Africa

It is not enough to heap all the blame for Africa's intractable economic crisis on the World Bank and the International Monetary Fund. Even if these institutions had not provided adjustment programs or tutelage, Africa's crisis would still persist because of the *approach*, traditionally taken by African leaders to resolve their economic difficulties. In *any* scientific resolution of a problem, there are four basic steps that must be followed:

Step 1: Identification and Public Exposure of the Problem. Generally, an economic malaise or societal problem is exposed by journalists, editors or the media (newspapers, radio, TV) as well as by intellectuals (teachers, university professors), writers, novelists, poets and so on. Exposing a problem (corruption, economic mismanagement, government wastes, inefficiencies) may be embarrassing. But the media and the writing profession perform a vital function for society by calling attention to a problem that might otherwise be ignored. To lavish praise upon a government when its tail is on fire performs a grave disservice not only to the government itself but also to the society at large.

Step 2: Analysis of the Problem. After identifying the problem, assuming the government is enlightened enough to permit such an exposure, the next step entails an analysis of *all* potential causes. For example, a chronic shortage of foreign exchange may be due to such *external* factors as low prices for an export crop, or to *internal* factors such as diversion of foreign exchange and overvalued currencies.

Steps 3 & 4: Prescription and Monitoring. After analyzing the causes of the problem, Step 3 requires a *prescription* of remedies and the final step, 4, a *monitoring* and *assessment* of the efficacy of the corrective measures. The final step is crucial since economic, political and other conditions change in the course of grappling with a problem.

Unfortunately, the manner in which many African leaders approached their economic problems was not only unscientific but crass as well. The media in much of Africa has been a government monopoly, owned or controlled by the state. It serves as a propaganda mouthpiece of the government, and naturally covers up problems embarrassing to the state. Usually, it is only after the government has been violently overthrown that the media engages in a debilitating and protracted analysis of "What Went Wrong?"

Even when African governments could no longer conceal a problem and had to admit its existence, they performed some rather strange quasi-Leninist gymnastics on the causes of the crisis: one step forward, two steps back. For example, in the early 1980s, the Marxist regime of Comrade Mengistu vehemently denied the existence of an imminent famine; when the regime finally admitted the threat of starvation, it blamed the drought, but not the inane civil war, disastrous agricultural policies, or insane government resettlement programs. Currently, at least 792,000 Angolans face starvation. Like its Marxist counterpart in Ethiopia, the Marxist government in Angola blames the drought, but not the 15-year-old civil war that has devastated the countryside and disrupted the lives and livelihood of peasant farmers.

This sort of intellectual astigmatism is not unique to Angola and Ethiopia alone. Most African government officials are imbued with a meretricious propensity to blame their economic difficulties on someone else, usually *external factors*: colonial legacies, American imperialism, a hostile international economic environment, and the avaricious proclivity of Western commercial banks to extract exorbitant interest premiums. They never considered the significance or the role of *internal factors*: senseless and endless civil wars which have produced an excess of 10 million refugees and cost Africa at least $8 billion annually in lost output; capital flight out of Africa (at least $15 billion is illegally siphoned out of Africa by the elites); wasteful military spending (African governments spend about $12 billion annually on the importation of arms and the maintenance of the military, just about the same $12 billion Africa receives in foreign aid each year from all sources).[2] The weapons are used not so much to establish order and stability, but to oppress and slaughter the African people.

Nobody denies the role of external factors in the causation of Africa's crisis. For example, the drop of cocoa prices on the world market caused Ghana to lose about $200 million in foreign exchange. Donor countries have been tardy in providing debt relief and cancellation of debts. Furthermore, aid resources, in some cases, have not flowed sufficiently to support current restructuring programs. But even so, more aid resources would make little difference in the *majority* of cases. Most Nigerians would concede that even if their country's $26 billion foreign debt were completely wiped out today, Nigeria would accumulate another huge foreign debt in less than two years. Clearly, analysts should also focus on the internal weaknesses of the government structure and its debt-creating afflictions. Clamoring for more debt relief is not enough.

African leaders need to take a critical look at their own policies and the *internal* causes of Africa's crisis. General Babangida remarked that African leaders have failed their people—a dramatic admission coming from a black African head of state. "In a widely reported speech President Babangida of Nigeria told the summit it was time Africa stopped behaving as if its survival depended on the charity of the developed countries" (*West Africa*, July 23-29, 1990; p. 2,147).[3] A bucket full of holes can only hold so much water for a while. Pouring in more water makes little sense if it will all drain away. To the extent that there are *internal leakages* in Africa (corruption, senseless civil wars, government wastes, capital flight, hideous tyranny, military barbarism, etc.), pouring in more foreign aid or debt relief won't save Africa. As a first order of priority, the leaks must be plugged.

But those Africans courageous enough to identify these *internal* factors and expose the leakages were persecuted, hounded and in many cases slaughtered. Say something an African government doesn't like and "Poof!" it is detention or the grave.

> One of the three Kenyan lawyers formally released from detention on Wednesday was arrested again and charged today with publication of a seditious magazine . . . The lawyer charged today was Gitobu Imanyara, editor in chief of *The Nairobi Law Monthly* . . . In its new proceedings against Mr. Imanyara, the Government cited as seditious the current issue of the magazine, which features a cover story titled "The Historic Debate—Law, Democracy and Multiparty Politics in Kenya." The issue includes a wide range of articles, including some for and against a multiparty system of politics and scholarly legal opinions. It also includes excerpts from speeches by President Moi.
>
> The magazine has a relatively small circulation, mainly among lawyers. But the current issue generated so much interest that its initial print run of 10,000 copies sold out. An extra 5,000 copies were printed and were being distributed on the streets of Nairobi as Mr. Imanyara was being charged in court.
>
> In the last two years, the Kenyan Government has shut down three magazines: a church publication, a financial and a magazine about development (*The New York Times*, July 27, 1990; p. A3).

Africa will *never* find solutions to its economic problems or develop in such an atmosphere of intimidation, harassment, detention and closure of newspapers and magazines that do not toe the government's line. It is this sort of intellectual barbarism on the part of "educated" African leaders that has kept black Africa in economic backwaters.[4] The supposedly "backward and primitive" chiefs of Africa show a far superior sense of intellectual maturity. The chiefs are not only tolerant of dissenting opinion but in fact solicit and encourage it as, by custom, they must rule by consensus. Decision-making by consensus, by its very definition, is the antithesis of dictatorship and intellectual repression.

Dictatorship was never part of the indigenous African political tradition. There were few despotic chiefs in traditional Africa. The African chief rules for life but he does not appoint himself. Nobody just gets up and declares himself "chief for life" and his village to be a "one-party state" in indigenous Africa.[5]

At an important February 1990 conference in Arusha, Tanzania, African leaders themselves recognized that repression impedes economic development. The conference adopted the *African Charter for Popular Participation in Development Transformation* which holds that the absence of democracy is a major cause of the chronic unemployment of Africa:

> We affirm that nations cannot be built without the popular support and full participation of the people, nor can the economic crisis be resolved, and the human and economic conditions improved, without the full and effective contribution, creativity and popular enthusiasm of the vast majority of the people. After all, it is to the people that the very benefits of development should and must accrue. We are convinced that neither can Africa's perpetual economic crisis be overcome, nor can a bright future for Africa and its people see the light of day unless the structure, pattern and political context of the process of socio-economic development are appropriately altered (*Africa Forum*, Vol. 1, No. 2, 1991; p. 14).

But as usual, African leaders failed to follow their pious pronouncements with action. In a blistering article, King Moshoeshoe II of Lesotho demanded: "Give Us Back Our Own Democracy":

> The important new content of current African mass democratic movements is the demand, by the grassroots, for radical change and reform . . . Meaningful African development cannot be attained without the consent and cooperation of the people, who must be assured not only that their governments' policies of development are being pursued in their interests, but also that their governments are continuously accountable to them. Only then can economic development gather the necessary momentum. . . .
>
> The continuing African struggle for independence from foreign domination is a liberation struggle for the right to determine a culturally derived political and economic ideology capable of delivering African economic and political development. Without such an *indigenous* ideology, which we failed to define at the time of our original independence, there can be little

or no progress towards regionizable development for the African majorities (*Index on Censorship*, April 1992; p. 10).

Ideology is irrelevant to Africa's needs. Africa had its own indigenous civilizations and ideology before the white man set foot on the continent. When Africa asked for its independence from colonial rule, it did not ask black neo-colonialists to destroy its indigenous institutions and impose "capitalism," "Marxism," "Shitoism," and other alien "isms" on its people. But that was exactly what most African leaders did after independence when they borrowed alien systems from Eastern Europe to impose on Africa. But when these systems collapsed in Eastern Europe, African leaders failed to draw lessons from them.

Lessons from Eastern Europe and Russia

The dramatic events in Eastern Europe and Russia have introduced new dimensions and vistas into how economic difficulties are to be resolved. In addition, geopolitical relations have changed, and it would be foolish for African heads of state to pretend they can do business as usual: clamor for more aid, and expect the West to rush to their assistance. Nor can they expect to play one superpower against the other.

One lesson from Eastern Europe and the Soviet Union is that half-baked economic reform measures do not work. In the Soviet Union, the Communist Party's stranglehold on the media was incompatible with Gorbachev's *glasnost* and his *perestroika* program of political and economic reforms. Other inconsistencies spelt doom. Gorbachev wanted a multiparty system, albeit one in which the Communist Party would continue to dominate. He also wanted to adopt free market devices in an economy which was fundamentally communist; a "regulated market economy," dominated by the state—a contradiction in terms.

Another lesson is that Marxists and statists do not reform themselves. They are booted out. Similarly, one cannot expect African elites to reform themselves by sharing political power or the largesse and subsidies they derive from the reins of power or by abolishing the present one-party state system from which they benefit immensely.

Other than a revolution, there is a less costly alternative: abandon attempts to reform the elite-controlled state sector and shift the emphasis to the *informal/indigenous* sector. Such a policy would make sense for several reasons. First, this is where the majority of the African people are. Most Africans are farmers, fishermen, artisans, bakers, traders, etc; they are not factory workers or civil servants. Second, a prosperous and growing informal sector will absorb workers laid off from the state sector. And third, rejuvenation of the informal/indigenous sector costs very little. For the most part it entails the removal of offensive regulations.

The final lesson that can be drawn from Eastern Europe pertains to the *sequence* of reform. Ideally, the sequence of reform should run from the intellectual to the political before economic reform. Economic reform alone is not sufficient. But then, how can there be political reform when there is no freedom of expression to discuss what political system is best suited to the people? Only intellectual freedom can establish the free marketplace of ideas from which political and economic reform can be crafted.

Furthermore, the two great revolutions of the West (American and French) were inspired by ideas freely espoused and exchanged across the Atlantic by such intellectual giants as Lafayette, Washington, Jefferson, Montesquieu, Voltaire and Rousseau, to name a few. In insisting upon economic reform first, many Western governments and aid agencies not only scoff at their own history but also put the cart before the horse. Intellectual freedom was the key to, and the trigger of, the epochal events in Eastern Europe.

There is no such *glasnost* in Africa. The media are still controlled and owned by the state. Newsprint into much of Africa is regulated by import licensing. A private newspaper or magazine which does not toe the government line is either denied an import license or banned. Hundreds of editors, journalists, professors and novelists languish in jail for writing something their governments did not like.

The print media is particularly important in the democratization process. It exposes human rights abuses, corruption, repression, economic mismanagement and a host of other ailments of a dictatorship. It is also in the print media where solutions to problems and ideas are identified, published, and exchanged. In fact, it can be said that nations that develop or advance are precisely those that permit a free exchange of ideas, and guarantee freedom of expression. But where do you have this freedom of expression in Africa today? What is needed in Africa at this stage is an information revolution that would break government monopoly over the media.

A free press is anathema to tyrants on both the left and the right. Freedom of expression is not alien to Africa but deeply rooted in its indigenous culture. Nobody was arrested by the chief or a council member for expressing their viewpoints. According to Dr. K.A. Busia (1967),

> The Asante provided opportunities for "commoners," i.e., those who were ruled, to express criticism, either through their lineage heads, or through a chosen leader recognized as a spokesman for the commoners; through him, the body of free citizens could criticize the government and express

their wishes when they thought that undesirable measures were being contemplated or enforced; in the last resort, they could depose their rulers (p. 26).

Give Africa back to its peasants and "primitive" chiefs and kings. These "backward" chiefs were far more intellectually and politically mature than many of the so-called "educated" African heads of state. Any peasant with a grievance against even a chief could see a Councillor, and get a fair hearing. Elders would negotiate conflicts between families; native courts would adjudicate disputes between individuals. Verdicts could be appealed; from the family court, the chief's court, and ultimately to the king's court of final appeal.

But, in much of "modern" Africa ruled by "educated" elites, no such processes of arbitration and conflict resolution prevail. Instead, we have kangaroo courts, military tribunals, arbitrary arrests, summary executions, government monopoly of the media, and denial of freedom of expression.

Africa's salvation lies in returning to its roots and building upon its own indigenous institutions, and on the tradition of reaching a consensus through open debates of issues and free expression of opinion. The argument that Western-style democracy is unsuitable for Africa, and would fuel tribalism, is pure nonsense. Africa should not copy blindly from any foreign country but must build on its own—exactly what Botswana did. It is not racked by civil war or tribalism but instead serves as a shining economic success story:

> Botswana built a working democracy on an aboriginal tradition of local gatherings called *kgotlas* that resemble New England town meetings; it has a record $2.7 billion in foreign reserves (*Newsweek*, July 23, 1990; p. 28).

To set the ball rolling on the rest of the continent, get the media out of the hands of incompetent and corrupt African governments, and let the African people speak. The peasants need real *blacknost* to do the *watusi*: one step back, two steps forward, while chanting *kirikiri* to their state houses, and demanding to see the "Swiss bank socialists."

The West can help in the democratization process by insisting that African governments sell off all organs of the mass media, which are *state owned* enterprises in most African countries, before receiving Structural Adjustment loans. The mass media ought to be the first strategic industry to be privatized in economic restructuring. Otherwise, there should be no loans for restructuring at all.

REFERENCES

Arhin, Kwame. *Traditional Rule in Ghana.* Accra: Challenge Enterprises, 1985.

Ayittey, George B.N. "A Blueprint For Africa's Economic Reform," *Journal of Economic Growth,* 1986, Vol 2, No. 3.

———. "Economic Atrophy in Black Africa," *The Cato Journal,* Spring; Vol. 7, No. 1, 1987.

———. "The Political Economy of Reform in Africa," *Journal of Economic Growth,* Spring, 1989.

———. *Africa Betrayed* (Forthcoming). Washington, DC: The Cato Institute, 1991.

———. *Indigenous African Institutions.* (Forthcoming). New York: Transnational Publishers, 1991.

Bundy, Colin. *The Rise and Fall of the South African Peasant.* Cape Town: David Philip, 1988.

Busia, K.A. *Africa in Search of Democracy.* New York: Praeger, 1967.

Kendall, Frances and Louw, Leon. *After Apartheid: The Solution for South Africa.* San Francisco: Institute of Contemporary Studies Press, 1987.

Koyama, Digby S. *Customary Law in a Changing Society.* Cape Town: Juta Publishing & Co., 1980.

Williams, Chancellor. *The Destruction of Black Civilization.* Chicago: Third World Press, 1987.

Duncan, David Ewing. "The Long Good-Bye," *The Atlantic,* July 1990.

World Bank. *Sub-Saharan Africa: From Crisis to Self-Sustainable Growth,* Washington, DC, 1989.

———. *Report on Adjustment Lending II: Policies for the Recovery of Growth* (Internal Report), Washington, DC, 1990.

NOTES

1. In 1992 only 9 black African countries (Botswana, Benin, Cape Verde Islands, The Gambia, Mauritius, Namibia, São Tomé & Principe, Senegal and Zambia)—out of the total of 45—allow their people the right to vote and choose their leaders. Five of the nine (Benin, Cape Verde Islands, Namibia, Sao Tome & Principe and Zambia) are recent additions to this tiny democratic club. Twenty-two are military dictatorships and the rest are one-party states. Several countries (Angola, Congo, Central African Republic, Ghana, Mali, Niger, Nigeria, Mozambique, Sierra Leone, South Africa, Togoland, and Zimbabwe) are however taking hesitant steps to open up their political systems.

2. For more on these malpractices, see Ayittey (1987 and 1989).

3. At the same summit, the newly elected Chairman of the OAU, President Yoweri Museveni of Uganda, declared: "We should not practice dictatorship under the guise of independence, because independence does not mean dictatorship.... Leaders must be elected periodically; they must be accountable. There must be a free press and there must be no restriction on who participates in the democratic process" *West Africa,* July 23–29, 1990; p. 2,147. It would be nice if President Museveni submits himself to a "periodic election."

4. It is even more maddening when these atrocities are meted out by African governments which have signed and ratified the Organization of African Unity's (OAU) Charter of Human and Peoples' Rights. For example, Cameroon did so in 1987, Ghana in 1989 and Malawi in 1990.

5. For more see Ayittey (1991).

Part V
Structural Adjustment and Employment

8

Structural Adjustment and the Labor Market

Norberto García
Jaime Mezzera

THE LATIN AMERICAN LABOR MARKET IN 1950–90[1]

Progress During Thirty Years: 1950–80

Economic growth, migration and the qualitative change in Latin American labor markets. During 1950–80, the region's labor force grew very fast, at an average rate of 2.5 percent a year, and labor supply more than doubled. With intense rural—urban migration, the urban labor force grew even faster: 3.8 percent a year, a tripling of urban labor supply. These simple facts lead to two main issues which are relevant to this chapter.

First, during those thirty years, Latin America underwent a massive transformation from a predominantly peasant society to a semi-industrialized urban economy, with all the attendant problems placed on social institutions, the economy and the labor market. Second, the incorporation of millions of new workers into urban jobs required intense long-term economic growth. Total GDP growth proceeded at an average rate of 5.5 percent a year, multiplying by a factor of five during the period. In turn, under the influence of industrialization policies and investment, nonagricultural GDP grew by 5.8 percent and industrial GDP by 6.2 percent a year, thus achieving a sixfold increase in 30 years.

Rapid economic growth led to massive changes in the composition of the labor force, as well as in the employment structure. The share of agriculture in the labor force, which was 55 percent in 1950, tumbled to only 32 percent in 1980, with the shares of both industry and the tertiary sectors increasing by 60 percent of their initial levels (data from PRE-ALC, 1982 and CEPAL, 1990a). In other words, by 1980 the Latin American labor problem had already become a predominantly urban question.

Urban modern-sector job creation. In the region as a whole, the urban labor force grew at 3.8 percent a year, nonagricultural employment did so by 3.9 percent, and formal-sector employment grew at 4.1 percent (PREALC, 1982 and García, 1982). At the same time, output per modern-sector worker grew by 2.2 percent a year, a doubling of productivity in thirty years (García, 1982).

Informality. We define the informal sector as the set of nonagricultural productive units with very limited access to capital and other inputs complementary to raw labor. Using the best available *proxy*, the share of the informal sector in the total labor force rose from 13 to 19 percent between 1950 and 1980, whereas its share in the urban labor force decreased slightly, from 31 to 29 percent (PREALC, 1982 and García, 1982).

Labor incomes. Unfortunately, although underemployment preeminent as a labor market problem, and therefore, incomes should be the main focus of analysis, there is no hard data for the region as a whole during this period. However, partial evidence of real wages increasing at the rate of productivity in the modern sector can be found and is reviewed in, for instance, Ramos (1972).

Though no information is available on the long-run informal-sector incomes per worker, it has been shown that total informal sector incomes increase at a rate close to that of the total modern-sector wagebill (Mezzera, 1990). Thus, incomes per worker in the informal sector must have increased too, since during 1950–80 the modern-sector wagebill increased faster than did labor supply to the informal sector.

Unemployment. In developing countries, unemployment is a predominantly urban modern-sector phenomenon; workers in agriculture and in informal sector are predominantly underemployed—in the sense of very low productivity and incomes—rather than openly unemployed. The regionwide average rate of open unemployment in urban areas fell slightly from 7.5 in 1950 to 6 percent in 1980 (PREALC, 1982 and García, 1982). Along with the persistence of informality, this almost constant rate of unemployment signals that, in spite of high growth during thirty years, by 1980 Latin America was still very far from achieving a near-total integration of its population into well-paid productive jobs. This is a major long-term weakness of the growth model, to which must be added that, for external-sector reasons, that model was no longer tenable, as is discussed next.

The main weakness of the growth model. Two related elements in Latin American economic and employment growth during these thirty years

were a matter of serious concern: the decrease in the role of exports as
an engine of growth, and the conceptually inseparable increase in the
external indebtedness of the region.

The region-wide foreign funding needs grew relatively slowly, from
2.2 percent of regional GDP in 1953–55, to 3.5 percent in 1970–75, but
then jumped by one more full percentage point in 1976–81. To a large
extent, this long-run increase reflects the stagnation of its primary net
exports, which were more than 10 percent of overall GDP in the mid-
fifties but fell to one-half of that figure in 1970–75, and the continued
negative balance of trade in manufactures.[2] The jump of the external
funding in the second part of the seventies was linked to the oil price
shock and the recycling of petrodollars, but is no more than an acceler-
ation of the long-term trend (Wells, 1987). The cumulative effect of these
trends was heavily felt in the region during the eighties, when fresh
loans ceased to be available.

Setbacks During the Eighties

From 1982 in most countries, the external crisis led to a strong reversal
of the trends of the three previous decades. The adjustment could not
be avoided, and the trade balance went from a negative figure of 30
billion dollars in 1981, to a surplus of almost 11 billion in 1983, a 40
billion dollar swing in only two years, that represented almost 4 percent
of its GDP and was achieved through import reductions (Wells, 1987).[3]
Such a severe economic adjustment led to a serious setback in the labor
market: thirty years of progress were lost in a decade.

Economic performance, 1980-89. The GDP growth rate fell from its
historical level of 5.5 to only 1.2 per year; nonagricultural GDP growth
(1.1 percent per year) followed suit, with industry growing by only 0.4
percent per year. As a consequence, per capita GDP fell during the
whole decade at an average annual rate of 1 percent every year. The
external crisis led to a very stringent foreign exchange constraint and
to severe short-term adjustment plans which in turn resulted in falls in
growth rates, in modern-sector employment creation, and in wages.
Also, the crisis and the adjustment plans in several countries led to a
large increase in inflation and to a severe reduction in investment as
savings fell and a large proportion of the remaining savings were used
to service the external debt.

Most of the impact took place during the 1982–85 period, when
average per capita expenditure fell, in real terms, by almost 17 percent
(Wells, 1987). From 1986, the downward trend became much less acute,
with some growth in some years and in some countries.

Modern-sector job creation. During the eighties, the rate of increase of
formal-sector employment was reduced to slightly under 3 percent.

However, the most intense fall in this rate was recorded within the medium and large-sized firms that had been the mainstay of modern-sector expansion up to 1980; jobs in that type of firm only grew by 0.5 percent a year between 1980 and 1989. As a result, very small firms; i.e., those employing up to 10 workers, expanded employment by 7.5 percent a year, and informal-sector employment grew by 6.7 percent a year.[4] In other words, very small firms and the informal sector (as proxied here) took up the slack of the excess urban labor that could not make it into modern-sector jobs. The consequent changes in the employment structure are shown in Figure 8.1, which also confirms that the main damage to the labor market took place during the comparatively short span of 1982–85.

Unemployment and informality. When the crisis exploded, in 1982–83, unemployment rates shot up by two full percentage points, then fell monotonically as displaced workers found "niches" in the urban informal sector and in small firms: in other words, the labor-market adjusted through underemployment. As defined, the share of the urban informal sector plus very small firms in total urban employment grew from 39 percent in 1980—when the modern sector was predominantly made up of large and medium-sized firms—to 51 percent in 1990, a time when half of the urban jobs are virtually informal.

Wages and other incomes. Within the modern sector, two segments can be recognized describing how wages behaved during the eighties. On the one hand, in large and medium-sized firms, real wages fell by close to 1 percent a year, thus reaching an index of 93 at the end of decade. On the other hand, the major setbacks in terms of real wages showed

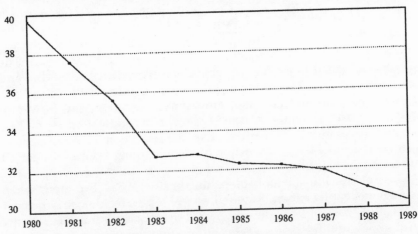

Figure 8.1   Non-Agricultural Labor Force Percent of Jobs in Large and Medium-Sized Firms, Latin America, 1980–1989

up, first, in very small firms of the modern sector, where real wages fell by almost 4 percent a year, thus reaching an index of 70 at the end of the decade. Second, in the public sector, real wages fell at same rate. Third, in the informal sector the real average income per worker tumbled almost 6 percent per year, producing an end-of-decade figure only 58 percent of its initial value (PREALC, 1991).

STRUCTURAL ADJUSTMENT AS A STRATEGY FOR THE NINETIES[5]

Introduction

According to CEPAL (1979, 1990) the share of manufacturing in total output went from 30 percent in 1950-55 to 37 percent in the second half of the sixties and to 36 percent by the late seventies. This strongly suggests that import substitution was successful up to the late sixties, but stagnated thereafter.

By 1965-70, the region as a whole, and most of the countries taken individually, had used heavy protection to build industrial structures which could have been the basis of an opening up based on manufactured exports. However, only a few countries began to follow strategies that included export promotion, Brazil, Colombia, Costa Rica and Uruguay among them.[6]

The crisis of the eighties has had the merit of bringing the foreign-exchange constraint back to its role as the foremost restriction to growth and employment creation.

Structural Adjustment

Adoption of a strategy. The U.N. Economic Commission for Latin America—reflecting a trend which is increasingly visible in several countries of the region—has taken a catalyst role in discussing the economic strategy for the nineties and beyond. What follows explores an interpretation of the notion of structural adjustment discussed in CEPAL (1990), one which is likely to proceed in the current decade, with a view to later assessing—in Section C—its impact on the labor markets of several economies of the region.

The process of structural adjustment has already begun in several countries. Chile started out along this path in 1975; Costa Rica, Mexico and Bolivia followed suit in the second half of the eighties. Argentina and Venezuela began their adjustment processes in 1989, with Brazil, Colombia and Peru doing so in 1990. In fact, Brazil had advanced in the modernization of its industry and infrastructure beginning in the seventies, while Uruguay took steps in the same direction at different times during the seventies and eighties. The above shows that, with the exception of Chile, the main impact of this process will be felt during the current decade, and is still too new to be evaluated.

Prospective analysis. The economic processes underlying the scenarios to be shown in Section C involve a reallocation of resources toward tradable-goods sectors in order to transit along the second phase of industrialization. This implies that investment, technological change, and the retraining of labor will be considerably more intense in tradable-goods activities, particularly in those geared to the production of exportable goods. Therefore, economic growth is expected to become increasingly oriented toward, and led by, exports, in order to achieve a significant and permanent relaxation of the foreign exchange constraint as well as to achieve a better insertion in the international economy.

In that context, investment in sectors producing tradable goods and in activities that support the former should expand more rapidly than in the other sectors. A similar trend is expected in terms of the efficiency of and returns on investment. One consequence of this process is the significant growth in productivity that would initially take place in the tradable-goods sector, and impact positively on the unit costs of exportables and on the growth of exports, particularly of nontraditional goods.

Structural Adjustment and Technical Change

The net impact of structural adjustment on the labor market goes beyond that of technological modernization, since, in addition to the latter's effects, it includes the impact of the liberalization of the economy on less competitive activities and their suppliers, the effect of restructuring the public sector in countries in which the level of public sector employment was very high, the restructuring of the private sector based on the criteria of external competitiveness, and a gradual change in the composition of production.

Two Phases in Structural Adjustment

It is important to distinguish between the short- and long-term effects on the labor market. In this regard, a distinction should be drawn between a transitional phase—in which the negative impact of the adjustment on the labor market will tend to be more strongly felt—from a later phase in which, following the consolidation of the economic changes, it should be possible to return to acceptable rates of growth and employment creation. This distinction between phases is related to the fact that, with limited resources, the initial impact of the set of policies aimed at the reallocation of resources causes a contraction in employment growth, particularly in the nontradable sectors, while time is required, on account of the different lags involved, to achieve greater growth in tradables, and for the latter to have a significant impact on employment. A corollary to this is that the effect on employment of a structural change will vary according to the phase of this process. It is important to bear this element in mind in order to understand some of the hypotheses underlying the 1991–2000 projections.

Finally, it should be recalled here that the process described above may involve different strategies, which range from a shock free-market policy, which focuses on the prompt achievement and maintenance of "the right relative prices," to more gradual strategies which also make use of sectoral restructuring programs, mitigate social consequences, etc. However, despite these differences, in Latin America there is a trend toward the adoption of strategies that assign a greater role to the market and to the competitive insertion in the international economy in a general context of scarcity of external and/or public resources.

THE CHALLENGE OF THE NINETIES IN THE LABOR MARKET[7]

Structural Adjustment, Employment and Income

For most Latin American countries the nineties present a twofold challenge. On the one hand, most of the countries of the region will face the need to achieve significant progress in the structural adjustment of their economies in this decade (CEPAL, 1990). On the other hand, they will have to do so without increasing the enormous social costs incurred in the eighties, and within a framework of greater equity. The performance of the labor market is crucial on both counts.

This section analyzes the expected evolution of the labor market, in the context of those changes which affect the supply of and demand for labor; it especially focuses on the results, by groups of countries, of the increase in employment and income by segments of the urban labor market. The analysis rests on the elaboration of scenarios based on 1990–2000 projections for a set of countries of the region.[8] Both the projections and their results must be understood as indications of the expected direction and intensity of the main phenomena examined in the light of certain hypotheses, and not as a forecast or statistical prognosis.

The specific features of the medium and long-term structural change adopted in each country will no doubt lead to different adjustment processes in the countries' urban labor markets. However, on account of the growing importance of temporary employment, part-time work, less protected jobs and occupations in the informal sector, greater flexibility and less stability in employment should be expected in most cases.

The areas that will be of greatest concern in the 1990-2000 projections are the impact of structural adjustment on the rates of labor absorption into modern segments, the increase in informal employment since, in terms of stylized facts, this is the key feature of an adjustment of the labor market in the Latin American countries, and the behavior of labor incomes by segments.

The Urban Labor Market in 1991-2000

The purpose of this section is to explore the evolution of the main features of the urban labor market in 1990-2000, in the context of an optimistic perspective of economic trends in Latin America during the decade. In other words, these projections are aimed at giving a "ceiling" for the labor market results that can be expected during the current decade.

Urban labor supply. The urban labor force is expected to continue to grow at a diminishing rate, and to average a growth rate of 3.2 percent over the decade in the region as a whole. However, some countries, basically those that have already advanced most in the rural-urban transition process, will exhibit much lower supply growth rates. This will play an important role in determining the outcomes of the projections.

CONTEXT AND MAIN HYPOTHESES.

Economic projections. The projected trends are optimistic for four reasons. First, they accept that net transfers of resources abroad will tend to decline, as a proportion of GDP, between 1990 and 2000, at a rate which would vary according to the scenarios described in later pages. Second, it assumes a rather dynamic performance of the export sector. This implies greater access to external markets than existed in the eighties, and a greater degree of integration among countries. Third, it projects, explicitly, a process of structural change in the majority of countries studied, assuming that economic policy is effective in achieving this as well as in gradually reversing the main macroeconomic imbalances—in terms of inflation and external deficits—inherited from the eighties, or in attaining structural changes with less pronounced imbalances than in the recent past. Fourth, largely as a consequence of the above, it assumes that the process of structural adjustment will advance at the rate determined by the availability of foreign exchange and/or public sector position. In this regard, those countries which embarked upon their process of structural change in the seventies and eighties—Chile, Costa Rica and Mexico—will continue their modernization during the nineties. Similarly, for those countries that initiated their changes in the late eighties or early nineties—among them Argentina, Brazil, Colombia, Peru and Venezuela—it is assumed that they will continue the effort toward change, particularly in the first half of the nineties. Finally, it is assumed that structural change is initiated during the nineties in Guatemala and Uruguay, the other two countries on which the projections are based.

As a result, the first half of the decade would witness a great effort toward gradual change in a large number of the countries studied, which will continue their modernization at a more moderate pace in the second half of the decade. This hypothesis is important because the negative effects of the transitional phase on the labor market will show up during the first half of the decade, while it is assumed that in the second half of the decade the more positive effects will be felt.

It should be pointed out that a reduction in the net debt servicing is required, through long-term negotiations, to restart the growth process. Such reduction is an assumption of these projections on the basis of which it not only becomes possible to increase the total investment rate but also—and possibly more importantly—to reorient a growing proportion of it toward tradable-goods sectors, thus inducing higher productivity and, through it, larger exports and the expansion of output at the speed of foreign exchange availability. In the labor market, productivity gains would make it possible to simultaneously increase wages and employment in the modern sector.

The rate of growth of investment varies according to the scenarios and in accordance with the rate of decline in net transfers of resources abroad in relation to output. Investment grows faster than does GDP, which represents a change with respect to the previous decade. In particular, the rate of increase in investment in the tradable sector is higher than that of total investment.

It is taken into account that, as pointed at in CEPAL (1990b), the increase in productivity must be a system-wide process in the sense that many nontradable activities that are closely related to tradable ones—typically services connected to foreign trade, but also nontraded production of inputs for tradable sectors—will have to undergo productivity increases consistent with those of the tradable-goods sector. No doubt, that implies that, in practice, the frontier of the tradable sector will become less well defined than what stems from simple theory, which ignores the internal heterogeneity of the non-traded goods sector.

Even assuming a gradual decline in the share of transfers of resources abroad in GDP, the required increase in investment demands even more rapid growth in domestic savings. A decisive factor for achieving that result is that real wages increase by slightly less than does productivity, in both the tradable and nontradable sectors. To the extent that real wages increase more slowly than productivity, there is an increase in the rate of savings and investment, of technological change, of productivity in the tradable-goods sector and, consequently, of exports, output and employment.

Projections of the labor market. The systematic increase in productivity in the tradable sector is crucial to the evolution of the labor market. In the first place, it reduces the conflict between the real exchange rate and wages, thus permitting the growth of the latter without real appreciation. Second, its effect on the generation of foreign exchange has a significant—albeit lagged—impact on employment. The latter aspect is clearly different from the framework of a closed economy that is not oriented toward the production of tradables.

Employment is projected in the form of two distinct segments: modern urban employment—both private and public—and informal urban employment. Employment in the public sector, even though autonomous, reflects the restructuring of the public sector which has already begun in different countries of the region. Modern private-sector employment is particularly sensitive to the rate of expansion in the respective activities. Growth in employment in the modern private sector will tend to be higher if real wages rise more slowly than productivity, not because labor demand is negatively sloped, but on account of the effect of that differential on the increase in domestic savings, the rate of investment and of exports, and, consequently, on its lagged impact on employment creation.

Employment in the informal urban sector is sensitive to the increase in the urban labor force unable to find employment in modern activities. The average income in the informal urban sector depends, on the one hand, on the performance of demand for their products—determined largely by the trend in wages and employment in the modern urban sector—and on the other, on the increase in employment in the informal sector (Mezzera, 1990).

Construction of scenarios. The main hypotheses described in the previous points were focused on the elaboration of scenarios for 1991–2000 for a sampling of ten countries of the region which represent more than 95 percent of the labor force and employment in Latin America, on account of which the results may be considered as representative of the region as a whole.[9]

The ten countries analyzed were in turn classified on the basis of two features:

1. countries with an expected growth in the urban labor force greater (lower) than the average for Latin America;

2. countries with a greater (lesser) degree of relative progress in the area of structural adjustment in 1991–2000.

Consequently, the following groups emerge on the basis of the above classification:

- *Group A*: Countries with a rate of increase in the urban labor force that is lower than the regional average and a lower degree of relative progress of structural adjustment. Group A includes Argentina and Uruguay.
- *Group B*: Countries with a rate of growth in the urban labor force lower than the regional average and with greater than average advance in structural adjustment. Group B includes Chile, Colombia and Costa Rica.[10]
- *Group C*: Countries with a rate of growth in the urban labor force that is higher than the regional average and with less relative progress in structural adjustment. Group C includes Guatemala and Peru.
- *Group D*: Countries with a rate of growth in their urban labor force that is higher than the regional average and with greater relative progress in structural adjustment. Group D includes Brazil, Mexico and Venezuela.

The scenarios were built from projections by countries for 1991–2000 using a simple macrosectoral and labor market model, able to capture structural changes. The country projections were then aggregated in order to obtain a scenario for each group and for the set of countries in the sample of Latin America.

Two scenarios were elaborated. The first of these, termed Scenario I or Basic, is characterized by the inclusion of optimistic hypotheses for the main variables of the external context and their impact on changes in domestic production patterns. Thus, on average, for the set of countries in the sample, it assumes a gradual decline in the share of net transfers of resources abroad in the GDP, from the approximately 3.8 percent recorded in the late eighties, to 2.8 percent in the year 2000. Similarly, for the same set of countries an increase of 5.1 percent per annum is recorded in exports, assuming constant terms of trade. It assumes a gradual shift in the composition of exports, toward nontraditional products. This external scenario is linked to steady progress in the structural change, which varies, as described before, by groups of countries, and therefore it assumes that efforts will be made toward increasing domestic savings, investment and productivity in both the tradable and nontradable sectors, consistent with the hypotheses on net transfers of resources and growth in exports.

The second one is Scenario II or of Rapid Growth. This was elaborated to determine the results on the labor market of rates of economic growth approaching those recorded by Latin America in the period 1950–1980, in the context of more open economies that are undergoing structural change, and with growth led by tradable-producing sectors. This scenario assumes a more rapid drop in the share in GDP of the net transfer of resources abroad, which for the sample of countries as a whole would decline from 3.8 percent at the end of the eighties to approximately 1.4 percent in the year 2000. Similarly, it allows for a more rapid increase in exports, at a rate of approximately 6.4 percent annually for the countries in the sample as a whole. In line with the above, it accepts an increase in domestic savings, investment and productivity, higher than the one recorded in the basic scenario. In particular, this scenario is also associated with a more rapid rate of change, in terms of a larger increase in investment in tradables and in technological change in those activities.

Results of Scenario I (Basic). Table 8.1 summarizes the results of Scenario I (Basic). The main conclusions are as follows: Latin American development should recover more "normal" relations between some of the variables that determine both economic and employment growth. During the crisis years of 1982–88 productivity of the modern sector remained constant while investment fell by about 3 percent a year. This implies that whatever growth took place was based on putting back into production some of the unused capacity that stemmed from the 1982–83 crisis. For the nineties, the projections imply that investment should grow faster than GDP, which should in turn expand faster than productivity, making room for employment in medium and large firms to grow much faster than the meager 0.5 percent a year registered during the eighties.

The average annual rate of economic growth being 4.3 percent, formal urban employment would grow at an annual rate of 2.3 percent, led by formal private employment growing at an annual rate of 2.6 percent; public sector jobs would, of course, increase slowly.

Results during the transitional phase are lower: the growth in private formal employment would be 2 percent in the first half of the decade and would increase to 3 percent in the second half. The employment/output elasticity of the formal private sector would be less than that recorded in 1950–1980 during the first half of the decade, and would be similar to those historical levels in the second half.

The composition of modern-sector employment would change toward modern nontradable activities, though output in tradables increases faster. Even though no distinction was possible in terms of employment by size of firm in the modern private sector, implicit in the results—particularly in nontradables—is that employment in smaller

Table 8.1 Projections of Urban Labor Market in Scenario I (Basic) (1)
1991–2000
(In percent)

	Annual increase in urban labor force	Annual growth in Gross Domestic Product	Annual increase in formal urban employment	Annual increase in private formal employment	Annual increase in public sector employment	Participation of informal employment (2) in urban labor force			Rate of open unemployment		Increase in productivity in the formal private sector	Annual increase in real average wages, formal sector	Increase in average income in the informal urban sector
						1991	1995	2000	1991	2000			
Latin America	3.2	4.3	2.3	2.6	1.2	31.4	34.0	35.6	5.4	5.9	1.9	1.5	-0.4
Group A (3)	1.2	2.8	1.3	1.9	-0.5	33.5	33.8	32.8	9.3	9.1	1.2	1.0	0.2
Group B (4)	2.7	4.4	2.7	2.8	1.7	28.2	28.6	28.0	8.8	8.9	2.0	1.7	0.6
Group C (5)	3.6	3.9	1.8	2.3	0.4	40.2	43.5	46.1	8.3	9.3	1.7	1.1	-1.0
Group D (6)	3.5	4.6	2.3	2.6	1.4	31.0	34.2	36.5	4.0	4.7	2.0	1.6	-0.5

(1) Assumes for the group of countries as a whole, a decline in the share of net transfers of resources in GDP from 3.8 % in 1990 to 2.8 % in 2000, and an increase in exports of 5.1 % per annum.

(2) Defined in restrictive terms as own-account workers, unpaid family members and domestic servants, on account of the non-availability of reliable information on informal sector micro-enterprises.

(3) Argentina and Uruguay; see text for definition.

(4) Chile, Colombia and Costa Rica; see text for definition.

(5) Peru and Guatemala; see text for definition.

(6) Brazil, Mexico and Venezuela; see text for definition.

Source: Preliminary estimates of PREALC

enterprises will increase faster than in large ones. This is due to the fact that economic growth in tradable activities is projected to be more intensive in productivity, as a consequence of the expected concentration of investment, technological change and skilled human resources in these sectors.

Since the rate of growth of formal employment for the period is lower than that of the urban labor force, the share of informal-sector employment will gradually increase from the 31.4 percent recorded in 1990 to 34 percent in 1995 and 35.6 percent in the year 2000. Consequently, one of the most important results illustrates that, despite the decline in the rate of increase of the urban labor force, the trend toward expansion of the informal sector will continue during the 1990–2000 decade (see Figure 8.2), although at a significantly slower rate than in the eighties.

It is important to point out that such result does not hold uniformly across countries, but only in those that belong to Groups C and D, the latter being Brazil, Mexico and Venezuela and thus dominating the regional average. In fact, countries in Groups A and B, where urban labor supply increases at a slower pace, show decreases in the share of informal employment, as is evident in Figures 8.3 through 8.6.

The rate of open urban unemployment should only show a slight increase in comparison to 1990, since in the medium term the labor market basically adjusts through changes in informal employment, as suggested by the trend over the past four decades.

Average wages in the modern segments would increase by approximately 1.5 percent annually, which suggests that the trends toward a

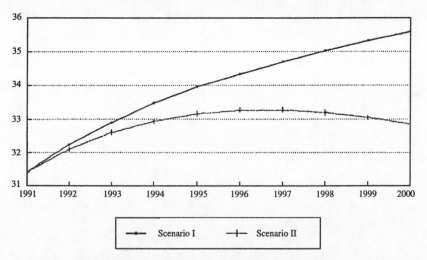

Figure 8.2 Projection of Informal Employment As Percent of Urban Labor Force — Latin America, 1991–2000

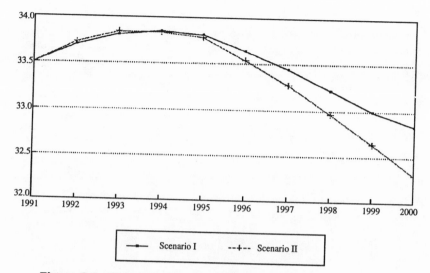

Figure 8.3 Projection of Informal Employment As Percent of Urban Labor Force — Group A, 1991–2000

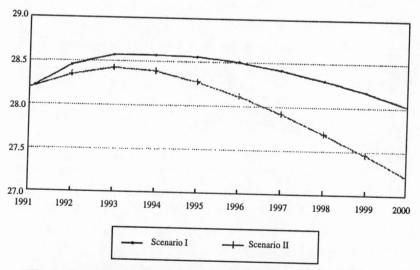

Figure 8.4 Projection of Informal Employment As Percent of Urban Labor Force — Group B, 1991–2000

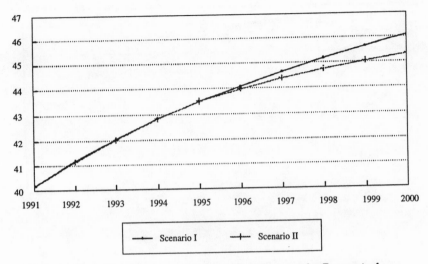

Figure 8.5 Projection of Informal Employment As Percent of
Urban Labor Force — Group C, 1991–2000

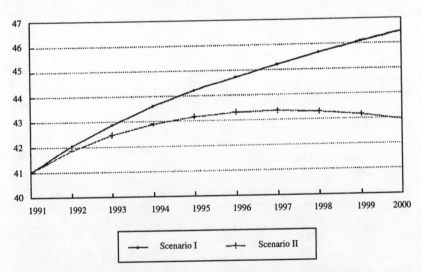

Figure 8.6 Projection of Informal Employment As Percent of
Urban Labor Force — Group D, 1991–2000

decline in real wages recorded in the decade of the eighties would be reversed. It should be mentioned that such an increase is associated with a rise of 1.9 percent annually in the productivity of modern sectors. The increase in real wages in tradable sectors is expected to be higher, but lower in the nontradable sectors, than that of the average of the modern sector, given that productivity in the tradable sectors would increase at much higher rates than in the nontradable sectors. Finally, the real average income in the informal sector would experience no growth, partly as a consequence of the steady increase in the sector's employment level. Even though there will be no recovery in this area, once more it does mean that there will be a change in the trend toward a sharp decline as recorded in the decade of the eighties.

It should be stressed that the results presented do not include specific employment policies analyzed in PREALC (1991) which are available to policymakers desirous to mitigate the negative effects of structural adjustment on the labor market. In this sense, they essentially reflect the trends linked with the spontaneous adjustment of the labor market.

The results of Scenario I by groups of countries are also illustrated in Table 8.1.

As expected, one of the most favorable results are those of Group B, which records expected growth rates in the urban labor force that are lower than the regional average and a greater relative advance in the process of structural change, growth in informal employment would be similar to that of the labor force, so that the share of informality remains constant at about 28 percent. Growth in real wages would be 1.7 percent per year[11]—in contrast with the 2 percent increase in productivity—and the real average income in the informal sector will increase at a rate below 1 percent per annum.

At the other extreme, the less favorable results are those of Group C, where the growth in formal employment is much lower than that of the urban labor force and consequently, the degree of informality would increase from the already high level recorded in 1990, 40.2 percent, up to 46.1 percent by the end of the century. Real modern-sector wages would increase at an annual rate of 1 percent, and real average income in the informal sector would decline by some one percent annually, as a result of its rapid expansion during the decade.

The results of groups A and D are strongly influenced by the different behavior which is expected of the labor supply. Thus, in group A—countries with very low rates of growth in the urban labor force and less progress in structural adjustment—the relative lack of progress toward structural change is offset by the lower rates of increase in the urban labor force. This explains why the degree of informality would decline slightly, in spite of the expected increase in GDP being among the lowest in the countries surveyed (2.8 percent per annum for the group). Similarly, the slow increase in real wages would be explained by the low increase in productivity. Finally, in this group real average incomes in the informal sector would grow very slightly, as a consequence of the reduction in the size of informal employment.

In group D the opposite should take place. Despite the greater progress toward external and internal adjustment, and the recording of the highest economic growth in the region, the very high increase in the urban labor force would lead to insufficient rates of absorption into the modern sectors. This would lead to a significant increase in the size of the informal sector by the end of the century, with its consequent impact on its average income. Nonetheless, since these are countries which have advanced most toward modernization, the increase in productivity and real average wages are among the highest in the sample: 2 and 1.6 percent per year, respectively.

It should be pointed out that the responsiveness of the results to the growth in urban labor force is connected with a number of factors. First, with low rates of economic growth, more sensitivity to labor supply behavior may be expected than with higher rates. Second, the projections arbitrarily end in the year 2000. If they had been continued, the results would have shown turning points and points of decline in the informal sector early in the next century. Third, the general evolution in Latin America is influenced by events in the larger countries of Group D, but, as shown in the group analysis, the trends vary across countries.

Results of Scenario II (Rapid Growth). As explained earlier, the Scenario II of more rapid growth was built to verify the labor-market impact of economic growth rates similar to those recorded for Latin America in 1950–1980.

The results of Scenario II may be analyzed in contrast with Scenario I. As illustrated in Table 8.2, economic growth in Latin America would rise to 5.3 percent per annum, one percentage point above the rate projected in the previous scenario. The increase in formal urban employment would be half a point higher than that of Scenario I, essentially on account of the increase in formal private employment, at a rate of 3.1 percent. In the second half of the decade, increase in formal private employment would be more rapid than in the first—approaching 3.7 percent—a result which would be rather closer to the employment/output elasticity of the period 1950–1980. In this scenario the degree of informality would increase, but more slowly than in the previous scenario: from 31.4 percent in 1990 to 32.9 percent in the year 2000 (see Figure 8.2). Even more important, informality would increase during the first half of the decade and then decline in its second half. Consequently, even though the trends of the eighties may not be completely reversed, they will slow down considerably. One very important consequence of this change is that some four million workers who, in

Table 8.2 Projections of Urban Labor Market in Scenario II (Rapid Growth) (1)
1991–2000
(in percent)

	Annual increase in urban labor force	Annual growth in Gross Domestic Product	Annual increase in formal urban employment	Annual increase in private formal employment	Annual increase in public sector employment	Participation of informal employment (2) in urban labor force			Rate of open unemployment		Increase in productivity in the formal private sector	Annual increase in real average wages, formal sector	Increase in average income in the informal urban sector
						1991	1995	2000	1991	2000			
Latin America	3.2	5.3	2.8	3.1	1.8	31.4	33.2	32.9	5.4	5.5	2.6	2.1	0.3
Group A (3)	1.2	3.4	1.4	2.0	-0.3	33.5	33.8	32.3	9.3	8.9	1.8	1.5	0.6
Group B (4)	2.7	4.9	2.9	3.0	1.8	28.2	28.3	27.2	8.8	8.6	2.2	2.0	1.2
Group C (5)	3.6	4.3	2.0	2.5	0.5	40.2	43.5	45.3	8.3	9.2	1.8	1.2	-0.5
Group D (6)	3.5	5.7	3.0	3.2	2.2	31.0	33.2	32.9	4.0	4.2	2.9	2.2	0.2

(1) Assumes for the group of countries as a whole, a decline in the share of net transfers of resources in GDP from 3.8 % in 1990 to 1.4 % in 2000, and an increase in exports of 6.4 % per annum.

(2) Defined in restrictive terms as own-account workers, unpaid family members and domestic servants, on account of the non-availability of reliable information on informal sector micro-enterprises.

(3) Argentina and Uruguay; see text for definition.

(4) Chile, Colombia and Costa Rica; see text for definition.

(5) Peru and Guatemala; see text for definition.

(6) Brazil, Mexico and Venezuela; see text for definition.

Source: Preliminary estimates of ECLAC.

Scenario I, would be engaged in activities in the informal sector, would find employment in the modern sectors, with the consequent increase in wages if Scenario II would hold. The rate of open unemployment in urban areas would remain almost constant, since, as described above, the long-term adjustment in employment would occur through changes in the size of the informal sector.

The most significant effect of the increase of one percentage point in economic growth would be on wages. On the one hand, a more rapid increase in productivity in the modern sectors (2.6 percent per annum) would permit greater growth in real average wages (2.1 percent per annum). On the other hand, the greater increase in demand and the slower expansion in the size of the informal sector explain the slight increase which now would be recorded in Scenario I in real average incomes in the informal sector, thereby reversing the trends of the eighties. It should be added that in this scenario the difference between the increase in real wages in the tradable and nontradable sectors would be even greater than in the Basic Scenario, because the difference in the growth in productivity between both sectors would also be higher.

In this scenario the differences between countries are sharper than before (see Table 8.2 and Figures 8.3 to 8.6). Group B would now record an increase in formal employment higher than that of the urban labor force, which explains why the degree of informality declines. On the other hand, greater progress in structural change, with a higher rate of economic growth, is associated with higher rates of increase in productivity, particularly in the tradable sector. This explains the higher rate of increase in real wages in the modern sector (2 percent annually). Greater economic growth and the decline in the size of the informal sector explain why average incomes in the informal sector would increase by some 1.2 percent annually.

At the other extreme, countries in Group C do not record any significant changes in the growth of the informal sector, which will continue to be very high at the end of the century, or in the growth of real wages—determined by the slow increase in productivity—nor in average incomes in the informal sector. This suggests that it would be necessary for the countries in this group to complete their structural adjustment more quickly in order to ensure more favorable results, or to accept a longer period before the same results are achieved.

In the other two groups, the different pattern in the labor supply continues to have a significant influence on their results. Thus, in group A, the higher rate of economic growth and the greater advance in structural adjustment—in comparison to Scenario I—leads to a slightly faster decline in the size of the informal sector and to a greater increase in productivity and real wages, although still at a relatively slow rate in contrast to the other groups. In group D, despite greater economic growth and advance in structural adjustment, the sharp increase in urban labor force continues to exert an upward pressure on the size of the informal sector and limits the growth of incomes in that sector, although less intensely than in Scenario I. Nevertheless, in the last few years of the decade, both trends would be reversed. The high rate of growth in productivity—particularly in tradables—would permit an increase in real wages of 2.2 percent per annum in 1991–2000, which would be higher in the second half of the decade.

An experiment with faster wage increase. As stated earlier, both scenarios share the tenet that, though real wages in the modern sector increase—in itself, a major change by comparison to the eighties—they do so while lagging behind output per worker in that sector.

This section carries out the experiment of having real wages expand at the same rate as productivity, whereas beyond the modern sector, informal-sector workers share in the sector's total incomes, as in the earlier scenarios.

The trade-off between wages and employment being simulated here is a modification of Scenario I; thus, it corresponds to an economy that opens up to foreign trade in which fast productivity gains lead to export expansion, and the consequently larger foreign exchange availability allows faster growth and more job creation.

When Scenario I is modified to allow faster growth in wages, the initial trade-off is that the consequently lower savings rate leads to less investment, smaller productivity gains—especially in sectors producing tradable goods—and, thereby, to less employment creation through a decreased availability of foreign exchange. Also, as productivity gains are reduced, so is the ceiling on real wage increases, and, in one country, this eventually translates into lower real wages as a result of the experiment.

During the limited period of the projections, real wages resulting from the new strategy actually drop below those of the Basic Scenario in one case, and a few others point in that direction; in most cases, the end of the decade signals higher real wages. However, in all cases, there is less employment creation in the modern sectors.

In all cases, reductions in net exports—by comparison to the Basic Scenario—lead to difficulties in terms of foreign exchange availability and net transfers to the rest of the world, which might entail severe problems which would become visible after the end of the projection period.

A comparison between Scenario I and the results of the experiment being reviewed here is shown in Table 8.3 for the aggregate of all ten countries. The Table suggests that the trade-off between higher real wages on the one hand and, on the other, the consequences on growth

Table 8.3   A Comparison of Projections Between the Basic Scenario
and its Modification
(In percent)

	Growth Rates		Yearly Averages		
	1991	2000	1991-1995	1996-2000	1991-2000
Gross Domestic Product					
original	3.87	4.58			4.32
modified	3.90	4.20	4.02	4.32	4.18
Gross Domestic Product, Manufacture Sector					
original	4.01	4.82			4.53
modified	3.95	4.37	4.12	4.48	4.30
Productivity					
original	2.37	2.07			1.93
modified	1.71	1.70	1.67	1.79	1.73
Exports					
original	5.09	5.85			5.60
modified	5.04	5.62	5.27	5.66	5.46
Manufacture Sector Employment					
original	2.17	2.72			2.55
modified	2.19	2.56	2.37	2.61	2.49
Urban Informal Sector Employment					
original	4.98	3.94	4.87	4.04	4.45
modified	6.02	3.94	5.42	4.17	4.79
Manufacture Sector Wages					
original	1.45	1.66			1.54
modified	1.71	1.70	1.66	1.79	1.73
Urban Informal Sector Income					
original	-3.03	-.025			-1.13
modified	-2.61	-0.28	-1.76	-0.32	-1.04

Source: Preliminary estimates of ECLAC.

and productivity, determines that in the medium term the initial improvement in wages will erode, and modern-sector employment generation will suffer as well. This, of course, adds to the loss in foreign
reserves which stems from the reduced rate of increase in exports.

On the whole, this exercise suggests that, in several countries, rapid
structural change through large productivity gains which are initially
concentrated in tradable goods producing sectors requires an investment effort which must be financed by wages increasing by slightly less

than does productivity. The phenomenon is especially clear for those countries where the modernization effort ought to be most intense to compensate for the rapid growth in urban labor supply, which in our case are Brazil, Mexico and Venezuela (Group D). Within this group, if the strategy of wages increasing at the rate of productivity is adopted, the reduction in modern-sector employment generation, though slight, is enough to lead to an increase in the share of informal employment, which, in turn, determines a fall in average informal income which is greater than in the Basic Scenario. In addition, open unemployment also increases faster. As stated earlier, in the Brazilian case the change in strategy leads to a reduction in real wages toward the end of the projection period. The lesser modernization effort assumed in the cases of Group A (Argentina and Uruguay) and Group C (Guatemala and Peru) allow that the informal-sector situation improves slightly, while there is no visible impact in the cases of the countries in Group B (Chile, Costa Rica and Colombia).

CONCLUSIONS

One of the main conclusions that emerges from the results of Scenarios I and II is that, even though they have been elaborated from an optimistic perspective, they do not show a reduction in the degree of informality in the urban sector of Latin America between 1990 and 2000, but quite the opposite. Since toward the year 2000, about 80 percent of the labor force in Latin America will be located in urban areas, this means that, even with a restricted definition of the informal sector as the one used, by the end of the century approximately 27 percent of the total labor force of the region will be engaged in that type of activity. For purposes of illustration, it should be recalled that, in the same year, total employment in the agricultural sector will be smaller: nearly 80 percent of informal urban employment. Such regional result is not, as pointed out earlier, valid in all countries, since several of them can expect, according to the above scenarios, to reduce informality over the current decade.

For the region as a whole, a period longer than a decade, or a rate of economic development and structural change more rapid than those simulated in the scenarios presented in this paper, would be necessary to achieve the turning-point of a reduction in the degree of urban informality. Thus, only for purposes of illustration, a third set of projections was elaborated to simulate a slight decline in the size of the informal sector by the end of the century. For Latin America as a whole, that result requires a rate of economic growth of approximately 5.7 percent with a more marked decline in the share of net transfers of resources abroad in the GDP, a sharper rise in exports, and a faster pace of structural change, by comparison with that of Scenario II.

The second conclusion is that the trends toward increasing the size of the informal sector identified in Scenarios I and II are a consequence of a growth in formal employment which, though significant, is not enough to absorb the increase in the urban labor force. The growth in formal private employment is, in particular, quite significant, while public employment suffers from the public sector restructuring process. The projections call attention to the impact of the transitional phase of the adjustment and, subsequently, to the influence of technological modernization and of the greater pace of growth in productivity, on the rates of labor absorption in the modern sectors.

The third conclusion is that even in Scenario I, the trend toward a decline in real wages in the modern sector recorded in the period 1980–1990 can be reversed. This is related to the greater increase in productivity—particularly in tradables—caused by modernization and with the capturing of at least a large fraction of that increase by wage earners in the modern sectors. In contrast, significant growth in the long term should not be expected in incomes in the informal sector, given the trend toward an increase in informality. However, this also suggests a partial reversal of the sharp decline recorded in this type of income in the decade of the eighties.

The fourth conclusion is that a process of modernization and transformation would tend to generate pressures on the urban labor market in the direction of a greater degree of heterogeneity in terms of opportunities and incomes, during a long period, before more homogenizing trends can be felt. This is also related both to the increase in the disparity of opportunities between the formal and informal sectors, and to the differences in the growth in income by sectors. As was seen, pressures may be expected for more rapid increases in wages in tradable sectors than in nontradable activities, and for an increase in wages in the latter activities that is greater than in the informal sectors. These pressures for differentiated rates of increase in remuneration for labor by sectors, are largely a consequence of the different rates of incorporation of resources and technology by sectors that are typical of a process of modernization and structural change. To this it should be added that both for reasons of incentives to investment (in the context of a greater internationalization of finance and a world of high interest rates), and on account of the need to stimulate rapid increases in domestic savings, there would be pressures for the rapid generation of profits and rates of profitability may tend to be high in sectors producing tradable goods. This will contribute to an increase in the degree of heterogeneity of incomes by social segments. Consequently, this fourth conclusion suggests the importance of introducing compensatory policies which, both through the labor market and through taxation, social expenditure and redistribution of incomes, would introduce a larger component of equity, particularly for the poorest urban groups and that portion of the urban middle class whose income has deteriorated most during the eighties.

Fifth, trends toward greater urban heterogeneity described in the previous paragraph are a result of events in each country. It is, however, important to note that the degree of heterogeneity among countries will also increase. Large disparities are projected in the situations that will be faced by the end of the decade by those countries which would have recorded the most rapid progress toward changing their production patterns and experienced less pressure from increases in their urban labor force (Group B), as against those which would have made less progress in structural adjustment and undergone very high rates of increase in their urban labor force (Group C). Consequently, the greater projected heterogeneity for Latin America as a whole is an expression of that expected within each country, and of the greater disparities among countries.

Nevertheless, the trends toward greater heterogeneity within each experience may correspond to a first—even though prolonged—phase of modernization. Once the point at which the absorption in modern strata exceeds the growth in the urban labor force is reached, then those trends may be expected to be gradually reversed.

These conclusions suggest an even more important role for policies to deal with labor market conditions, the situation of incomes and urban poverty, since in the course of the next decade, these will constitute the main problem.

Finally, it is important to point out that even in Scenario I, by the end of the century, far-reaching changes would have taken place in the region in terms of its capacity to achieve insertion in an international economy which, while more competitive, will also prove more beneficial to the region, insofar as it will force it to make better use of its potential for growth. In this sense, the process of structural change simulated in the nineties, would generate better preconditions for the creation of employment and incomes after the year 2000.

REFERENCES

CEPAL, (1979a). *Series históricas del crecimiento de América Latina*, Santiago, CEPAL, 1979.

———(1979b). *El balance de pagos de América Latina, 1950-77*, Santiago, CEPAL, 1979.

———(1990a). *Anuario estadístico de América Latina y el Caribe, 1989*, Santiago, CEPAL, 1990.

———(1990b). *Transformación productiva con equidad*, Santiago, CEPAL, 1990.

N. García. "Absorción creciente con subempleo persistente," in *Revista de la CEPAL*, diciembre, Santiago, CEPAL, 1982.

N. García and V.E. Tokman, 1985 *Acumulación, empleo y crisis*, Serie Investigaciones sobre empleo # 25, Santiago, PREALC.

E. Kritz. "Microempresas y pequeño crédito en Lima metropolitana," in PREALC, *Lecciones sobre crédito al sector informal*, Santiago, PREALC, 1990.

J. Mezzera. *Crédito y capacitación para el sector informal*, Serie Investigaciones sobre empleo #29, Santiago, PREALC, 1987.

J. Mezzera. "Gasto del sector moderno e ingreso en el sector informal," in PREALC *Ventas informales: relaciones con el sector moderno*, Santiago, PREALC, 1990.

PREALC. *Mercado de trabajo en cifras*, Santiago, PREALC, 1982.

——. *Employment and equity: the challenge of the 1990s*, Santiago, PREALC, 1991.

J. Ramos. *Labor and development in Latin America*, Columbia University Press, 1972.

J. Wells. *Empleo en América Latina: una búsqueda de opciones*, Santiago, PREALC, 1987.

NOTES

1. The data on which this chapter is based come from Chapter I of PREALC *Employment and equity: A challenge for the nineties*, Santiago, PREALC (1991). That chapter was prepared mainly by our PREALC colleagues Ricardo Infante and Emilio Klein.

2. By far the largest proportion of the decline in the role of primary net exports comes from the deterioration of their relative price, since at constant prices the fall is very slight. However, the long-term deterioration of terms of trade for primary-goods exporters was already pointed out by CEPAL in the late forties.

3. When the regionwide average of 1976–81 is compared to that of 1984, that swing amounts to almost 6.5 percent of GDP.

4. To a very large extent, the "expansion" in small firm job creation represents the shrinking of firms that used to employ more than 10 workers.

5. This section uses the data and closely follows the reasoning of parts of Chapter I of PREALC *Employment and equity: a challenge for the nineties*, Santiago, PREALC (1991), which was prepared by the authors of this paper.

6. In fact, at the time export promotion was often seen as a subsidy-led export growth within the import substitution strategy.

7. The data on which this section is based come from Chapter II of PREALC *Employment and equity: A challenge for the nineties*, Santiago, PREALC (1991). Those figures were prepared by Victoria Contreras working under the guidance of the authors of this paper. The computation of the model on which this chapter is based was performed by Christian Herrera. In preparing the model itself, the authors greatly benefited from a consultancy by Osvaldo Larrañaga.

8. The scenarios by countries focus on the urban labor market, partly for reasons of information, but mainly because it is the market in which more than 75 percent of the region's labor force will be seeking employment in the current decade.

9. The information on growth of the labor force and employment in this section refers to the ten countries of the sampling. Consequently, there are slight discrepancies with the figures for Latin America as a whole.

10. Although Colombia embarked upon its economic modernization program in 1990, its much lower indebtedness and inflation rates, and better performance in terms of exports suggest that, in comparison to many other countries in the region, it is in a better position to experience a shorter transition period and a faster progress in structural adjustment.

11. Here again growth in real wages in those sectors producing tradables would be much higher than that in the nontradables sectors, given the respective productivity growth differentials.

Part VI

Implementation
of Structural
Adjustment Programs

9

Implementation and Sustainable Adjustment

The Management of Policy Reform

Richard J. Moore

INTRODUCTION

The past decade has seen a dramatic decline in the capacities of nations in the Third World to cope with the demands and requirements of economic growth and development. This decline affects not only the long- and medium-term, but even the day to day necessities of organized social, political, and economic life. The economic crises of the 1980s have led to a fiscal crisis and also to a crisis of confidence in the ability of these nations to manage development.

More than a decade after the inception of structural adjustment policies, we are confronted with the reality that the implementation of sustainable structural adjustment efforts requires more focus on the institutional and human resource environment of reform. It is widely recognized that development and economic growth require more than economic resources. The improvement and efficient utilization of human capital is crucial to national development efforts, both in the public and in the private sector. However, this is not just an issue of training individuals and improving individual skills for formulating and implementing policy. Nor is it ultimately just an issue of strengthening a given government organization or department, or a particular private enterprise to respond to extant problems. To achieve sustainable development also requires the development of institutional capacity for transferring specific skills, for building human resources, and for providing for appropriate programmatic responses to a constantly changing policy environment. Recognition of this need to focus on institutional development and implementation is increasingly evident in the donor community. The Operations Evaluation Division of the World Bank noted in its 1989 *Annual Review of Performance Evaluation*:

> [I]n a large number of unsatisfactory operations, the principal determinants of performance were institutional. . . . In some cases, institutions at the national and project levels were weak, and their capacity was overstretched by the Bank-supported operations. Often, difficulties stemmed from poor management. . . . Other difficulties arose when project designs turned out to be based upon an inadequate understanding of the surrounding culture, rural social and institutional structures, and behavioral norms. . . . These findings call for a more careful assessment of the institutional aspects of proposed operations. (p. vi)

In a recent analysis of 84 Board-approved projects, we found further evidence of the need for a stronger focus on institutional development for successful implementation, particularly in adjustment lending. In our sample, while treatment of the need for institutional development was evident in half of all investment project lending, in most SALs and SECALs treatment of institutional needs in the design of lending operations was systematically weak (Gray, Khadiagala, and Moore, 1990).

The tragedy of this lack of focus is that demands for restructuring institutional relationships in the Third World are at the base of policy reform and structural adjustment efforts. However, the assumption has often been made that sustainable reform initiatives are relatively automatic once the negotiated acceptance of them was established and monitored conditionalities were put in place. In Korten's (1986) words, many reform initiatives were assumed to require only the "stroke of a pen," that there was no distance between word and deed. Implementation as a potential problem was assumed away or was presumed to be resolved by the mere presence of technical assistance . . . until recently.

Even where more care has been taken to assure effective implementation, the record shows several key fallacies in approaches taken. First, many reform efforts have viewed the policy process itself as "linear" (Thomas and Grindle, 1990: 1164). That is, it is assumed that reforms get on the government agenda, a decision is made, and implementation follows. If implementation is unsuccessful, the tendency has been to assume that the reason is simply because of weak political will or a weak implementing institution. A second approach, linked to this linear perspective, assumes that institution building is primarily a technical exercise and technical assistance (TA) for a given institution becomes the answer. More often than not, the "solution" involves the imposition of technical expertise (usually expatriate), of technical systems (budgeting, information, monitoring, etc.) that are often not adapted to local contexts, or the creation of whole new units (PIUs or economic policy advisory units) that are linked to the immediate demands of SALs but may not be integrated or internalized for the longer haul.

In both of these approaches the major shortcoming of reform efforts is the failure to see implementation as an interactive phenomenon, requiring concern for implementation in different modes and at different stages of the policy process. As Lamb and others have noted, reform requires institutional strengthening at key strategic locations in the policy implementation process. Often, limited groundwork is done with regard to a realistic understanding of the complexity of the institutional, political, and economic impacts that inhere in policy reform.

IMPLEMENTATION AND REFORM

The implementation of policy reform initiatives is like the weather: everyone talks about it, but no one does anything about it. Under the best of circumstances, the implementation of the policy reform "package" encouraged by the multilateral and bilateral donor community has been problematic throughout the Third World. In this paper, I argue that the successful implementation of policy reform is limited in part because of the absence of a clear understanding of the institutional and administrative requirements for sustained and sustainable reform efforts.

These institutional requirements are lacking not only in the environment of the host country, but within the donor community. A great deal of effort has been expended on the design and analysis of the macroeconomic policies that support the dominant orthodoxy of structural adjustment. However, very little research has been conducted on the implementation and management of policies, or on the systematic evaluation of the linkages between policies and programs, on the one hand, and implementation, on the other.[1] Notes Lamb:

> work on strengthening policy institutions within developing countries is less developed . . . Developing the institutional capacity for timely and flexible policy response is clearly central to successful policy reform and structural adjustment . . . moreover, reform initiatives must often deal with institutions which, though powerful and relatively competent, may have become part of the policy reform problem rather than the means for its solution" (Lamb, 1987: 3).

Even when there has been a focus on the implementation issue, rarely do analyses go beyond examining administrative apparatuses and procedures, particular management skills, or the characteristics of bureaucrats. Little attempt is made to link the internal dynamics of administration or administrators to the contextual issues of organizations in social, economic, and political milieus.[2]

Part of the problem of this limited analysis may inhere in the current policy reform orthodoxy itself. Because one principal tenet of the orthodox model is the stimulation of the private sector and market forces *at the expense* of public sector action, little attention is paid to the requirements of the governing process. In fact, the orthodoxy assumes a minimal role for government as an outcome of the reform process itself. Policy reform is perceived as a painless political choice. As a result, the inability of governments to carry out reforms effectively is "blamed" on the victim. In the worst case scenario, it is argued that political leaders are ignorant of and unresponsive to "appropriate" policies; in the best case scenario, governments are seen as naive newcomers to the positive long-term effects of the reform initiatives. In either scenario, the "established" wisdom is suspect.

Technical assistance adheres closely to the orthodox assumptions of the model, perceives government as a compounding and perverse factor in development, and frequently underestimates the need for a clear understanding of the "grounded" issues of governance, political interests, and bureaucracy.[3] The ultimate irony, however, is that much of the activities of the donors requires a strong state role. For example, efforts to improve monitoring capabilities, or to improve the process of data gathering, or to improve policy analysis requires strengthening, not dismantling, the state's role. Similarly, the multiplicity of sectors involved directly or affected indirectly by reform initiatives presumes a coordinating capability within government (and one might add, among donors). Thus, there would seem to be a contradiction among attempts to remove or reduce the state apparatus, the preexistence of a weakened administrative state, and demands by donors for a "lean and mean" state apparatus to carry out the mandates of reform.[4]

Another factor that has limited the successful implementation of reform initiatives is closer to home: the fields of development administration and development management themselves still have not geared up adequately for the dramatic shifts that have occurred in development assistance strategies. Most approaches still focus on institutions within which managers work; training needs, skills, and organizational design issues are examined within the behaviors of managers in specific predetermined institutions. Some recent approaches attempt to move toward a more adaptive and programmatic response, however, but they have not gone the extra step of focusing on policy-based institutional consequences of implementation (Lamb, 1987).

How are we to know that these institutions are the relevant "sites" of management and implementation problems associated with particular policy reform initiatives? While training needs assessment is critical, a prior determination of "training for what?" is essential. A first stage must be a mapping of potential implementation problems that emanate from specific policy and programmatic decisions, which may be contained within a given institution, or which may cut across institutions. Focusing on specific institutions and specific projects alone will not lead us to improved performance of the management of policy reform initiatives.

This failure to identify policy decisions as the locus of actions on the part of the study and practice of development management is reflected in the practices of the donor community. As institutions, many of the multilateral and bilateral members of the technical assistance community have not geared up to policy-based technical assistance.[5] Even with the issuance of the tremendously important "Management in Development" section in the 1983 WDR, there has been, until recently, limited translation of much of that message into institutional or policy-based interventions. In a recent analysis by the author and others (Moore, 1989; Gray, Khadiagala, and Moore, 1990) of projects presented to the Board of the Bank in 1988, we found strong evidence that concern for ID work was often an afterthought, the amount of technical expertise in ID in project design was relatively weak, and that those projects with strong ID work in project design were a consequence of strong background and experience in ID by members of the design/appraisal team. In addition, policy reform initiatives must be seen as process; the failure to focus on ID at all stages of the project cycle often assures implementation problems. The recent expansion of research and operational activity in public sector management at the Bank (in the Latin American and African regions and in the country economics department) and increasing focus on midterm evaluations for institution building are positive signs.

Ironically, the issues of complexity in the policy design process and the need for coordination among reform initiatives have an inverse, indeed perverse, relationship to the need for reform itself. The greater the need for reform in a given country, and often the poorer the country, the more complex the package of reforms that are introduced, and, as a result, the more difficult the sustainability, complementarity, and coordination of reform efforts. This complexity is often translated into "front-loading" of institutional conditionalities that exacerbate the problem of weak managerial capacity and lead to the inefficient implementation and institutionalization of reforms. Further, policies of stabilization find themselves inextricably tied to policies of adjustment, even though the double-barreled effect of pursuing both simultaneously may have an even more intensive political consequences. Sustainability of a viable political context during implementation is made more difficult.

A STRATEGIC MAPPING OF IMPLEMENTATION

There is a need to focus explicitly on the issue of implementation and the management of reform. What may be required for "success" may not be *additional* reform initiatives nor new conditionality agreements; rather, success may require concerted effort to focus on the sustainability of previously initiated reforms, less ambitious institutional reforms, and the strengthening of management at key policy decision points, in the implementation process. It is at these key decision points in particular policy reform initiatives, that bottlenecks to implementation may occur. The task of strategic mapping or tracking exercises, then, is to provide a means for preempting these potential bottlenecks in implementing reform, across and within institutions. Management improvements, organizational changes, and developing policy analytic capabilities should be provided at these "sites."

Lamb (1987) offers a useful beginning when he argues for a "policy enclave" approach, and provides key questions we need to ask in order to proceed analytically:[6]

1. What are the key components of "policy" decision-making?
2. Which institutions or entities control critical aspects of the decision process?
3. How can policy choices be made less demanding on institutions, i.e., reducing tensions, providing signals, altering the range of stakeholders affected, etc.?
4. What are the potential politics of policy decisions in a given policy area?

Elsewhere I have offered a more complete version of a possible approach to this strategic mapping and how it may provide us with a "first stage needs assessment" (Moore, 1988a). Here I would like to simply offer the basic elements of that approach toward resolving implementation problems. The argument can be broken down into several series of statements.

1. There are different types of reform initiatives and they can be categorized in that they:

   - have identifiable theoretical objectives, and are therefore "targeted;"
   - engender specific actions because of the theoretical basis for the achievement of their objectives;
   - involve differing time frames for the expected achievement of results, both in terms of the expected time necessary to accomplish the theoretical goals empirically, and in terms of the ap-

propriate sequencing of the initiation and implementation of actions.

The literature recognizes the distinctions among types of reforms in terms of their economic rationale, noting, for example, the distinctions among expenditure reducing, expenditure switching, and institutional reforms. Cornia, et al (1987) refer to distinctions among macro, meso, and micro reforms. Others, such as Hirschman (1986) and Grindle and Thomas (1987) point to distinctions between "chosen" and "pressing" reforms.

In each of these taxonomies, distinctions among types of reforms imply distinct requirements for implementation. For example, Hirschman's pressing reforms involve high-stakes issues of macroeconomic adjustment, and are politically intense rather than administratively intense. Here the principle issues are regime stability, political consensus building and commitment, regime maintenance, and whether reforms are ambiguous or focused in order to generate consensus (Grindle and Thomas, 1987). Key institutional sites are few in number and high level. Thus, there are few implementation issues beyond agenda setting and maintaining commitment. However, the consequences of failed consensus can bring down the entire reform. Decisions about who will implement reform are guided by (a) sites that generate political consensus, (b) sites that accomplish high-level decisions, and (c) sites that are linked in an information flow to leadership.[7]

2. Different categories or types of reforms systematically have different kinds of implementation obstacles that occur at different stages in implementation and in different locations. (A location should be thought of as an institution, bureau, office, or process of decision-making.) Thus, different types of reforms follow different (but identifiable) paths for their achievement.

   •Some reforms are theoretically "prior" to others and must be in place before others can be accomplished, either because of an economic rationale or for reasons of political and institutional capacity (i.e., sequencing and timing of reforms count);[8]
   •The siting of reform, in terms of the paths through institutions, interests affected, and the most "appropriate" place for focusing implementation efforts, is central to effective management of the reform process.

3. If reforms can be grouped by some guiding theoretical purpose or goal, and if their purposes suggest or direct us to systematic and consistent sets of actions that ought to be taken, then there may also be consistent implementation requirements necessary for their achievement.

- •Certain kinds of reforms may require greater (or lesser) institutional apparatuses for their achievement or implementation (administrative/institutional complexity (or AC);
- •Certain kinds of reforms may require greater (or lesser) amounts of political will and leadership for their successful implementation and accomplishment (political intensity and stakes or PI);
- •Reform initiatives cannot be treated as discrete projects. They interact, they create externalities which affect other reforms, and they are not mutually exclusive;
- •Different reforms may pull institutions and processes in different, and possibly contradictory directions; some are containable (C) in one institution, others are not;
- •Different donors, as well as different stakeholders within the country context, have different agenda, and these agenda need not be—and often are not—mutually reinforcing or supportive donor match (or DM).

4. The environment (E) in which reform is introduced and in which reform is implemented is critical. Different environments, different behavioral modes and responses, different institutional settings, different regime goals . . . all of these affect the paths toward implementation and the viability of reform and carry with them different learning requirements (L). The dynamics of implementation do not occur outside of the context of the country in which reform is being conducted.

5. If we can identify ex ante and theoretically, and if we can identify empirically, those potential obstacles that affect implementation, then we may be able to design interventions that will assist in the alleviation of some of the implementation problems, prior to their appearance or in response to their appearance. This process of identification will assist in making both strategic choices and strategic management interventions.

Thus, there are a series of strategic choices that must be made during the design and implementation process: choices regarding program design, institutional setting, analytic capabilities required, impact of and on beneficiaries or stakeholders, and timing of initiatives. Different reforms will involve different strategic choices. Therefore, there are different "paths" of implementation for reforms dependent on the content of the reform. As a result, different potential implementation issues become relevant. A schematic representation of these issues suggests itself: Different reforms have different theoretical objectives ——> different prescriptions ——> different instruments of action ——> different implementation problems arise ——> different types and sites of interventions.

While our intention here has not been to provide either an exclusive or an exhaustive characterization of potential implementation issues, we are concerned with those that are the most salient. We have identified nine such factors that may affect implementation (I):

1. Political Intensity (PI);
2. Administrative Complexity (AC);
3. The number of sites of decision-making (S);
4. The degree of bureaucratic routinization or change required ($\blacktriangle$);
5. The degree of sequencing or timing required (T);
6. The containability of reform initiatives (C);
7. The amount of organizational learning and information required (L);
8. The relatedness of reform to the larger context or environment (E); and
9. The match of donor for the intended reform in terms of organization, skills, and goals (DM).

Thus, the potential for bottlenecks in the implementation of a specific reform or a package of reforms is a function of the degree to which these factors are relevant: $I = f(PI, AC, S, \blacktriangle, T, C, L, E, DM)$. One can think of the strategic management of policy reform as the effort to account for these potential implementation pitfalls in the design and conduct of reform. Strategic management requires the design of management interventions that respond to implementation obstacles as these are manifest in different reform initiatives.

Our ability to "forecast" or diagnose the potential pitfalls of implementation is related to our ability to determine how a given reform type moves along the path toward implementation and the degree to which these implementation bottlenecks are relevant. The identification of these linkages in the implementation process is a process of strategic mapping. Strategic mapping requires the identification of "locations" where either potential or manifest implementation obstacles appear as places for designing interventions.

This mapping for planning strategic interventions for implementation is incomplete. In fact, much of the "filling in" is contextual; this is not intended to provide a blueprint for management interventions. However, it is argued throughout this paper that the success of implementation requires a "needs assessment" focusing on the institutional requirements of reform initiatives. Strategic management and management interventions during implementation are mediating forces between organizations and their environments, involving the identification of streams of organizational decisions that respond to and structure environment and policy goals (Backoff, 1987; Mintzberg, 1979; Moore, 1986).

	Liberalizing the Economy			Institutional Reforms		
	A REDUCE DEMAND	B EXPAND SUPPLY	C SECTORAL REFORMS	D CIVIL SERVICE REFORM	E PARA- STATALS (SOEs)	F ALTER PUBLIC SECTOR
Specific reforms:	devalue	raise producer prices	marketing boards	redundancy	divest SOEs	reorganize ministry
Potential implementation issues:						
Political Intensity(PI):			Eg.: How does an issue (devalue) affect PI, where when, who?			
Administrative Complexity (AC)						
Number of Sites (S)						
Salience of Contextual Issues (political climate, bureaucratic interests, etc.) (E)						
Organizational Learning (L)						
Containability (C)						
Donor Match (DM): predilections, comparative advantage, existing activities						

Figure 9.1 Matrix of Reform Initiatives and Implementation Problems

In Figure 9.1, I attempt to provide a matrix for the examination of these relationships between categories or clusters of reform and potential implementation issues. The horizontal axis provides a categorization of various objectives of reform. The vertical axis provides a typology of the potential bottlenecks of implementation. The argument here is that some of the cells in the matrix are more important as potential implementation pitfalls requiring actions to minimize their impact. For example, under macro policies aimed at liberalizing the economy through the reduction of demand, the potential for problems of heightened political intensity are of great salience. Thus, instruments for ameliorating these tensions are appropriate strategies for intervention. Similarly, reforming the civil service may have repercussions at various levels and at various times. Ultimately, however, the implementation of civil service reform requires the establishment of bureaucratic procedures for determining civil service needs, qualification systems, testing procedures, mechanisms for the release/retirement of personnel, pension and other in-kind remuneration schemes. All of these, and other issues, are ones of administrative intensity and complexity. Yet, the potential of civil service personnel to form a salient stakeholding force with the capacity to make demands is an issue of political intensity. Resolution of the issue, therefore, may require action at both levels (Moore, 1988b; 1990).

LESSONS FROM IMPLEMENTATION EXPERIENCES

The effort here has been to suggest that concern with implementation needs to focus on the policy process and not simply on a given institution or set of institutions. As is evident from the matrix, the strategic mapping of interventions to assist in implementation is no mean feat. Indeed, one of the first lessons that can be learned from the institutional dynamics of the implementation record for SALs to date is that the design, supervision, and monitoring of implementation and institution building for implementation is a very labor-intensive process. For the Bank, the implication is that more staff time needs to be allocated to supervision than currently is the case.

A second lesson is the need for greater focus in technical assistance and perhaps in adjustment lending itself. Too often, technical assistance in support of SALs has been overly ambitious, loosely designed TA that has not been successful in creating sustainability (Moore, 1991). More focused TA, fewer and better prioritized institutional conditionalities are appropriate. The move toward SECALs offers an opportunity and much promise in this regard as a means for creating cumulative institution building and organizational learning (Nunberg, 1990). In addition, early success in implementation on relatively focused institutional objectives can help to build credibility and the legitimacy of reform itself.

Further, the timing and sequencing of TALs may not mesh with the time horizons of SALs, and this needs to be recognized. Institution building is a long-term process and may not fit the short-term horizon of SALs or the often crisis management style of TALs supporting SALs to date. In some TALs, supporting the adjustment process technical assistants and consultants contracted to carry out systemic or institution wide reforms (eg., implementing a performance budgeting system or a debt management system), have found themselves caught in the day-to-day operational management of departments rather than longer-term institution building for which they have been contracted (Moore, 1991).

One of the increasingly evident institution-strengthening mechanisms in SALs or associated TALs has been the effort to create or strengthen core policy or advisory groups to give clear policy direction. However, efforts must be made to ensure both the integration of these groups into the policy decision process and their coordination with technical activities in line ministries. The creation of "policy enclaves" unlinked to operational activities may drain talent from existing institutional management and may have exactly the opposite effect: the longer-term weakening of key institutions. Again, it is critical to remember that the purpose of implementation of SALs and related technical assistance is sustainable reform and long-term institution building.

Recent improvements in the capacity to design, monitor, and evaluate institutional needs for implementation are evident in the donor community. However, what still remains to be done is to transfer and institutionalize these capabilities in host governments such that real policy dialogue can occur.

REFERENCES

Ahohe, Emile. "Stabilization and Adjustment Policies: Principles and Implementation Problems." Paper presented at the African Studies Association meetings, Chicago, Illinois, 1988.

Backoff, Robert. "Strategic Management: Its Origins and Development." Paper presented at the Annual Meeting of the Association of Public Policy and Management, Bethesda, Md., October 1987.

Balassa, Bela, Gerardo Bueno, Pedro-Pablo Kuczynski, and Maria Henrique Simonsen. *Toward Renewed Economic Growth in Latin America.* Washington, DC: Institute for International Economics, 1986.

Bates, Robert H. *Markets and States in Tropical Africa.* Berkeley, CA: University of California Press, 1981.

Berg, Elliot. "Issues and Problems in Structural Adjustment Policy." Lecture given to the Society for International Development, Washington, DC, April, 1987.

Blejer, Mario, and Sylvia Sagari. "Sequencing the Liberalization of Financial Markets." *Finance and Development,* 25, 1 March 1987, pp. 18–21.

Callaghy, Thomas M. "The Politics of Economic Stabilization and Structural Change in Africa: Ghana, Zambia, Nigeria." Columbia University, Draft Paper, October, 1987.

Cleaves, Peter and Martin Scurrah. *Agriculture, Bureaucracy, and Military Government in Peru.* Ithaca, NY: Cornell University Press, 1980.

Cornia, Giovanni Andrea, Richard Jolly, and Frances Stewart. *Adjustment with a Human Face: Protecting the Vulnerable and Promoting Growth.* Oxford: Oxford University Press, 1987.

Daland, Robert T. *Brazilian Planning: Development, Politics, and Administration.* Chapel Hill: University of North Carolina Press, 1967.

Edwards, Sebastian. "Sequencing Economic Liberalization in Developing Countries." *Finance and Development,* 24:1, March 1987, pp. 26–29.

Estman, Milton J. "Development Assistance in Public Administration: Requiem or Renewal." *Public Administration Review,* September—October 1980, pp. 426–431.

Gellar, Sheldon. "Public Sector Reform and Private Sector Expansion in Mali." Report prepared for USAID, June, 1985.

Gray, Cheryl W., Lynn S. Khadiagala, and Richard J. Moore. "Institutional Development Work in the Bank: A Review of 84 Bank Projects." PRE *Working Paper #437,* June 1990.

Graham, Lawrence, Clarence Thurber, and Edgardo Boeninger, eds. *Development Administration in Latin America.* Durham: Duke University Press, 1968.

Grindle, Merilee. *Bureaucrats, Politicians and Peasants in Mexico: A Case Study in Public Policy* Berkley, CA: University of California Press, 1977.

———. "Policy Content and Context in Implementation." *Politics and Policy Implementation in the Third World.* M.S. Grindle (ed.), 1980, pp.3–39.

Grindle, Merilee and John Thomas. "The Political Economy of Policy Reform in Developing Countries," Mimeo. Cambridge, MA: HIID, 1987.

Gulhati, Ravi. "Who Makes Economic Policy in Africa and How?" *World Development* 18,8, 1990: pp. 1147–1161.

Hayter, Teresa and Catharine Watson. *Aid: Rhetoric and Reality,* London: The Pluto Press, 1985.

Hirschman, Albert O. *Rival Views of Market Society and Other Recent Essays.* New York: Viking, 1986.

Hood, Ronald D., Judith McGuire, and Martha Starr. *The Socioeconomic Impact of Macroeconomic Adjustment.* Report prepared for USAID, January 1988.

Korten, David. "Micro Policy Reform." *NASPAA Working Paper #12.* Washington, DC: NASPAA, 1986.

Israel, Arturo. *Institutional Development: Incentives to Performance.* Washington, DC: Johns Hopkins University Press for the World Bank, 1987.

Lamb, Geoffrey. "Managing Economic Policy Change." *World Bank Discussion Paper #14,* June 1987.

Mintzberg, Henry. *The Structuring of Organizations.* New York: Prentice Hall, 1979.

Montgomery, John D. "Bureaucratic Politics in Southern Africa." *Public Administration Review,* Sept/Oct, 1986, 46:5, pp. 407–413.

Moore, Richard J. "Report on the Seminar on the Restructuring of the Ministry of Commerce and Industry, Panama," August, 1986.

———. "Management Training and Policy Analysis in LDCs: Recent Issues and NASPAA's Response," December, 1987.

———. (1988a) "Policy Reform and Implementation: A Zambian Case Study. *NASPAA Working Paper #16,* March 1988.

———. (1988b) "Report on Civil Service Reform Programs and their Impacts." Prepared for the USAID/Liberia Mission, August 1988.

―――. "The Treatment of Institutional Development Issues in LAC Projects (1987-1989)." World Bank, PSMU/LATHR, May 1991.

―――. "Project Completion Report: Peru." Prepared for the Public Sector Management Division, LAC, The World Bank, March 1991.

Moore, Richard J., et al. *Contracting Out in Honduras.* Report Prepared for USAID/Honduras, June 1987.

National Association of Schools of Public Affairs and Administration (NASPAA) *.Improving Management in Southern Africa: Final Report to the Regional Training Council of the Southern African Development Coordination Conference.* Washington, D.C.: NASPAA, 1985.

Nelson, Joan. "The Political Economy of Stabilization: Commitment, Capacity, and Public Response," 1984, *World Development* 12: 10, pp. 982–1006.

―――. *Fragile Coalitions: The Politics of Economic Adjustment.* New Brunswick: Transaction, 1989.

―――. *Economic Crisis and Policy Choice.* Princeton: Princeton University Press, 1990.

Nunberg, Barbara. *Public Sector Management Issues in Structural Adjustment Lending.* World Bank Discussion Paper #99. Washington, DC: IBRD, 1990.

Paul, Samuel. *Strategic Management of Development Programs.* Management Development Series No. 19. Geneva: International Labor Office, 1983.

―――. *Institutional Reform in Sector Adjustment Operations: The World Bank's Experience.* World Bank Discussion Paper # 92. Washington, DC: IBRD, 1990.

Picard, Louis A. *The Politics of Development in Botswana: A Model for Success?* Boulder, Colorado: Lynne Reinner Publishers, Inc., 1987.

Picard, Louis A. and N. Lynn Graybeal "Structural Adjustment, Public Sector Reform, and the West African Political System." Paper presented at the 1988 African Studies Association meetings, Chicago, Illinois, 1988.

Please, Stanley. *The Hobbled Giant: Essays on the World Bank.* Boulder, Colorado: Westview Press, 1984.

Ravenhill, John. *Africa in Economic Crisis.* New York: Columbia University Press, 1987.

Steedman, David. "Capacity Building for Policy Analysis in Sub-Saharan Africa: A Review of the Experience of Selected Donors." Report prepared for the World Bank, April 1987.

Streeten, Paul. "Structural Adjustment: A Survey of the Issues and Options." *World Development,* 15,2 December 1987, pp. 249–262.

Thomas, John W. and Merilee S. Grindle. "After the Decision: Implementing Policy Reforms in Developing Countries." *World Development,* 1990, 18, 8: pp. 1163–1181.

Vengroff, Richard. "Policy Reform and the Assessment of Management Training Needs in Africa: A Comparative Perspective." Paper presented at the African Studies Association meetings, Chicago, Illinois, 1988.

White, Louise. "Implementing Economic Policy Reforms: Policies and Opportunities for Donors." *World Development,* 1990, 18, 1: pp. 49–60.

World Bank. *World Development Report.* Washington, DC: The World Bank, 1983.

World Bank. *Lending for Adjustment: An Update.* Washington, DC: World Bank, 1988.

World Bank. *World Development Report.* Washington, DC: The World Bank, 1988–90.

NOTES

1. A number of sources are exceptions to this statement. Increasingly, USAID and World Bank staff have become cognizant of the links between macroeconomic policy, microeconomic policy, organizational change, and implementation. See the work done by Lamb (1987) for a clear analysis of the linkages between policy and management in the context of adjustment. Work done by Grindle (1979) and her colleagues provided early recognition of these linkages. More recent work (Thomas and Grindle, 1990; White, 1990; Gulhati, 1990; Moore, 1989; Gray, Khadiagala, and Moore, 1990) reinforce the need to understand these linkages. Several other notable exceptions include Steedman (1987); Please (1984); Paul (1990); Nunberg (1990).

2. This argument is central to the work of Grindle. See, for example, Grindle (1979), Grindle and Thomas (1987) and Thomas and Grindle (1990). There are, of course, a number of exceptions in the literature on development administration, including Graham (1968); Cleaves (1974); Daland (1967); Picard (1987). Also, see the work done by Robert Bates (1981).

3. It is ironic that the Lagos Plan, which offers a strong endorsement of a dependency approach and an equally strong critique of the World Bank approach, is weak on a discussion of domestic governing factors as well. See John Ravenhill (1986: pp. 1–35).

4. See Picard and Graybeal (1988), Callaghy in Nelson (1990).

5. Recent evidence of the recognition of this can be seen in the efforts of USAID to provide workshops for its midlevel and senior personnel in the area of structural adjustment. One such effort, conducted for USAID by the Development Studies Program, is an interdisciplinary seven-week workshop to provide this "gearing up." Similarly, in 1990 the World Bank conducted a one-week workshop on institutional development for professional staff.

6. Recent work by Arturo Israel (1987) at the Bank adds insight into the issues of the requirements of institutional development.

7. A more detailed discussion of these distinctions is provided in Moore (1988a).

8. The argument that adjustment policies have a theoretical sequencing is accepted wisdom from an economic perspective. In fact, the logic of stabilization policies prior to adjustment policies is based upon this assumption. See Edwards (1987) and Blejer and Sagari (1988) for discussions of the sequencing issue in liberalization policies. However, little attention has been paid to the political or organizational issues of sequencing.

Part VII

Policy Reform
for the 1990s

10

The Political Economy
of Reform

Paul Streeten

INTRODUCTION

In this chapter on policy reform in the developing countries, my emphasis will be on policies in the social or human sectors of the economy, i.e., principally public expenditure on nutrition (food subsidies), health, and education; and it will be on the political economy rather than on narrowly economic factors determining reform. The reason for discussing the political economy is that it is by now pretty well known what ought to be done in this area, yet not much is being done. The main question: Why does human neglect continue? is important to anyone interested in reform, and points to political obstacles and inhibitions.

BEYOND STATISTICS

We devote financial and fiscal resources to the provision of education, health, nutrition and family planning. But in the supply of these social services the links between resource "inputs" and "outputs" or results, reflected in a full, healthy and long life, are even more tenuous than the links between inputs of labor and capital and the production of turnips, shoes or sausages. There is a wide range of outcomes, as reflected in a healthy population, for a given amount of money spent on primary health care, or a family planning program for given resources devoted to it. Without money, hardly anything can be done. But even large amounts of money can have little impact. What then are these determinants of the effective use of funds for social purposes? They can be grouped under five headings: (i) institutions, (ii) skills and aptitudes, (iii) attitudes, (iv) levels of living, and, (v) policies.

Institutions determine the organizational basis from which the energy, commitment and enthusiasm of the beneficiaries can be enlisted.

The skills and the aptitudes of the teachers, village workers and health personnel will make all the difference in the delivery of these services.

Attitudes are less easily measured than time spent on education, but the fact that they cannot be counted should not lead to the conclusion that they do not count. Human development is not just a question of literacy and numeracy, but of what might be called operacy, the skills of doing. They are concerned with choosing objectives and priorities, adopting valuations, alternatives, making decisions, resolving conflicts, and accommodating other people's views. They spring from self-discipline, pride in work well done, willingness to cooperate.

Levels of living, normally considered to be consumption and not regarded as being productive, are at low levels crucial in determining the efficiency of work done. The dedication and commitment to work on a health or education program is more likely to be forthcoming from a well-nourished, alert, healthy group of people.

Policies are more fully discussed elsewhere in this paper. It is plain that the right division of labor between different levels of government, nongovernmental organizations (NGOs) and the market (and the family) will be a crucial influence on the impact of social reforms.

Each of these five factors, which themselves interact, can be positive or negative from the point of view of human development. Progress in human development is both a condition and a result of human development. This explains why it is so difficult to get started on human development. But there is also a message of hope in it; for once the process does get started, it becomes self-enforcing and cumulative.

Whether the five variables work in a positive or negative direction will also depend on political pressures, political constituencies, political obstacles and political inhibitions.

POSITIVE AND NORMATIVE POLITICAL ECONOMY

The political economy of financing human development is concerned with two sets of questions: first, what interests, pressures and inhibitions lie behind current policies for human development, particularly those that appear neither compassionate nor sensible, either because they conflict with declared aims or because they pursue them in an ineffective way; and second, what changes in political pressures, in coalitions and alliances, can lead to reform?

The first set of questions has been explored by the self-interest, or public choice, school. The so-called new political economy asserts that citizens, politicians, bureaucrats and states use the authority of government to distort economic transactions for their own benefit. Citizens use political influence to get access to benefits allocated by government; politicians use government resources to increase their hold on power; public officials trade access to government benefits for personal reward; and states use their power to get access to the property of citizens. The result is an inefficient and inequitable allocation of resources, general impoverishment and reduced freedom.

Unfortunately, there is plenty of evidence that some regimes operate like this. Trujillo in the Dominican Republic, Somoza in Nicaragua, Amin in Uganda, Marcos in the Philippines, Mobutu in Zaire, the Duvaliers in Haiti, are examples of naked self-interest dictating policy.

On the other hand, there are examples of political regimes that represent and promote the interests of the poor. In Malaysia, political power lies with the poorer Malays, while economic power lies with the Chinese and Indian communities. As a result, Malaysia has implemented policies that benefited the poor Malay community. In Zimbabwe, after power had shifted from a white to a black government, numerous measures were taken that favored human and social objectives. For example, the share of primary education in total educational expenditure rose from 32 percent in 1980 to 58 percent in 1984, and real expenditure per head on primary education doubled.[1] In Malaysia and Zimbabwe influence does not go with affluence.

Even if it were true that we all always pursue only our self-interest, this is open to different interpretations; some of these may be in conflict with one another and with the interests of others, other interpretations may be in harmony. There may, for instance, be a conflict between smaller present and larger future gains; or between "hot," impulsive and "cool," deliberated interests; or between concentrated smaller and more widely dispersed larger gains; or between certain smaller and uncertain larger gains; or, perhaps as important as interest conflicts between groups, the conflict between perceived smaller and actual but nonperceived larger gains. In particular, when perceptions of interest by one group are in conflict with those of others, while real interests are in harmony, or when short-term interests conflict, whereas there is convergence in the long term, wise policymakers can use the areas where there is an identity of interests to overcome resistance and opposition.

The new political economy that emphasizes the self-interested motivation of all agents has been a healthy corrective to an earlier view, according to which a benevolent government, like Platonic or Fabian guardians, always promotes the general welfare. Just as, according to this view, the government can do no wrong, according to the new view, the government can do no right. The old view called for government intervention whenever there was market failure; the new view calls for minimum government intervention, ascribing all ills to government failure.

The principle of social impoverishment through competitive, short-term, self-interested political action by pressure groups that attempt to frustrate the working of Adam Smith's Invisible Hand has been aptly called the "Invisible Foot." The policy problem consists in finding ways to prevent the Invisible Foot (of political rationality) from trampling on and destroying the beautiful work of the Invisible Hand.

But surely this picture is at best incomplete. Governments sometimes transcend individual and group interests and free themselves from the political pressures that make for allocation of scarce resources to the privileged and powerful. If there is one thing that is abundantly clear from historical evidence, it is that they can and do act in the common interest, or in the interest of the poor, the weak, the unemployed, and that they can act rationally. Otherwise, how can we account for the fact that measures are taken to protect children and future generations, who have no votes and no power? Such poor countries as Sri Lanka, Costa Rica, China and Jamaica have achieved spectacular results in longevity and health through public interventions.

A more plausible theory of the state, supported by a wealth of evidence, sees most governments as neither monolithic nor impervious to moral or social (or aesthetic) motivation and appeals, or to appeals to economic rationality. According to this view, the obstacle to progress is neither solely ignorance nor solely political self-seeking. There are large areas in which a better analysis, a clearer sense of direction, and a mobilization of the poor and their trustees and of the guardians of rationality would help, just as there are other areas where it is fairly clear what should be done, but vested interests (political and professional) prevent it from happening. Political action, according to this view, is not necessarily destructive but can be a way of resolving conflicts. Action for the poor and for improving the human condition is helped by democracy and a free press; and human development, even when it occurs in a dictatorship, eventually leads to the call for civil and political freedom, as we have recently seen.

SUCCESSFUL RESTRUCTURING OF SOCIAL SERVICES

There are examples of successful restructuring of the social services toward the poor. Zimbabwe redirected public expenditure to primary education and health services after independence between 1979 and 1985. The new ruling party, the Zimbabwe National Union, led by

Mugabe, was widely accepted and had a wide and largely rural support base. Political debate was intense, the press was relatively free and played an important role in keeping the government alert to social problems.

Free health care was available for those earning less than 150 dollars a month, and the immunization and diarrheal disease control programs expanded rapidly. A children's supplementary feeding program was instituted, providing a daily meal to undernourished children in rural areas. Similar restructuring took place in education, with communities participating in contributing labor. Health expenditure rose by 70 percent between 1980 and 1982; a growing proportion of this increase was devoted to preventive rather than curative services.[2] A quite different picture is presented by Chile under Pinochet. It enjoyed a rapid improvement in infant mortality and the health status of the poor. Chile had a long historical record of social services, and benefited from continued expansion of female education and reduction in fertility. But there can be no doubt that government policy contributed to the success by expanding public support measures. Some have explained this as an attempt to check popular discontent at a time of political repression. "The expansion of targeted nutrition and health programs also has an obviously populist ring in a country where popular expectations of public provisioning are very high, and the Chilean government has indeed consistently endeavoured to build political capital from its achievements in the area of child nutrition."[3] Important lessons about political pressures and the search for popular support, even in an authoritarian regime, can be learned from Chile's achievements.

Indonesia in the 1980s restructured social expenditure to primary village schools, largely in order to reduce the risks of rural uprisings. Reforms in Morocco and Ghana also were intended to expand and improve rural primary education and to eliminate subsidies to middle-class university students, and in Ghana to pupils at the upper secondary level. Most of the resistance to these reforms was directed at the withdrawal of benefits from university students and limits on enrollment. In Ghana student protests occurred in 1987 and 1988, leading to a closing down of the universities. In Morocco, enrollments were increased again in response to political pressures.[4] Both Ghana and Morocco continue to attempt restructuring in spite of middle-class opposition, which appears to be even stronger in this field than to eliminating food subsidies for the middle class.

Plentiful external assistance helps such efforts. After 1988, Jamaica benefited from funds from the World Bank for a broad-based Social Adjustment Program that had wide political support. Its small size was an advantage in getting aid. Larger countries have much greater difficulties in getting such aid.

In addition to targeted subsidies and restructuring of the social services, there are numerous other measures a government can adopt to improve the condition of the poor. Channeling credit to poor people has been highly successful and has met with little opposition. If the high-jacking of subsidized credit by rich and powerful borrowers can be avoided, credit gives the poor access to productive assets, enabling them to earn higher incomes; it engages them in the productive process, thereby making them agents of change; and it enables them to acquire the education and skills for further raising their earning power. It also gives them self-esteem and the social recognition that is important to all of us. It is for reasons such as these that Professor Yunus, the founder of the Grameen Bank in Bangladesh, has written of credit as a basic human right.[5] The creation of efficient, small-scale, labor-intensive work opportunities is another promising area in which the interests of the better off and the poor can be made to coincide, if the activities are made complementary rather than competitive with the larger firms.

NORMATIVE POLITICAL ECONOMY

Turning to the normative side of political economy, one frequently hears of complaints that the "political will" for certain desirable reforms is lacking. But this is not a helpful way of analyzing political constraints and political action. One does not have to be a behaviorist to believe that behavior is the manifestation of will. If the action is absent, to say that the political will is lacking does not really add anything. If the will to action is absent, there is no point in asking for the will to have the will. Nevertheless, political will can be subjected to analysis, pressures, harnessing, mobilization and channeling. But it is more useful to think of the construction of a political base for reform. In view of the large literature on the positive theory of private interest (the public choice school), it is surprising how little thought has been given to the normative application of power constellations: how to build constituencies for a human development strategy, how to form coalitions and alliances in favor of improving the nutrition, education and health of the poor; how to harness and organize support for rational social policies that benefit everyone in the long run. Instead of speaking of the need for political will, this approach would be concerned with bargains, pacts, alliances, coalitions, compromises, compensations and accommodations of conflicting interests. The focus would shift from empty phrases to an analysis of the political constituencies for successful reforms that are both efficient and compassionate. A possible reason for the failure, in the past, of the recommendations for human development and poverty eradication, the main principles of which have been known for a long time, is the neglect of heeding political constraints and of the need to create a constituency for reform.

Illustrations of such mobilization of interests for the benefit of poor people in developing countries can be found in the interest of bankers in advanced countries in liberalizing markets for labor-intensive imports from developing countries; or in the interest of independent retail chains or consumer groups in low-cost imports; or in the interest of U.S. export lobbies in debt relief for the developing countries. Alliances of this kind can build on the interest of some groups in advanced countries to improve the lot of weaker and poorer groups.

Any attempt to include a political analysis is faced with a dilemma. Either recommendations are confined to what is regarded as politically feasible, and end up in a sterile perpetuation of the status quo; or the recommendations, free of any political constraint and utopian, end in frustration because of their lack of realism. There is, however, something to be said for utopianism in policy analysis. First, it can be useful as a framework for thinking, in the same way that physicists assume a vacuum. The assumption would not be useful for the design of parachutes, but can serve other purposes. Second, utopianism provides a sense of direction, even if the full ideal is not realized. Third, it avoids getting stuck in the status quo, often the result of an excessive preoccupation with political constraints. Fourth, as recent experience has abundantly illustrated, the conjuncture of circumstances sometimes changes quite unexpectedly and dramatically, and unless we are prepared with detailed reform proposals quite recently thought to be unfeasible, the reforms will go by default. Fifth, the utopian reformers themselves can constitute a pressure group, countervailing the self-interested pressures of the obstructionist groups. For these reasons it is useful to speculate about the kind of society we want, unencumbered by the inhibitions and obstacles of political constraints.

On the other hand, there is a danger that the best becomes the enemy of the good, the optimum an obstacle to improvements. To be successful, it is essential to have a feel for the politically possible, and, more than a feel, to make a careful analysis of actual and potential power constellations. It can be argued that past failures of human development are the result of the neglect of the analysis of how to mobilize pressures for its realization. A principal message of this chapter is to emphasize the need to include political feasibilities in the recommendations for human development, without losing the vision of a better society.

In the political economy of human development in general, in promoting and financing the well-being of the poor in particular, and in embarking on restructuring social services to the poor, six areas are worth exploring:

1. Common or shared interests between rich and poor.
2. Mutual interests and bargains between rich and poor, including the payment of compensation.
3. Interest conflicts within the ruling groups that can result in benefits for the poor.
4. Empowerment of the poor and participatory forms of organization.
5. Organization of distinct "trustees for the poor" and "guardians of rationality."
6. International pressures and support.

These six sources of a political power base can be directed at (1) raising the ratio of public expenditure to national income, or (2) raising the ratio of social expenditure to public expenditure, or (3) raising the ratio of priority social expenditure (for low-income countries, basic education, health care, water for the rural poor) to social expenditure; or (4) making any given ratio more effective in achieving its objectives, by improving institutions, skills, attitudes, and levels of living.

Obviously, these goals should be achieved in the context of a growing national income, growing public expenditure, and growing social expenditure, or at least not declining ones.[6] In addition to the obvious reason that there would be no point in raising these ratios by shrinking income, public expenditure or social expenditure (the three denominators), it is politically easier to raise tax rates and reallocate funds from, say, military to social expenditure, and from, say, higher education to primary education, when total income and public expenditure are growing than when they are constant or declining. In addition, much of public expenditure, such as interest payments, is committed and not available for reallocation. In the following sections some successes and failures are discussed.

Common Interests

It is fairly universally recognized that the government has to play a strong role in financing certain basic health and education services. Immunization and vaccination against infectious diseases, and spraying to protect all residents from vector-borne diseases such as malaria, are almost pure public goods. So-called "merit goods," that is goods to which all citizens have a basic right (primary health and education), irrespective of their ability to pay, fall into the same category. The universal desire that no child should die of hunger or malnutrition can be similarly regarded as a public good, a concern of the whole community.

Some of these measures cost very little. For 10 cents per child oral rehydration can save children from dehydration, the result of diarrhea, the biggest killer today. Instruction in washing hands, boiling water and sanitary practices prevents this illness. Immunization for life against the six leading child-killing diseases in poor countries can be achieved by spending 50 cents. In spite of this, these diseases kill 10,000 children a day.[7]

The pharmaceutical companies do not spend money on research into vaccines against malaria and other tropical diseases because these account for only 1 percent of their profits. These diseases cause half the world's illness but receive only 3 percent of medical research funds [UNDP and WHO Report 1990]. Neither common nor mutual interests can activate profit-seeking agents to devote efforts to the solution of these problems.

One reason for the neglect of relatively cheap, preventive health services in favor of expensive, curative ones has nothing to do with interest conflicts or special political or professional interest groups. The preference for curative over preventive health services is partly a matter of perception. A disease suffered is felt by some individual and those who care for him or her. An illness prevented is a mere shadowy statistic. The bias in favor of curative health services is, partly, a matter of human fallibility, especially where it could be shown that prevention would be in almost everyone's interest. Although the difference between a visible and felt ill and an invisible possibility remains, education and training can help to change such perceptions.

Even here, political participation can overcome resistance. Intended beneficiaries of a health project in Lesotho were going to traditional healers rather than government health workers because the healers offered curative remedies whereas the health workers had prepared only lectures on preventive health. The traditional healers were then integrated into the formal health system and government health workers provided also curative remedies. As a result, the impact of the preventive service improved.[8]

The interests of some nonpoor groups can be enlisted for the benefit of the poor, if these groups gain from the propoor measures. For example, raising the productivity of small farmers and small businesses may lower the prices of the goods and services they produce. Of course, there should also be some increase in their incomes to avoid the productivity gains being too widely diluted. The buyers of these goods and services, and those who employ workers who buy them, will benefit and support the measures. Similarly, when the real incomes of the poor rise, the interests of those who gain from their higher purchases can be enlisted. Much of what the poor buy will be produced by the poor, and what the poor produce will be bought by them. To this extent, productivity-raising propoor policies will have multiplier effects. But some of these effects will spill over to the nonpoor, and this will be a source of political support by the nonpoor.

Mutual Interests and Compensation

Financing a service must be distinguished from its provision. Social services may be wholly privately, or wholly publicly, provided and financed. But these services may also be financed by the state and provided privately; or they may be provided by the state but, through user charges, privately financed. Governments can issue vouchers for private schools to deprived parents, unable to pay for them, who are then free to choose the school for their children. University students may receive loans which are repaid out of the higher income the education enables them to earn.

Some health and education programs, as has been seen, are almost pure public goods. Others are almost entirely private goods, such as an appendectomy or a pain reliever. Most services combine features of public and private goods. A person treated for tuberculosis benefits, but the people who might otherwise have been infected also benefit. Family planning services benefit both the parents and the community. The public goods aspects fall under the previous heading of common interests, the private goods aspects imply that a benefit to one may mean a loss to someone else. Paying for services by those who can afford it does, of course, still leave benefits for those who pay and relieves the government of losses.

There are three ways of combining the virtues of markets and decentralization with those of the government in the finance and provision of public goods: the use of selective user charges (public provision, private finance); decentralization of health care (greater responsiveness and accountability of public provision and public finance to the needs of the poor); and government use of private-sector providers (public finance, private provision), both profit-seeking and NGOs. Each of these has merits and drawbacks. User charges which exempt the poor require means tests. Decentralization can be more responsive to needs and more accountable to the beneficiaries, but local tax capacity is often weak and central grants are required; these present a dilemma between automaticity and conditionality to prevent their use for local political purposes. Private providers paid out of government revenue present problems of quality and cost control.

Compensation can take two radically different forms. First, in the process of implementing austerity measures or other policies that hurt the poor, particular groups of the nonpoor may have to be compensated or "bribed" into accepting the policies; secondly, particularly vulnerable groups may be insured against deprivation, irrespective of their political power, as a matter of public policy.

Various "targeted" subsidies, food aid, employment schemes and the redirection of social services to these groups fall into the second category. In Costa Rica, during the stabilization policy 1982–83, the government set up a temporary food aid program which distributed food to 40,000 families, about 1 in 12 households, designated as needy by local committees. In Chile employment programs were expanded during the depression of 1983, and nutrition, health and subsidy programs for poor children and mothers were strengthened.[9]

These palliatives, often temporary, can be interpreted in two different ways. They can be seen either as sops for the poor that keep them quiet and prevent the fundamental, structural measures that would permanently and substantially improve their lot. Or they can be regarded as part of a piecemeal campaign that, like numerous termites in the rotting woodwork, undermine the structure of an old system, or, like pioneers, demonstrate the way and build the constituencies that eventually lead to its replacement by an improved order. The chances of compensatory measures leading to long-term reforms are better if the measures protecting the poor are not, as it were, stuck on after the event, but are built as an integral part into the adjustment program from the beginning.

So far, compensation to poor losers has been discussed. The other type of compensation may have to be paid to comparatively better off losers when progressive, propoor reforms are implemented, either because equity requires it, or, in spite of the fact that compensation would be inequitable, or otherwise undesirable, because political opposition has to be overcome. These compensation payments can be particularly important in periods of transition, in order to conciliate opponents, maintain coalitions and appease hostile antagonists. Since urban wage earners are often the losers in periods of adjustment, wage increases, redeployment payments or retraining schemes to these vocal and powerful groups may be necessary. When overstaffed bureaucracies have to be reduced, civil servants, particularly in Africa, also suffer from dismissal. Temporary subsidies for specific goods and services, investment in certain types of infrastructure projects, public housing, or, as in Turkey, rebates paid to consumers on value-added tax are other examples of compensation payments.[10]

In implementing compensation payments, policymakers will have to consider seven questions. First, are the losses for which compensation is considered real or only perceived? The Repeal of the Corn Laws in 1846 was feared to lead to the death of British agriculture; in fact it flourished; the factory laws were thought to lead to the death of British industry; in fact it prospered. The imposition of antipollution legislation has often led to the discovery of new, previously unexploited, profit opportunities that arise from the commercial use of substances previously discarded.

Second, are these payments politically necessary? Would not persuasion or weakening of the political opposition do? The answer will depend on the strength of the government and its commitment to the reform.

Third, is the compensation deserved? This is a moral or humanitarian question, the answer to which is likely to conflict with that to the previous one. It is the weak, powerless, poor and inarticulate who are likely to be the most deserving, though they are also most likely to benefit directly from the reforms.

Fourth, can the payments be afforded? Information and administrative costs may be excessive, or the effects on incentives and the allocation of resources may be undesirable.

Fifth, do they have undesirable side effects that cancel the benefits? In addition to the blunting of incentives and allocational distortions, they may lead to capital flight, to strikes, to sabotage, or even to coups d'état.

Sixth, can compensation be offered in noneconomic forms? In Peru in 1976, President Morales Bermudez offered the restoration of civilian democratic rule for acceptance of his stabilization measures. Similar attempts were made in Argentina, Brazil and Algeria after food riots in October 1989 and in Jordan after riots in the spring of 1989.

Seventh, can the policy makers rely on support by the international community? This question will be discussed later.

The first type of compensation, targeting subsidies to the poor, and the second type, overcoming opposition of the nonpoor, are combined when a targeted scheme is broadened. Narrow targeting of, say, food subsidies on low-income groups should aim at covering all the poor, but only the poor. If it achieves this objective it has the advantage that it saves scarce budgetary resources and meets priority needs. But it has two great defects. First, while it avoids the leakage to the nonpoor, it is bound to have another, possibly worse, leakage: some poor will be left out. Second, it does nothing to recruit the self-interested support of at least some nonpoor. For both these reasons it is therefore better to err on the side of excess coverage than deficient coverage. In this way some of the beneficiaries who are not in dire need will support the scheme. Some of the benefits may then be recouped, e.g., by a tax on tobacco or alcohol, which does not hit children.

SOME COUNTRY EXPERIENCES

Sri Lanka switched in 1978–80 from a general rice subsidy and ration scheme (including occasionally free rations) to a targeted food stamp program aimed only at the poor. In spite of favorable circumstances, the reforms showed both the political pressures to cover many nonpoor, and the failure to reach many poor. It also involved considerable administrative costs. In 1978 the subsidy was removed from the richest part of the population. In 1979 the rations were converted into non-indexed food stamps and an attempt was made to target somewhat larger benefits to the poorest third. The share of food subsidies in GNP fell from about 5 percent in the mid-1970s to 1.3 percent in 1984.[11] Subsidized rice rations were given to half the population. Subsidies to other food items, such as wheat and sugar, were available to all, and benefited the high-income households.

The government attempted to check the incomes of claimants, but parliament repeatedly opposed it successfully, although special measures for the very poor were adopted. Aiding the poor is politically acceptable; cutting benefits to the middle classes is not. The objective of benefiting all the poor and only the poor is impossible to achieve; excess coverage is preferable, both for political and administrative reasons, to deficient coverage.

In Morocco, as in Sri Lanka, subsidies on food items were removed between 1985 and 1988, and the impact on the poor softened by "food for work" programs. Only the subsidies on flour, sugar and cooking oil remained. But the grade of flour that remained subsidized had accounted for about 80 percent of all flour milled before the reforms. Again, as in Sri Lanka, a good part of the middle-income groups had to be included among those covered by the reduced subsidies. Covering only the poor proved politically unacceptable.[12]

In Argentina, Chile, and Peru tax reforms that benefited the poor depended on the agitation of middle-class professionals, white collar workers, small and medium-sized businessmen and bureaucrats, who shared in the transfers that were primarily intended for the poor.

In some cases narrow targeting has been more successful. The Colombian food stamp program of 1978–82 and the Philippine food price discount of 1983 have successfully combined geographic targeting with additional indicator targeting based on the nutritional status of pre-school children.

The lessons from these experiences, particularly for attempts to restructure services to the poor, are four. First, the administrative costs of narrow targeting are high, and as costs rise the targeting becomes even narrower. The less efficient the bureaucracy, the stronger the arguments are against a targeted antipoverty program. Second, targeting is very difficult because the poor are heterogeneous and hard to identify, and their composition and location changes in time. There is, therefore, a substantial risk that some poor people will be left out. Third, if small children in poor households are to benefit, the transfer to these households has to be substantial. Fourth, and most important in the present context, the interests of at least some groups among the nonpoor, especially the urban, middle-income groups, must normally be mobilized or appeased, if measures intended to help the poor are to be successful. These conclusions point to the need for a broad coverage, unless special circumstances make narrower targeting advisable.

Interest Conflicts within Ruling Groups

Conflicts within powerful groups can often be used for the benefit of the poor and powerless. The improvement of the living conditions of the British working class in the nineteenth century was the result of a conflict between Tory landlords and skilled operatives, on the one hand, and capitalist industrialists, on the other. Before the poor were permitted to organize themselves in trade unions, before they had the vote and before they had access to free public education, their fate improved as a result of the factory laws which introduced safety regulations, shortened the working day, and got women and children out of the mines, and of the repeal of the Corn Laws, which reduced the price of food for urban workers. The capitalists predicted that the factory laws protecting the poor would be the death of British industry; the landlords said that the repeal of the Corn Laws would be the death of British agriculture. In fact both industry and agriculture flourished for a quarter of a century. It shows how self-interest can be misperceived and how benefits can accrue from measures judged at the time to be harmful. The same is likely to be true for measures improving the condition of the poor in most developing countries. The long-term interests of the rich, properly perceived, are not likely to be harmed.

Similarly, rich farmers have an interest in higher prices for their agricultural products, which benefit poor growers too, if they grow and sell the same crops, or if the higher prices affect all crops. There may be common interests in rural schooling and health services, rural infrastructure, and improved varieties of crops. On the other hand, the urban middle class, students, the military and civil servants want low food prices, from which the urban poor also benefit. The urban sector will gain strength in postagrarian societies, although by reason of collective action it can be very strong while its size is still quite small.

The impact of some policies, such as tariff reductions or exchange rate devaluations or food pricing reforms, does not follow divisions between rich and poor, but cuts across them. Higher import prices benefit both rich and poor producers of domestic substitutes, lower import prices benefit both rich and poor consumers of these imports.

Sometimes regional (or ethnic) lines can define interest alignments. Pressure for irrigation in a district in India, if successful, can raise the productivity and incomes of both rich and poor. An increased flow of resources to the Northeast of Brazil benefits the landowners there and, with higher employment, also benefits the landless laborers.

There can be a harmony of interests between the providers of social services and their beneficiaries. Although it has been seen that some of these professional interest groups can interfere with basic needs by insisting on overqualification and excess standards, others can be recruited to the effort. Primary school teachers, paramedical personnel, nurses, social workers, and extension workers all stand to benefit from an expansion of services, and are often better organized and more vocal than the recipients of their services. Kenya and Sri Lanka have powerful teachers' unions, both the result and the cause of the large amount of resources devoted to primary education in these countries. In Peru the expansion of primary education was largely the result of efforts by political parties to win teachers' votes.[13]

Empowerment and Participation

The poor, like the rich and powerful, are a heterogeneous group. Action to reduce the poverty of one group, such as the urban poor, may increase the poverty of another group, such as the rural poor. One useful distinction among the chronically poor (as contrasted with those who are poor only temporarily) is that between the "working poor" and those who are excluded from the labor force. The "working poor," who sell the product of their unskilled labor and, perhaps, a few small assets, can organize themselves in order to raise the returns to these assets. The second category of poor cannot participate in the labor force either because they are old, infirm or otherwise incapacitated, or because they are excluded by social or economic discrimination. The alleviation of their poverty has to be sought through pressures for social services and transfer payments, and elimination of the discrimination. In the short run conflicts may arise. In the long run, poverty reduction of both groups can be in the general interest of society, by both raising productivity and lowering desired family size.

The most obvious way in which political pressures can be used to benefit the poor is the vote in democracies. Although this may not help the poorest, coalitions between them and some better-off groups, both self-interested and altruistic, are frequent, and the poorest 40 percent have fared well in countries with multiparty systems and free elections: Costa Rica and Chile in the 1960s and early 1970s in Latin America, Botswana, Mauritius and Zimbabwe in Africa, and Sri Lanka in Asia. The standard prescription for improving the condition of the poor is, of course, first, their combination in organized pressure groups for more vocal representation of their interests and concerns, and, second, self-help, "bottom-up" and "people-centered" development through participatory organizations. The former may be backed by withholding their labor in strikes as a bargaining weapon. For the latter, various participatory forms of organization and self-help by the poor also can reduce their dependence, add to their power, help formulate policies, make them more self-reliant and provide some of the resources they need.

Participation and decentralization are sometimes used more as slogans than as a thought-out strategy. Participation can be both an end in itself and a means to the efficient provision of goods and services. It can take many different forms, such as codetermination (as in German factories), shop floor participation in workers' councils, financial profit sharing, collective bargaining, Swiss canton–like voting, representative elections, cooperatives, etc.

Some have claimed that even the market is a form of participation. And small village markets certainly can be, though large anonymous markets are less likely candidates for direct participation. On the other hand, it should be remembered that free, competitive markets, in conditions in which assets are fairly equally distributed and production is conducted in an efficient, labor-intensive manner, do create demand for labor and therefore raise its bargaining power. As the economy progresses, there is growing demand for upgrading skilled labor and this, again, adds to the power of workers.

Some forms of participation are compatible with undemocratic government. Mussolini's and pre-Hitler Austria's fascist states took the form of corporate states, in which workers, employers, and farmers participated, being represented in separate chambers. Yugoslavia's Tito got the idea for his worker-managed enterprises from Mussolini's fascist state. Taiwan and South Korea, both authoritarian regimes, have practiced successful participation. Democratic government, in which unrepresentative "representatives" are elected, can be a far cry from participatory government.

If participation goes together with decentralization, the result is often increased regional inequalities. This happened in Chile under Pinochet, and in China under the communes. Poorer municipalities could afford only inferior services.

Most forms of participation require central government support. The paramedical personnel chosen from among the villagers need training at the center. Central legislation is needed to get access to education, health, credit. Without it, local power elites tend to take over decentralized participatory organizations and central countervailing power may be needed to combat them. Finance for participatory institutions often depends on central government.

West Bengal has one of the more successful antipoverty programs. Its Communist state government maintained strong central control and replaced local leaders with its own cadres, while simultaneously pursuing a strategy of decentralization. It is a good example of the combination of centralized and decentralized state action.[14]

Another example is the civil rights movement in the USA. Here was indeed a grass-roots movement, with heavy involvement of volunteers. But it depended for its success on strong support by the central government and the Supreme Court. Anyone concerned with the fate of the blacks in Mississippi would not want to decentralize power to the state of Mississippi. Control by local elites would not be a force for liberation or prosperity. But mobilization of the blacks themselves, with the support of central legislation and judicial rulings, can advance their cause.

In other cases, however, the interests of local elites coincide with those of the poor, and decentralization will then lead to reform. In India, communities have joined forces to protect themselves against invasion by outsiders who wanted to denude their forests and pollute their rivers. Their defense cut across class lines and decentralization worked for the benefit of the poor.

In small-scale enterprises such as those that have grown up in the informal sector of some developing countries interest alignments do not follow the lines of workers against employers, but buyers against sellers. What has come to be known as flexible specialization has presented quite new constellations of interest, different from those appropriate for the age of mass production.

A unity of interests also exists for educational and health reforms, from which the whole community benefits. But when the allocation of scarce goods is at stake, such as a land reform, agricultural credit, or the distribution of fertilizer, the local elites will tend to undermine the reforms. Even here, however, short-term interests of the rich and their long-term interests, or their perceived and real interests may be in conflict. In the longer run the higher productivity and production of the poor can benefit the rich, just as an alert, educated, skilled, healthy labor force is beneficial to its employers. Empowerment of the poor can therefore be in the real (as opposed to perceived), and long-term (as opposed to short-term) interest of the rich and powerful.

There is another area in which participation has to be modified. Highly technical decisions, such as those about whether to change the exchange rate (or leave it as it is), or about a weapons system, cannot be left to participatory organizations but must call on experts who, of course, should be accountable to the public. But experts, doctors, scientists, engineers, and bureaucrats also constitute a power group that can be hostile to human development.

In spite of these qualifications and limitations of participation, it is highly desirable to involve the beneficiaries of projects and policies in decisions that involve their lives and work, for at least three reasons, which are also three aspects of human development: participation is an end in itself and expresses the autonomy of the citizens; it makes the projects and policies more responsive to real needs; and it reduces the costs of constructing and maintaining them.[15]

The benefits of participation, and the need for government or donor support, are now beginning to be well understood. It is no longer believed that, for social reforms to occur, it is necessary and sufficient to seize the central power of the state. But the precise level for specific decisions (central, province, local or participatory), the combination of government, markets, NGOs and self-help organizations, the allocation between financing and providing the goods and services, and the precise division between central, external, and locally generated finance, the blend between cooperation and conflict, the need for accountability and democratic control, and the phasing of the decisions, raises complex questions, the answers to which will vary from case to case.

Guardians of Rationality and Trustees for the Poor

The state is normally neither monolithic nor impervious to outside pressures (including pressures for rational and altruistic policies). Governments consist of many departments, ministries and agencies, and many layers, from central government via provincial (or in a federation state) government to village and town councils. Power is divided between the legislature, the judiciary and the executive. Each of these pulls in a different direction and the final outcome is the resultant of these forces. Pressure groups can influence these outcomes. Economists, and other professional groups committed to certain standards, action groups, the churches, and voluntary organizations can constitute themselves as both "guardians of rationality" and "trustees for the poor."[16] In the former capacity they exercise influence on policies aiming at reducing poverty; in the latter on policies that do not waste resources in an attempt to distort their allocation in favor of special interest groups. It is not their function to acquiesce in the results of the free play of market forces.

Sometimes showing that the interests of a group can be more effectively pursued by other, more benign means can win acceptance. The military may not be convinced of the greater social value of village pharmacies than that of tanks, but it may be persuaded if its own objective, viz. security, can be achieved with fewer weapons. Channeling expenditure from swords to plough shares, and from tanks to baby food, can be achieved by showing that national security is served better by a smaller military budget, and then redirecting the resources saved to the social sectors.

In a democracy, if all always acted and voted exclusively in their individual, economic self-interest, the poorest 49 percent of voters would lose. For, in order to get a majority, it is necessary to bribe only the middle 2 percent of voters to vote with the top 49 percent to achieve a majority of 51 percent. And the top 49 percent have more money for this purpose than the bottom 49 percent.[17] Of course, the example is highly artificial, because they do not act like this, because people do not know to which percentile they belong, and because redistributive policies cannot be targeted precisely. Nevertheless, there is some evidence that, in democracies, there is, indeed, redistribution toward the middle, but little redistribution toward the poor, except in times of war. But the assumption of purely selfish voting is too unrealistic, and many quite well-off citizens, at least as voters, do show concern for the poor and vote for measures that reduce their poverty. "Welfare payments" may have acquired a bad name, but reducing the number of malnourished children or helping single mothers has great general appeal, as the 1990 Economic Summit on children showed.

International Support

The international community can be mobilized both as a pressure group and as a source of finance for human development. Feeding and educating deprived children has a powerful appeal to human beings everywhere. A well-designed human development program in a poor country can count on support from citizens of all countries. Eliminating hunger and starvation in the world can be regarded as a public good, and providing each human born into this world with the potential for the full development of his or her capacities is part of the enlightened self-interest of mankind.

The United Nations Children's Fund (UNICEF) has been a highly successful pressure group for protecting the poor, particularly children and pregnant women, in the adjustment processes that were initiated in the 1980s. Through its book, *Adjustment with a Human Face*, and through its dialogues with the International Monetary Fund and the World Bank, its propoor advocacy influenced the policies on conditionality of these two institutions and other donors away from a merely technical, economic approach for stabilization and balance of payments corrections, toward a more humane, compassionate approach, concerned with the human and social dimensions of stabilization and adjustment. It also drew attention to the need and the political advantages of protecting the poor (by a form of compensation) from the burdens of adjustment. There were, of course, groups inside these institutions, and in some developing countries, that had been responsive to propoor policies and that had continued the traditions of the basic needs strategy of the 1970s.

The success of UNICEF in getting governments to restructure their expenditure has been due not only to the general appeal of improving children's health, but also to the low costs at which substantial improvements can be achieved, to external financial support for these measures, and to the fact that they included many children in the middle-income groups. The political benefits to governments of the special campaigns that accompanied these drives may not be applicable to other areas with less public appeal, more narrowly targeted to the poor, fewer resources contributed by other sectors such as the military, and less external finance.

Donors have funded programs that compensate the poor during adjustment periods. The best known are the Bolivian Emergency Social Fund (ESF), started in 1986, and the Ghanaian Program of Action to Mitigate the Social Costs of Adjustment (PAMSCAD), which started in 1988. These are programs of employment creation through local public works, credit creation and social services. They are mainly intended to be temporary, designed for workers dismissed from the tin mines in Bolivia and from the overstaffed public sector in Ghana. Local communities and NGOs play an important part in proposing and designing these programs. Bolivia's ESF, in particular, involved minimum government involvement and full delegation of responsibility to local communities and private contractors. The World Bank is planning similar programs for many other countries.

The Bolivian and Ghanaian programs have been criticized because the foreign funds were not additional to other aid, and were, in any case, quite small compared with Bolivia's debt service and the drop in the world price of Ghana's principal export, cocoa. A second ground for criticism is that the poorest among the dislocated did not benefit. However, in countries like Bolivia and Ghana, with so many poor people, it is hard not to benefit some poor people with almost any scheme. A deeper criticism is that both projects are remedial to adjustment measures, whereas the most desirable policy would incorporate human concerns right from the beginning, in the very structure of the adjustment process.

If a country that has neglected human development in the past now intends to adopt reforms that promote it, it runs into short-term problems. These may take the form of heavy burdens on the budget and on administration, or of political discontent and riots by those who are likely to lose from the reforms. If there is redistribution of income to the poor, there is likely to be an additional impetus to inflation arising from the sectors producing goods (especially food) on which the poor spend their money, because their supply is inelastic in the short run. This may be accompanied by unemployment in the trades that had previously catered to the rich, because it takes time to shift resources. There may be a reduction in productive investment, and balance of payments problems caused by additional food imports and capital flight, as the rich try to get their money out of the country. If the reform-minded government replaces a dictatorship, previously oppressed groups will assert their claims for higher incomes, with additional inflationary results. If some groups become disaffected, they may organize strikes, sabotage or even coups d'état. All these are familiar troubles for reform-minded governments that wish to change the course of policy in favor of the poor.

In such critical situations the international community can help make the transition less painful and disruptive, and more likely to succeed. It can help to overcome an important obstacle to reform—the fear that the cost of the transition to more appropriate policies is too high. It can add flexibility and adaptability to otherwise inert policies set on a damaging course. Structural adjustment loans have come to be accepted in other contexts, such as the transition to a more liberal international trade regime and more market-oriented domestic policies. By an extension of the same principle, adjustment loans should be given to the transition to a more human-development–oriented regime. They can take the form of financial or technical assistance to a land reform, or a tax reform, or of well-designed food aid or of international food stamps. An international economic order built on international support of domestic efforts for human development is more sensible and more likely to succeed than one built on the hope of trickle-down effects.

THE POLITICAL ECONOMY OF PHASING THE TRANSITION

Should the transition from a wasteful, repressive, inhuman regime to a strategy of rational allocation and human concerns be sudden or gradual? Shock therapies have recently been recommended to East European countries in their transition from centrally planned to market economies. It has been said it would not be wise to attempt jumping over an abyss in two successive steps. It is certainly true that the shock approach can be appropriate in an economy that responds quickly and flexibly to changes in policies, one in which signals are speedily heeded and incentives work in desirable directions, that has provisions to look after its victims, in which external assistance is plentiful, and the demand for its exports is high and expanding. If there is spare capacity in the sectors into which workers are to be redeployed, if foreign capital is rapidly repatriated, and if cuts in consumption can soon be reversed or in which those worst affected can be rescued, shock treatment may well be best. This is not the case, for instance, in most African economies.

It is also true that sudden shocks may lend credibility to government intentions, without which the measures may not be sustainable, and that gradual and slow reforms provide more scope for oppositions to be formed, for hostile coalitions to be organized, and for opportunities for evasion to occur. But sometimes there is stronger opposition to sudden and large changes. There have been massive protests, riots and coups d'état in response to sudden and large cuts in consumption, employment, and output. Gradual change can be carried out with less pain and less opposition. If general food subsidies are to be reduced in order to concentrate them on the poor, a gradual phasing out will be accompanied by increases in the supply of food, so that the sufferers from the price increase are somewhat cushioned. The avoidance of deprivation and extreme hardships will also reduce the chances of racial, ethnic and religious strife, and will contribute to a more peaceful society.

Restructuring for reform imposes strains and costs on some people. They may become unemployed and lose their source of income and self-respect, while the society loses their productive contribution. If the society does not have a social safety net to catch these victims of the reform process, suffering can be great, and political opposition to the reforms can mount. The effects of economic policies are never certain, and a gradual approach makes it easier to reverse course when errors are made. International support is often crucial in deciding on the speed of change. It has to be large enough to induce leaders to accept the risks of reform, but not so large as to make them avoid the necessary domestic measures. The reforms in Sri Lanka in 1977–1979 provide an example of how aid, combined with favorable economic conditions, can permit reforms towardmore targeted policies to be carried out successfully.[18]

THE POLITICS OF AID

Aid policies, just like domestic policies, are motivated by political pressures, national interests, idealism and human solidarity. Military security, altruistic and Machiavellian motives or profit-seeking export interests can inspire foreign assistance policies. Business interests are behind the provision of inappropriate, capital-intensive technologies, and the interests of consultancy and training firms behind the provision of inappropriate technical assistance. Denmark and Sweden have bought off the business lobby by earmarking a fixed percentage of the aid program for programs of interest to businesses and the donor country.[19] The answer to the pressures from consultancy firms and training institutions lies in decentralizing technical assistance pro-

grams to the donor offices in the developing countries. The local representatives who are in continual touch with the needs and people of the
recipient countries are more likely to choose the right local people.

The interests of banks that had lent to developing countries and are
eager to have their debts serviced are clearly partly behind the switch
in donor policies from project aid to program lending. The policy
conditionality that accompanies such lending is often based on the
premature crystallization of flawed orthodoxies. Unfortunately or for-
tunately, depending on whose point of view one takes, policies, like
projects, are substitutable for one another, and it is sometimes not
difficult to evade the conditions imposed.

It is often said that aid is inevitably given in the national self-interest
of the donor country; it is just a branch of foreign policy. A lot depends,
of course, on how narrowly or broadly national self-interest is interpreted. It is, however, noteworthy that countries like Holland, Sweden, and
Norway, whose aid programs are inspired by moral concerns of human
solidarity, have given more aid, and of a better quality, than countries
like the USA and the UK, which have defended aid in terms of national
self-interest. Australia conducted a public opinion survey which
showed that people regard aid as an expression of human solidarity.

Frequently NGOs and action groups agitate for more and better
quality aid. Expanding the role of NGOs would help in reducing the
bias in favor of large projects that create few jobs, and might raise aid
effectiveness. To some extent this has occurred. But NGOs might object
to becoming too dependent on government funds and government
objectives.

The obstacles to restructuring aid policies to the priority sectors often
do not lie with outside pressure groups, but have to be sought within
aid ministries. Reducing conditionality would reduce the amount of
work to be done by the donor, but would also reduce leverage. It could
be replaced by actually giving aid only to those who have shown a
commitment to human development policies. Quiet signaling can be
more effective than hamfisted conditionality.

An objection to supporting human development programs consisting
of primary education, primary health, and family planning, that has
sometimes been raised by aid ministries, is that they involve supporting
recurrent expenditure, with the complaint that they present a bottom-
less pit, or indefinite donor commitment. The answer should lie in
designing strategies with gradually growing recipient contributions, or
with self-liquidating cost-recovery over a specified period. This may be
accompanied by jointly working out new sources of tax revenue to
finance the human development projects, for which cost recovery
would be wrong.

Combining development aid with conditions for policy reform, poverty alleviation, social objectives and political freedom has become popular among bilateral and multilateral donors. The concessionary component in the assistance buys, as it were, the policies that a purely commercial lender cannot insist on. It is controversial how desirable and feasible such conditionality is. Some observers have said that conditions can be imposed only if the recipient government is, in any case, committed to the policies. Complaints have been voiced that conditionality imposed by foreigners is intrusive, incompatible with national sovereignty, and can be counterproductive if it discredits domestic groups aligned with such reforms. It can also be evaded by substituting other undesirable policies for the ones eliminated by conditionality. The same objectives can be achieved by adopting a quieter style than by imposing performance criteria, by supporting regimes determined to promote human development, withdrawing aid from those that do not, and thereby signaling unobtrusively to all the conditions for receiving aid.

THE STRUGGLE FOR HUMAN PROGRESS

It has taken the more enlightened, advanced societies three centuries to achieve the civil, political, and social dimensions of human development. The eighteenth century established civil rights: from freedom of thought, speech and religion to the rule of law. In the course of the nineteenth century political freedom and participation in the exercise of political power made major strides, as the right to vote was extended to more people. In the twentieth century the welfare state extended human development to the social and economic sphere, by recognizing that minimum standards of education, health, nutrition, well-being and security are basic to the civilized life, as well as to the exercise of the civil and political attributes of citizenship. These battles have not been won easily or without resistance. Each progressive thrust has been followed by reactionary counterthrusts and setbacks.[20]

The struggle for civil liberty was opposed after the French Revolution by those fearful that it could lead only to tyranny; in the fight for political participation that it would bring about enslavement of the masses. We are now witnessing one of these counterattacks on the economic liberties of the welfare state, and, on some fronts, partial retreat. The arguments again are that the opposite of the intended results is achieved. Just as civil liberty was said to lead to tyranny, and political liberty to slavery, so compassionate public concern for the poor, it is now argued, can lead only to their pauperization. It is, however, not inevitable that in the war on poverty, poverty should win.

Well-designed public expenditure programs can contribute substantially to improving the human condition.

NOTES

1. *Adjustment with a Human Face*, edited by Giovanni Andrea Cornia, Richard Jolly, Frances Stewart. Clarendon Press, Oxford, 1987, pp. 292–293.

2. *Adjustment with a Human Face*, edited by Giovanni Andrea Cornia, Richard Jolly, Frances Stewart. Clarendon Press, Oxford, 1987, pp. 123–124.

3. See Jean Dreze and Amartya Sen. *Hunger and Public Action*, Clarendon Press, Oxford, 1989, p. 239.

4. See Joan Nelson, "The Politics of Pro-Poor Adjustment," in *Fragile Coalitions: the Politics of Economic Adjustment*, Joan M. Nelson and contributors, Transaction Books, U.S.-Third World Policy Perspectives No. 12, Overseas Development Council, New Brunswick (USA) and Oxford (UK), 1989, p. 108.

5. There are arguments against credit as a top priority. First, at very low levels of development, food and health come first. At higher levels, education and training in vocational skills may make credit unnecessary. Credit, with its debt burden, can also blunt incentives to work, as the worker thinks he is earning for his creditor.

6. At the same time, in the face of declining denominators (national income, public expenditure, social expenditure), it is to be commended if priority expenditure is maintained, so that the social priority ratio rises.

7. James Grant, Comment on Nancy Birdsall's essay: "Thoughts on Good Health and Good Government" in *A World to Make, Development in Perspective*, edited by Francis X. Sutton, Transaction Publishers, New Brunswick (USA) and London (UK), 1990, p. 115.

8. Lawrence F. Salmen. "Popular Participation and Development," Washington, DC: The World Bank, mimeo, n.d.

9. See Joan Nelson, "The Politics of Pro—Poor Adjustment," in *Fragile Coalitions: the Politics of Economic Adjustment*, Joan M. Nelson and contributors, Transaction Books, New Brunswick (USA) and Oxford (UK), 1989, p. 101.

10. See John Waterbury, "The Political Management of Adjustment and Reform," in *Fragile Coalitions: the Politics of Economic Adjustment*, Joan Nelson and Contributors, Overseas Development Council, Transaction Books, New Brunswick (USA) and Oxford (UK), 1989, p. 41.

11. See Neville Edirisinghe, *The Food Stamp Scheme in Sri Lanka: Costs, Benefits, and Options for Modification*, International Food Policy Research Institute, Research Report 58, Washington DC, March, 1987.

12. See Joan Nelson, "The Politics of Pro—Poor Adjustment," in *Fragile Coalitions: the Politics of Economic Adjustment*, edited by Joan M. Nelson and contributors, U.S. Third World Policy Perspectives, No. 12, Overseas Development Council, Transaction Books, New Brunswick (USA) and Oxford (UK), 1989, pp. 106–107.

13. See the excellent essay by Laurence Whitehead, "Political Explanations of Macroeconomic Management: A Survey," *World Development*, volume 18, number 8, August 1990, pp. 1133–1146.

14. See Kamla Chowdry, "Poverty, Environment, Development," in *A World to Make, Development in Perspective*, edited by Francis X. Sutton, Transaction Publishers,

New Brunswick and London, 1990, pp. 137–150 and Judith Tendler's comments, pp. 152–154.

15. For World Bank experience in this regard, see Michael Cernea, "Farmer Organizations and Institution Building for Sustainable Development," Regional Development Dialogue, Nagoya, Japan; U.N. Center for Regional Development, Vol. 8 No. 2, Summer 1987, pp. 1–19. See also Norman Uphoff's assessment of the World Bank's integrated rural development projects in Nepal, Ghana, and Mexico, "Fitting Projects to People," in Michael Cernea, ed. *Putting People First: Sociological Variables in Rural Development*, New York, Oxford University Press, 1985, pp. 359–395.

16. The expression "guardian of rationality" for the economist is due to Kenneth Arrow, *The Limits of Organization*, 1974, p. 16; that of "trustees for the poor" to Gerald M. Meier, *Emerging from Poverty, The Economics that Really Matters*, Oxford University Press, Oxford, 1984, p. 4.

17. See Robert Nozick, *Anarchy, State and Utopia*, Basic Books, New York, 1968, pp. 274–275. As Nozick points out, other coalitions are possible.

18. See Joan M. Nelson, "The Political Economy of Stabilization: Commitment, Capacity and Public Response," *World Development*, volume 12, number 10, October 1984, pp. 1000–1005.

19. See Paul Mosley, "Increased Aid Flows and Human Resource Development in Africa," UNICEF International Child Development Center, Innocenti Occasional Papers Number 5, August 1990.

20. See Albert O. Hirschman, *The Rhetoric of Reaction; Perversity, Futility, Jeopardy*, The Belknap Press of Harvard University Press, Cambridge, Mass., 1991.

11

Democracy and Economic Growth

Stephan Haggard

The wave of political liberalization washing across the developing world and Eastern Europe has once again raised basic questions about the relationship between democracy and economic growth. The first set of issues is how economic conditions influence politics. Do the level of economic development or growth rates help account for political outcomes, including democracy? Are certain development strategies, economic policies, or conditions more conducive to the consolidation of democratic politics than others?

The second set of questions concerns the relationship between democracy and economic growth. Are stable democratic institutions, the rule of law, and respect for human rights necessary preconditions for growth? Or, as some pessimists have argued, does an expansion of participation and interest group activity inevitably drag down economic performance by increasing demands for consumption and entrenching various inefficiencies? Is there an inevitable trade-off between democracy and development?

These are big questions, and as with most big questions, simple answers usually have to admit to numerous exceptions. This chapter surveys the terrain, summarizes what is known and not known, and raises some questions for debate. The chapter is divided into four parts. The first looks at the relationship between economic development and democracy in the long run, the second looks at the short-run economic constraints on democratic politics.[1] This exercise is repeated with reference to the influence of democracy on growth, looking first at the long run before examining the capacity of democratic governments to initiate and sustain the economic reforms required to achieve long-term growth.

Several general findings emerge. I state them here baldly, developing the qualifications below.

1. Viewed over the long run, there is a strong association between the *level* of economic development and democratic institutions, political rights and civil liberties. It is difficult to define thresholds exactly; this is a source of some hope since it suggests that the relationship is not rigidly deterministic. Below some minimum level of income per capita, however, democracy is rare.

2. Poor economic conditions probably contributed to the wave of democratic transitions we have seen in the last decade. But economic crises have also been associated with the collapse of democratic regimes in the past. Severe economic crises will weaken whatever regime is in power if they exacerbate other political and social cleavages and lead to social polarization.

3. Over the long run, there is no conclusive evidence that the economic performance of democracies is either better or worse than the economic performance of authoritarian regimes. This suggests that the transition to democracy will not necessarily improve economic performance, and could possibly worsen it, though it is likely to change the distribution of gains from growth. In analyzing these outcomes, however, much depends on political factors not related directly to democracy per se.

4. There is no evidence that the domestic private sector in the developing countries, particularly in manufacturing, is a strong, consistent, or principled supporter either of democracy or the market. Rather, their support for both has tended to be instrumental, depending on country-specific and policy-specific factors.

5. Some types of authoritarian regimes have been able to undertake economic reforms that would have been highly unlikely under democratic rule. Yet given the difficulty in distinguishing performance between the two types of governments over the long run, it seems more fruitful to explore the importance of political factors that move beyond the simple distinction between democratic and authoritarian rule. These include the political orientation of the party in power, electoral and interest-group constraints, and the organization of the state itself.

6. Contrary to what is often thought, the transition to a more market-oriented economy demands greater governmental capabilities in a number of areas, as well as the forging of new institutions. A focus on institutional development has the advantage of strengthening the prospects for economic development, while avoiding some of the possible pitfalls from external assistance that will be viewed as unwanted intervention.

ECONOMIC DEVELOPMENT AND DEMOCRACY:
THE LONG RUN

Sociological interpretations of politics have linked successful democratic development with features of the social structure. Only a small step was required to connect the social structure to economic development, producing an economic theory of democracy. Democratic institutions, it was argued, rested on certain "preconditions" such as literacy and mass communication that could only be met at a certain level of development (Lipset 1959). Higher levels of development were also generally associated with increasing income equality and particularly the emergence of middle classes, which were seen as critical carriers of democratic values. Historically, it was argued, the middle class opposed the status hierarchies associated with traditional forms of rule, sought to check the growth of arbitrary state power through law, and supported ideologies that drew parallels between the benefits of economic and political competition. In the current historical context, it could be argued that middle classes in the developing world are more cosmopolitan and more open to external ideological influences than other strata. As Barrington Moore (1966: 418) argued succinctly for an earlier period of European history, "no bourgeoisie, no democracy."

Table 11.1 provides some recent evidence on the hypothesis that level of development and democracy are linked; I will call this the Lipset thesis. Following a World Bank classification scheme, 119 countries have been grouped into four categories on the basis of dollar income per capita in 1987: high income, upper-middle income, lower-middle income, and low income. Two Freedom House scales have been used to measure the extent of political rights and civil liberties in the same year on a scale from 1 to 7, with a score of 1 given to those countries with the most extensive guarantees of these rights and liberties, and a score of 7 to those in which these rights are most restricted.

The table shows the distribution of political scores by income group. There are some interesting exceptions to the Lipset hypothesis. Several low-income countries, including India, maintain relatively high scores in terms of political and civil liberties. A few high-income countries are also outliers. Kuwait and Saudi Arabia are not surprising in this regard, but Singapore poses a more serious anomaly. Nonetheless, the findings are strongly supportive of the Lipset hypothesis *at the extremes of the income scale*. Low-income countries tend to have much weaker institutionalization of political rights and civil liberties than high-income countries.

The middle-income countries do not conform to Lipset's expectations. Both subgroups are bi-modally distributed, and the upper-middle-income countries have a weaker record of protecting political liberties

Table 11.1   Per Capita Income, Political Rights and Civil Liberties, 1987
(Number of Countries/Percentage in Income Group)

	Low Income (<$500)		Lower-Middle Income ($500-2000)		Upper-Middle Income ($2000-6000)		High Income (>$6000)	
Political Rights								
1. *	0	0	2	6.1	3	16.7	19	79.2
2.	1	2.4	10	30.3	4	22	1	4.2
3.	2	4.8	4	12.1	0	0	0	0
4.	3	7.1	2	6.1	1	5.5	1	4.2
5.	8	19.0	8	24.2	4	22.2	1	4.2
6.	18	42.9	6	18.2	4	22.2	2	8.3
7. **	10	23.8	1	3.0	2	11.1	0	0
Average		5.7		3.6		4.1		1.8
Civil Liberties								
1. *	0	0	1	3.0	2	11.1	15	62.5
2.	0	0	3	9.1	5	27.8	5	20.8
3.	1	2.4	9	27.3	0	0	0	0
4.	2	4.8	6	18.2	2	11.1	0	0
5.	12	28.6	8	24.2	2	11.1	3	12.5
6.	17	40.5	5	15.2	5	27.8	0	0
7. **	10	23.8	1	3.0	2	11.1	1	4.2
Average		5.1		4.2		4.1		2.0
	N-42		N-33		N-18		N-24	

* Most Extensive
** Least Extensive

Source: World Bank, World Development Report, 1989 (New York: Oxford
University Press, 1989); Raymond Gastil, Freedom in the World:
Political Rights and Civil Liberties: 1986-87 (New York:
Greenwood, 1987).

than the lower-middle-income countries. I have run a more comprehensive test on 30 middle-income countries, using data from 1972 through 1986. A bivariate regression of GDP per capita on political rights and civil liberties shows no relationship. On the other hand, it might be expected that there would be greater ambiguity in the middle-income cases, which constitute a "zone of transition" between more and less restrictive polities.

These general results are also supported by more sophisticated tests. Cross-national statistical studies have routinely found significant correlations between level of development and democratic rule, even when tested against other hypotheses (Bollen and Jackman 1985). Conversely, there appear to be close correlations between GNP per capita and coup attempts (Londregan and Poole 1990).

These findings are sobering, and call into question the optimistic hope that democratic governance can be exported widely. Critics of the Lipset hypothesis point to the exceptions, such as India, to argue that countervailing factors can offset the liabilities associated with low income. Among those that are of relevance to the Indian case are a British colonial heritage and the absolute, rather than relative, size of the middle class. Yet the general hypothesis of an association between level of development and democracy is not disproved by a single outlier, even a large one. Viewed over the long run, and for most countries, the achievement of some minimum level of economic development appears to be a necessary if not sufficient condition for democracy.

I draw a somewhat controversial policy implication from this discussion. It is certainly desirable to bring pressure to bear in low-income countries to limit human rights abuses, expand the flow of information, and encourage the development of civic associations. If the Lipset hypothesis is correct, all efforts should be made to accelerate the economic development of low-income countries. Nonetheless, those arguing for the transplant of democratic institutions to extremely poor countries, for example, through the organization of "free and fair elections," should be asked why they expect such institutions to take root now if they have not done so in the past.

ECONOMIC GROWTH AND DEMOCRATIZATION:
THE SHORT RUN

The Lipset hypothesis fell on hard times beginning in the 1960s as a number of bureaucratic-authoritarian installations occurred in the developing world. The "new authoritarianism" afflicted not only the poorest developing countries, but relatively advanced ones in which the level of industrialization was high. Brazil (1964), Argentina (1966 and 1976), Chile (1973), and Uruguay (1973) were the paradigmatic cases, but reversals of democracy also took place in Korea (1972) and Turkey (1970 and 1980). As we have seen, the middle-income countries present the greatest difficulty for the Lipset hypothesis. There is no evidence that the upper-middle-income countries were more democratic than the lower-middle-income ones, casting doubt on any simple evolutionary model of the spread of democratic norms.

These cases also raised the question of whether Lipset's cross-sectional observation could be given a dynamic interpretation. Lipset's hypothesis drew the relationship between the *level* of economic and political development and made no mention of growth *rates* or other economic variables that might operate on politics in the short run. As Mancur Olson noted in a provocative essay, rapid growth might itself be politically destabilizing.

The nature of the debate about the relationship between economics and politics shifted from an analysis of long historical patterns toward a better understanding of how short-run economic conditions affected politics. This work focused initially on trying to locate the economic correlates of the breakdown of democratic regimes. Several interrelated arguments came out of this new debate, which was heavily influenced by the dependency thinking then coming out of Latin America. Most of these arguments had a functional form: certain development strategies "demanded" the control of labor and the left. In Peter Evans's pithy statement, "in the context of dependent development, the need for repression is great while the need for democracy is small" (Evans 1979: 35).

Perhaps the most specific argument, one associated with Guillermo O'Donnell (1973), concerned the economic requirements of secondary import substitution. Authoritarian rule was most likely to occur at a critical phase in the process of Third World industrialization. To maintain forward momentum in the production of consumer durables and to generate adequate investible resources to finance these relatively capital-intensive ventures, it was "necessary" to compress wages and concentrate income. This could not be accomplished under democratic auspices. As economic propositions, these claims have been subjected to close scrutiny and wide criticism (Collier 1979). Nor is it likely that militaries knew about or accepted such arguments, and it is even less likely that they were a primary motivation for political intervention.

A second line of argument looked at the need to attract foreign capital. Authoritarian installations, it was argued, occurred at that stage of development when extensive foreign investment is deemed necessary. Multinationals, banks, and even multilateral institutions such as the IMF and World Bank (Broad 1989) are more likely to invest where labor and the left are controlled.

This is not implausible, and constitutes an important challenge to the assumption that the private sector is necessarily democratic in its political orientation. Business, both foreign and domestic, may be attracted to authoritarian solutions in countries where they see strong threats from labor or the left to their economic viability or basic property rights. The most recent examples have come from the East Asian newly industrializing countries. The business community was actively opposed to more democratic politics in Hong Kong, publicly silent on the issue in Korea, and largely irrelevant to the process in Taiwan (Haggard 1990: ch. 5).

Yet business may also accept or even spearhead democratic forces where continued authoritarian rule is itself the cause of political instability and uncertainty or where democracy would improve business access to government and reduce unwanted state intervention. This was true in Brazil in the late 1970s and in the Philippines in the early 1980s, when business broke openly with authoritarian governments and helps explain the growing popularity of the Partido de Acción Nacional (PAN) in Northern Mexico, the most economically open part of the country.

A more plausible political-economic explanation of the breakdown of democratic regimes would focus on the contribution of economic crises to broader political and class conflicts (Wallerstein 1980; Cohen 1987). Military intervention is more likely to occur in response to political crisis or stalemates during which contending forces are sharply polarized, including over economic issues such as property rights, the distribution of income, or the appropriate development strategy. Recession and inflation exacerbate such conflicts by providing incentives for groups to mobilize to protect their income shares. Economic conditions, even if they are not the immediate cause of democratic breakdowns, contribute to the level of political conflict and polarization. This pattern is visible in virtually all of the cases of bureaucratic-authoritarian installations cited above: Brazil (1964), Argentina (1966 and 1976), Turkey (1971 and 1980), Chile (1973) and Uruguay (1973).

As the world turned in the 1980s, and more countries became democratic, the academic debate shifted once again to the role economic factors might play in *facilitating* democratic transitions. Ironically, the poor economic conditions of the 1980s appeared to be a powerful stimulus to democratization. Economic crisis undermined the legitimacy of authoritarian governments, which was often based on economic performance, and compounded the political problems governments had by acting as a spur to protest.

To explore the plausibility of this hypothesis, I have examined trends in per capita private consumption in a number of transitional cases for which comparable data is available. I have distinguished between two periods: a "transition" period, which includes the year of the transition itself and the two previous years, and a "pretransition" period that reflects a decade-long trend. These comparisons are vulnerable to obvious criticisms. The exercise does not prove that economic factors were dominant, or even central, to the political dynamics of the democratic transitions in question. Moreover, I have not compared the transitional countries with nontransitional ones. There are clearly a number of countries that experienced poor economic performance in the 1980s and did *not* democratize, particularly in the Middle East and Africa.

Nonetheless, it is striking that periods of democratic transition were periods of relatively poor economic performance when compared with trend. In a number of cases, private consumption declined quite sharply. This is true for five of the six Latin American cases and three of the four Asian cases. The proposition also holds for Hungary, and were data available on economic conditions in Poland in 1989, they would no doubt demonstrate the proposition to hold for that case as well. There is not comparable data for the "pretransition" period in Portugal and Spain, but the transition periods were characterized by low consumption growth in both countries when compared to the relatively prosperous period of the early 1970s.

Does the observation of a link between economic distress and democratization hold when we examine the transitions in more detail? Economic crisis played a role in undermining authoritarian rule in a number of countries, including Argentina, Bolivia, Peru, Uruguay, the Philippines, Poland, and more recently, Nicaragua. In each case there were also quite distinct political grievances, and the catalyst for change was frequently some political event, such as an election or plebiscite; this was true in the Philippines, Uruguay, Nicaragua and Poland. Nonetheless, economic grievances were clearly important in garnering support for the opposition.

There are several interesting exceptions. In Turkey, the economic reforms implemented by the military from 1981–83 were generally popular, and though the military's handpicked candidate did not win the election in 1983, Turgut Ozal ran on a platform of market-oriented policies that he had overseen for the military during 1981 and 1982. In both Korea and Chile, the transition occurred under relatively good economic performance, and the reaction against the two leaders was largely political. Nonetheless, it is also the case that both Chun and Pinochet had undertaken dramatic economic reforms in the period prior to the transition and that these were politically costly. It is also interesting, however, that there has been a fair degree of continuity in economic policy in these three cases. Incoming civilian governments by and large defended the basic economic orientation for the outgoing military governments.

Recent discussions of democratization often assume a certain inevitability to the process. Such enthusiasm needs tempering. Though economic crisis may have contributed to democratization, there is no reason to believe that the political wheel might not once again turn away from political liberalism. The fact that economic crises in the 1980s have advanced political liberalization cannot be used to dismiss the proposition linking economic difficulties with authoritarian installations. It is probably more accurate to argue that deep and sustained economic crises create problems for *whatever* sort of government is in power, authoritarian or democratic.

In the hardest-hit countries, the economic crisis of the 1980s has produced severe social strains, including rapid downward mobility for members of the middle class, political polarization, and a general erosion of faith in the capacity of government. Economic difficulties usually have differential effects across different groups, and thus exacerbate class, ethnic and regional cleavages. Data is poor, but the debt crisis has probably widened income inequalities in the heavily indebted countries, and these countries were already among the most unequal in their distribution of income (Sachs 1989).

If these cleavages are severe and polarized enough, they can easily overwhelm the consolidation of democratic values and institutions. If new governments are unable to reignite growth, or are lured toward policies that generate new economic crises, antidemocratic social forces on both the left and the right could quite easily expand their influence, and the current trend toward democratization could reverse. The clearest risk of this occurring is in Peru, but the Philippines, Romania and Nicaragua also face daunting problems of democratic consolidation.

The Middle East poses a somewhat different set of problems. The strains associated with rapid economic transformation have been one factor contributing to the emergence of fundamentalist movements. This was true in Iran, and it is now evident in Egypt and Tunisia. These groups have seized the banner of "democratization" to oppose existing authoritarian governments, but their commitment to liberal pluralism as it is understood in the West is uncertain at best. The first test case is likely to be Pakistan, where Benazir Bhutto faces challenges not only from ethnic groups, but from political forces that might be considered restorationist.

It is not my intention to argue that economic factors are the underlying determinants of social conflict or political structure. Some countries are capable of managing quite severe social conflicts while retaining a democratic structure: India, again, provides an example. My objective is simply to underscore that economic conditions can have important political repercussions. This leads quite naturally to the next set of questions this chapter seeks to address. How will the trend toward political liberalization in the developing world affect economic policy and performance?

DEMOCRACY AND DEVELOPMENT: THE LONG RUN

The debate about the relationship between democracy and economic growth is an old one, and plausible stories may be told that are diametrically opposed. On the one hand, it has been argued that democratic institutions are conducive to growth, while authoritarian rule undermines it; this is the core of classic, contractarian liberalism. Democracy is associated with the rule of law and the guarantee of individual rights, including that in property. Law reduces uncertainty and the costs of transacting, and guarantees contract. Individual rights, particularly in property, are crucial for development; without property rights, there is no incentive for risk taking and capital accumulation and innovation suffer accordingly. More indirectly, democracy is associated with the free flow of information, which also contributes to growth.

A recent AID document introducing the "Democratic Pluralism Initiative" is worth quoting as some length since it is strongly representative of this perspective:

> By and large, economic development and political freedom throughout the world have been mutually reinforcing in modern times. Open societies, through legally guaranteed freedoms of speech, press and association, as well as through free elections and a system governed by the rule of law, allow the unrestricted flow of ideas and the expansion of a private sector that is an important counterweight to state power. Open markets, in turn, promote political diversity by providing employment outside of government, allowing individuals to maintain their livelihood independent of the state (United States Agency for International Development, Asia and Near East Bureau. 1989. "Democratic Pluralism Initiative [DPI]: Open Markets—Open Schedules." [Processed.]).

Authoritarian rule, by contrast, is associated with arbitrariness, the absence of law, and uncertainty. Tyrants can use their monopoly over the use of force to skew property rights in their favor, undermining any incentive to productive activity, and are more likely to intervene in the economy in various unproductive ways. Authoritarian governments are likely to be corrupt, since they are not subject to scrutiny and criticism. By limiting the flow of information and the scope of public debate, authoritarian governments are more likely to become rigidified.

The opposite view has been summarized neatly by Huntington and Nelson, and has come to be known as the "incompatibility hypothesis" (1976: 26): "The liberal model of development avoided the problem of choice by claiming that all desirable values could be maximized. But it has turned out not to be a realistic or relevant choice for most modernizing societies." Democracies permit the flourishing of interest groups, which almost by definition are concerned not with public welfare but with seizing the largest share of the social pie for themselves (Olson 1982). Democracies generate demands on the state, and on total resources, which are likely to be met by expanding consumption at the expense of investment; democracies are myopic. Finally, democracy also generates its own uncertainties. It is true that democracy is associated with the rule of law, but laws can also be changed as governments change; indeed, uncertainty is a central feature of democratic governance.

Conversely, authoritarian rule has its advantages. Authoritarian governments place restraints on self-interested actions through rules backed by sanctions; the collective action dilemmas that are so characteristic of development can be resolved by command. Authoritarian rule gives political elites greater independence from distributionist pressures, and increases their ability to extract resources, provide public goods, and impose the short-term costs associated with efficient economic adjustment (Haggard and Moon 1990).

As might be expected where such conflicting views exist, the evidence is contradictory and inconclusive. Gerald Scully (1988) has offered one of the more comprehensive and direct statistical tests of the two competing propositions, using Gastil's Freedom House indicators and data on 115 market economies over the period from 1960 to 1980. Scully finds evidence of a large growth differential, 2.53 percent per annum vs. 1.41 percent, in favor of politically open societies. Yet there are methodological problems with Scully's analysis, including the omission of nonmarket economies, a failure to distinguish adequately between political and economic liberties, and the construction of indicators in a way that reduces the weight of the rapidly growing middle-income countries in the sample, many of which are authoritarian. Other studies support Scully's conclusions, however. Barro (1989) and Kormendi and Meguire (1985) find that a political rights variable is positively associated with growth in large cross-sectional analyses, and Dick (1974) and Kohli (1986) both raise doubts about the claim that authoritarianism promotes growth.

In another large cross-national comparison, however, Erich Weede (1983) finds no relationship between democracy and economic growth in the developing world taken as a whole. There is a relationship in those countries in which state intervention in the economy is high, though; in these economies democracy retards growth. Jackman (1976) also finds no systematic evidence that military regimes are either successful modernizers, nor that they retard economic development. Finally, a number of cross-national studies have found evidence that authoritarianism does in fact promote economic growth (Adelman and Morris 1967; Huntington and Dominguez 1975; Marsh 1979).

Methodological criticisms of these studies are numerous. Even where there are results, the associations are usually weak. The methods are generally quite crude. With a few exceptions, most of the work in this area to date has been done by political scientists, and as a result, it does not rest on plausible economic models of the growth process. The appropriate methodology is to introduce political variables into the existing economic models, thus establishing adequate controls for the other determinants of the outcome in question, whether growth, inflation or investment (Scully 1988; Barro 1989; Haggard, Sharif and Webb 1990).

Yet there is another, more compelling reason why these studies yield poor results: they are conceptually flawed. The distinction between authoritarian and democratic systems, and even more nuanced measures of democracy or pluralism, are not necessarily the political variables that are most relevant for explaining economic performance. We can therefore expect quite disparate performances among governments with similar ratings on a democratic–authoritarian scale.

It is therefore possible that the transition to democracy will improve economic performance, but this is by no means a foregone conclusion. Three examples might be cited. Haggard and Kaufman (1989a) have noted that a distinction can be drawn between "strong" and "weak" authoritarian regimes. The former have organizational characteristics that are conducive to rapid growth, such as centralized decision making and meritocratic bureaucracies. Korea, Taiwan, and Singapore are examples. While none of these governments were by any means laissez-faire, they were more oriented toward the market, and toward exports in particular, than most other developing countries. Moreover, they achieved this market orientation under authoritarian auspices (Haggard 1990). Zaire and Haiti, by contrast, are examples of "weak" authoritarian regimes that are penetrated by networks of patron-client relations and corruptions and are unable to pursue any coherent policy.

A second example might be drawn from Africa. If democratization there is accompanied by an increase in violence, perhaps associated with new ethnic tensions, it could quite easily lead to a worsening of economic performance (Wheeler 1984). On the other hand, if democracies do succeed in avoiding these pitfalls and acting as a check on arbitrary decision making and extensive state intervention, then economic performance could improve.

In Latin America, finally, a number of authors have noted that populist governments pass through a predictable policy cycle (Dornbusch and Edwards 1989; Sachs 1989). Newly elected populist governments, often responding to past periods of wage compression limitations on labor activity, seek to redistribute income to the urban popular sector through expansionist fiscal and monetary policies and generous wage contracts. These policies prove unsustainable, leading to large fiscal and balance of payments deficits, inflation, and eventually a painful stabilization. The terms of debate on economic policy have fundamentally changed in Latin America in the last ten years in the direction of greater economic liberalism, but it is premature to dismiss populism as a thing of the past; witness the popularity of Cárdenas in Mexico, Lula in Brazil, and Alan Garcia in Peru. The election of Menem in Argentina, Andres Pérez in Venezuela, and Manley in Jamaica did not result in a turn toward populism, but all three were elected in part because of their identification with policies responsive to the plight of the "little guy." Vargas Llosa's campaign in Peru, by contrast, was severely damaged by his promise to launch difficult adjustment measures if elected. If democracy means a return of populist political forces and the political polarization that frequently accompanied them, then economic performance will suffer.

The broader analytic point is that a number of political variables are important for explaining growth, and these can cut across the authoritarian-democratic distinction. Among them are the orientation of the party in power, the stability of the government, and the degree of state intervention in the economy. I now turn to an analysis of how some of these factors might affect the prospects for economic reform in new democracies.

DEMOCRACY AND ECONOMIC PERFORMANCE IN THE SHORT RUN: THE POLITICS OF ECONOMIC REFORM

In seeking to promote growth, governments face two, somewhat different, policy challenges. The first is to achieve or maintain macroeconomic stability. Where inflation is already high, this means painful stabilization measures: reducing expenditures, raising taxes, and controlling the growth of the money supply and wages. Short-term balance of payments problems also demand exchange rate adjustments. The long-term challenge is to liberalize the economy. Liberalizing measures include reducing trade barriers, reforming pricing policy, reducing intervention in financial markets and reforming or privatizing the state-owned enterprise sector.

At the broadest level, these reforms face two types of political barriers; I will call them the coalitional problem and the time-inconsistency problem. The first arises as the result of the balance between negatively and positively affected groups in the reform process. Though economic theory tells us that these reforms are superior for society as a whole, they can have substantial costs for some groups. Public attention is captured by "IMF riots" that accompany the lifting of food subsidies, but powerful groups within the private sector are likely to be equally vociferous opponents of market-oriented reform; such opposition is by no means limited to the government itself. Among those negatively affected by structural adjustment are traders and commercial interests with privileged access to foreign exchange and imports, consumers of subsidized inputs from state-owned enterprises, recipients of subsidies, and both labor and management in protected firms in the import-sub-stituting sector. In most developing countries, the nontraded goods sector benefits from an overvalued exchange rate in comparison with the traded-goods sector. Moreover, these groups are likely to be rela-tively powerful compared to the beneficiaries of reform efforts. They are, for the most part, located in the urban areas and benefit from greater opportunities for organization. Economic reform must, therefore, be treated as a problem of coalition management; successful reform means compensating or finessing losers, while building a new base of support among the gainers (Waterbury 1989; Nelson 1989, 1990). Some of the cleavages that are likely to emerge in this process are summarized in Figure 11.1.

The second difficulty arises out of the time horizon of the politician. The benefits of reforms may take some time to unfold, but the time-ho-rizon of the politician is sometimes quite short as a result of electoral or other political constraints.

These two problems suggest the following hypothesis: reform is most likely when political elites are temporarily or permanently freed from political constraints. This might happen in several ways. The first is through the exercise of dictatorial powers. The most heated and long-standing debate in the literature on the politics of stabilization and structural adjustment concerns the relative capacity of authoritarian and democratic governments for instituting reforms (Skidmore 1977; Sheahan 1980; Remmer 1986; Haggard 1986; Haggard and Kaufman 1989a). Clearly, authoritarian governments have been able to launch quite extensive adjustment initiatives in some cases; Chile, Korea, Tur-key, Ghana provide recent examples, and Mexico, with its corporatist organization of interest might also be added to the list.

Yet, as we have seen above, there does not appear to be any convinc-ing link between regime type and growth over the long run. This apparent contradiction can be reconciled by giving greater attention to the broader political setting in which conflicts over economic policy are played out. In settings where partisan alignments are severely polar-ized or fragmented, regime type *has* made a difference, and incoming military governments have "solved" economic policy problems that democratic governments could not.

A recent collective research project on the politics of adjustment finds, however, that the willingness of governments to initiate new economic policies is more closely associated with *changes* in government than it is with the type of regime (Nelson 1990). Governments facing upcoming electoral challenges, not surprisingly, have been reluctant to impose unpopular programs. Interestingly, this is found to be true of both democratic and authoritarian governments. As military governments seek to negotiate an exit from government, political constraints resurface powerfully. This was true in Argentina and Brazil during the transition period, and has proven a major constraint on economic reform in Nigeria.

Incoming governments, by contrast, can capitalize on honeymoon periods, particularly where the opposition is weak and its policies discredited. Dramatic stabilization efforts were launched by Paz Estenssoro in Bolivia, the new Solidarity government in Poland, by Collor in Brazil and by Menem in Argentina. Where economic conditions have been deteriorating and the ruling party's policies have been discredited, democracies have launched quite substantial structural reforms as well. Examples include Colombia in the late 1960s, Sri Lanka in the late 1970s, Costa Rica and Jamaica in the early 1980s, and at least in some regards, by Aquino in the Philippines, including tax reform, trade liberalization, and the reform of agricultural pricing policy.

If politicians are politically positioned to launch reform efforts, there remains the problem of their technical ability to do so. Reforms vary in their organizational intensity and the nature of the skills required to implement them. Dismantling some interventions is simply a matter of issuing cease and desist orders; of getting bureaucracies to stop doing what they have done in the past. Where bureaucracies are centered entirely around interventions in the market that are no longer deemed necessary, such as marketing boards or boards of investment that dispense licenses, the bureaucracy itself might simply be dismantled.

Yet it is frequently overlooked that many economic reforms demand administrative and technical capabilities that are in short supply in poor countries: adequate education among middle- and low-level personnel; specialized training for higher-level and technical staff; and information processing, gathering and communication capabilities. Miles Kahler (1990) has called this the "orthodox paradox": liberalization itself demands a strengthening of the state's capabilities and an ability to reconcile conflict claims within the bureaucracy itself.

Examples abound. The control of public expenditure requires the establishment of multiyear public investment programs, the capacity to monitor projects once launched, and institutional mechanisms to make

Policy	Favored Interests	Neutral or Uncertain	Threatened Interests
I. Short-Term Measures			
A. Devaluation	Traded goods sector Holders of foreign assets	Workers, peasants (depends on traded goods/ consumption)	Non-traded sector Holders of foreign assets
B. Reduced expenditures	Foreign creditors		Public sector workers Suppliers Recipients of subsidies, services and transfers
C. Increased revenues		Depends on incidence of taxes	
D. Monetary contraction	Liquid asset holders Non-indexed groups Traded goods sector (fixed exchange rate) Foreign and domestic creditors		Debtors Non-traded goods sector (fixed exchange rates)

Figure 11.1   Policy Coalitions and Cleavages

expenditures transparent and permit a smooth reconciliation of spending and revenue decisions. Trade reform is often seen simply as a process of removing restrictions, but successful export promotion involves more extensive interventions, such as drawback and exemption schemes for exporters, the provision of overseas market information, and the management of export-processing zones. Other reforms demand the establishment of modern economic institutions that are frequently underdeveloped. For example, successful privatization in Eastern Europe and elsewhere will rest on the ability to develop capital markets on which shares can easily be traded, and the regulatory apparatus to oversee them.

Policy	Favored Interests	Neutral or Uncertain	Threatened Interests
II. Structural Adjustments			
A. Trade liberal- ization	Importers Exporters Consumers Purchasers of protected capital and intermediate goods		Import substituting local and foreign labor in ISI sectors Agriculture where protected
B. Domestic price reform	Depends on whether group is net seller purchaser of liberalized good		
C. Financial market reform	Savers Borrowers w/out access to subsidized credit Foreign banks and investors	Banks (depends on portfolio structure)	Informal financial sector (curb market) borrowers Borrowers with access to subsidized credit
D. Privatization of state-owned enterprises	Large domestic and foreign investors Consumers of SOE goods where monopolized Competitive private-sector firms		Workers and management of SOEs Privileged suppliers Consumers of SOE goods where subsidized

Figure 11.1 Policy Coalitions and Cleavages (*continued*)

There is a useful policy lesson to be drawn from this discussion. Some political parameters, such as the timing of elections and the nature of the party system, are not manipulable, but knowledge of their consequences can be useful in timing assistance or the launching of initiatives. The structure of interest groups might appear to be a relatively fixed component of the political landscape, but this is not true. It might be possible for outside donors to assist in the organization of those groups who would benefit from reform. Yet it should be understood that this is a risky business. As the Peruvian election campaign shows once again, reformers can be delegitimated by their connections with outside agents. Moreover, from the perspective of economic reform, more powerful interest associations may or may not be a good thing; it all depends on the orientation and interests of the groups in question. Strengthening the institutional capabilities of governments does seem relatively risk-free, though, and, for the low-income countries, is likely to make an important contribution to economic reform.

CONCLUSION

A discussion of the full range of political factors that might impinge on economic policy once democracy is established is far beyond the scope of this chapter. Given the relatively recent arrival of democratic institutions in the developing world, there is much we do not know about how new political structures will work and what their effects on economic reform will be. For example, do parliamentary systems have certain advantages over presidential ones? How will legislative-executive relations affect economic policy-making? Just as partisan differences result in different policy outcomes in the advanced industrial states, so we can expect that different governments in the developing world will also develop different policies. How will the party structure affect the consolidation of economic reforms? Are different internal bureaucratic organizations more conducive to sound policy, for example, the combination of budgeting, finance, and planning functions?

For the purpose of assisting new democracies, these questions are the most important ones; unfortunately, we don't now have many answers to these questions.

It is clear, however, that there has been a substantial amount of painful social learning over the last decade. When the debt crisis broke in 1982, it was seen mainly as a short-term problem that could be solved through a combination of relatively quick adjustment measures, economic recovery in the advanced industrial states, and a rescheduling of external obligations. By the middle of the 1980s, the view of the crisis had changed. While the debt overhand remains a critical problem today, there is a broader recognition that many problems are the result of development models which date to the 1930s and 1940s in some Latin American countries, and to independence in Africa and South Asia. In seeking to assist the positive changes that are taking place, it is important to keep in mind that fundamental reorientations in development strategy cannot be expected to take place swiftly.

REFERENCES

Adelman, Irma, and Morris, Cynthia Taft. *Society, Politics, and Economic Development*. Baltimore: Johns Hopkins University Press, 1967.

Agency for International Development, Asia and Near East Bureau. n.d. "Democratic Pluralism Initiative (DPI): Open Markets—Open Societies." (Processed.)

Barro, Robert. "A Cross Country Study of Growth, Saving and Government." National Bureau of Economic Research Working Paper No. 2855, 1989.

Bollen, Kenneth A., and Jackman, Robert. "Economic and Non-Economic Determinants of Political Democracy in the 1960s." In *Research in Political Sociology*. Greenwich CT.: JAI Press, 1985.

Broad, Robin. *Unequal Alliance: The IMF, the World Bank, and the Philippines.* Berkeley: University of California, 1988.

Cohen, Youseff. "Democracy from Above: The Political Origins of Dictatorship in Brazil." *World Politics* 40, October, 1987: pp. 30–54.

Collier, David, ed. *The New Authoritarianism in Latin America.* Princeton: Princeton University Press, 1979.

Dick, G. W. "Authoritarian vs. Non-Authoritarian Approaches to Economic Development." *Journal of Political Economy* 82, July/August 1974: pp. 817–827.

Dornbusch, Rudiger, and Sebastian Edwards. "The Macroeconomics of Populism in Latin America." World Bank, PRE Working Paper, 1989.

Evans, Peter. *Dependent Development: The Alliance of Multinational, State, and Foreign Capital in Brazil.* Princeton: Princeton University Press, 1979.

Haggard, Stephan. "The Politics of Stabilization and Structural Adjustment." In *The Politics of International Debt.* Edited by Miles Kahler. Ithaca: Cornell University Press, 1986.

——. *Pathways from the Periphery: The Politics of Growth in the Newly Industrializing Countries.* Ithaca: Cornell University Press, 1990.

Haggard, Stephan, and Robert Kaufman. "The Politics of Stabilization and Structural Adjustment." In *Developing Country Debt and Economic Performance. Vol. 1: The International Financial System.* Edited by Jeffrey Sachs. Chicago: University of Chicago Press, 1989a.

——. "Economic Adjustment in New Democracies." In *Fragile Coalitions: The Politics of Economic Adjustment.* Edited by Joan Nelson. New Brunswick: Transaction Books, 1989b.

——. "The Political Economy of Inflation and Stabilization in Middle-Income Countries." World Bank PRE Working Paper, June.

Haggard, Stephan, and Chung-in Moon. "Institutions and Economic Growth: Theory and a Korean Case Study." *World Politics* 42, 1990: p. 2.

Haggard, Stephan, Karim Sharif and Steven Webb. "Political Determinants of Inflation." World Bank, 1990. (Processed.)

Huntington, Samuel, and Jorge Dominguez. "Political Development." In *Handbook of Political Science. Vol. 3: Macropolitical Theory.* Edited by Fred Greenstein and Nelson Polsby. Reading, Mass.: Addison Wesley, 1975.

Huntington, Samuel, and Joan Nelson. *No Easy Choice: Political Participation in Developing Countries.* Cambridge: Harvard University Press, 1976.

Jackman, Robert W. "Politicians in Uniform: Military Governments and Social Change in the Third World." *American Political Science Review* 70, December 1976.

Kahler, Miles. "Orthodoxy and its Alternatives." In *Economic Crisis and Policy Choice: The Politics of Adjustment in the Third World.* Edited by Joan Nelson. Princeton: Princeton University Press, 1990.

Kohli, Atul. "Democracy and Development." In *Development Strategies Reconsidered*. Edited by John Lewis and Valeriana Kallab. New Brunswick: Transaction Books, 1986.

Kormendi, R.C., and P.G. Meguire. "Macroeconomic Determinants of Growth." *Journal of Monetary Economics* 16, September 1985: pp. 141–63.

Lipset, Seymour Martin. "Some Social Requisites of Democracy: Economic Development and Political Legitimacy." *American Political Science Review* 53, March 1959: pp. 69–105.

Londregan, John, and Kenneth Poole. 1990.

Marsh, Robert M. "Does Democracy Hinder Economic Development in the Late-comer Developing Nations?" *Comparative Social Research* 2, 1979: pp. 215–248.

Moore, Barrington. *Social Origins of Dictatorship and Democracy*. Boston: Beacon Press, 1966.

Nelson, Joan. *Fragile Coalitions: The Politics of Economic Adjustment*. New Brunswick: Transaction Books, 1989.

———, ed. *Economic Crisis and Policy Choice: The Politics of Adjustment in the Third World*. Princeton: Princeton University Press, 1990.

O'Donnell, Guillermo. *Modernization and Bureaucratic Authoritarianism: Studies in South American Politics*. Berkeley: Institute for International Studies, University of California, 1973.

Olson, Mancur. *The Rise and Decline of Nations: Economic Growth, Stagflation, and Social Rigidities*. New Haven: Yale University Press, 1982.

Remmer, Karen. "The Politics of Economic Stabilization: IMF Standby Programs in Latin American, 1954–1984." *Comparative Politics* 19, October 1986: pp. 1–24.

Sachs, Jeffrey. "Social Conflict and Populist Policies in Latin America." NBER Working Paper No. 2897, March 1989.

Scully, Gerald W. "The Institutional Framework and Economic Development." *Journal of Political Economy* 96, June 1988: pp. 652–62.

Sheahan, John. "Market-Oriented Economic Policies and Political Repression in Latin America." *Economic Development and Cultural Change* 28, January 1980: pp. 267–91.

Skidmore, Thomas. "The Politics of Economic Stabilization in Postwar Latin America." In *Authoritarianism and Corporatism in Latin America*. Edited by James M. Malloy. Pittsburgh: Pittsburgh University Press, 1977.

Wallerstein, Michael. "The Collapse of Democracy in Brazil: Its Economic Determinants." *Latin American Research Review* 15, 1980: pp. 3–40.

Weede, Erich. "The Impact of Democracy on Economic Growth: Some Evidence from Cross-National Analysis." *Kyklos* 36, 1983: pp. 21–39.

Wheeler, David. "Sources of Stagnation in Sub-Saharan Africa." *World Development* 12, January 1984: pp. 1–23.

NOTES

1. When referring to "democracy" and "democratization," I will limit myself to the political rules governing national politics. Democratic regimes are those in which

free speech and organization are guaranteed, leaders are chosen by competitive elections, and governments are not systematically subject to the veto or control of nonelected individuals or institutions. Increasingly sophisticated scales have been devised for the measurement of political liberalization and democracy. Though these are used in the paper, I generally limit myself to the dichotomous distinction between democratic and nondemocratic governments. My emphasis is therefore subtly different from a focus on the relationship between human rights or participation and economic development, and does not examine the effects of the extension of democratic reforms and principles beyond the central government, for example to the workplace.

I also limit myself largely to a discussion of economic growth seen as expansion of national output. I do not address the important question of equity or the ability of the government to meet other economic targets, such as managing inflation, except insofar as they are seen as contributing to economic growth.

12

Structural Adjustment for the 1990s

Daniel M. Schydlowsky

STRUCTURAL ADJUSTMENT IN STYLIZED FORM: CAUSES AND CURE

A country needing structural adjustment is, at bottom, a country that has a structural maldistribution of its productive resources. Its capital was put in the wrong place and, in consequence, its labor force is also deployed in the wrong activities.

Capital was put in what now appears as the wrong place for one or both of two main reasons. One reason would be that the capital simply was put in place in a different time, under different circumstances. Times have changed and the external conditions facing the economy have changed. Thus, while good decisions were made in the past, these now look wrong because conditions have changed. This is a cause of structural maladjustment external observers don't normally focus on, while countries' domestic decision makers do. In any case, the maladjustment resulting from changes in external conditions facing an economy may require as much change and be just as painful as maladjustment due to other causes.

The second main reason for maladjustment is wrong decisions made in the past. Erroneous policies were adopted in the past and now the consequences are coming home to roost. This is the cause of structural maladjustment that external observers mostly focus on and that domestic decision makers like to ignore. What is more, the particular kind of policy that is chiefly blamed for structural adjustment problems is import substituting industrialization. ISI was THE big mistake. Now countries have to pay for it. This is the main conventional diagnosis of the causality of structural maladjustment.

It naturally follows that if resources are in the wrong place, they should be reallocated to the right place. They need to be moved from where they are to where they should be. That involves reallocating labor to new tasks, reassigning land to different uses, and reallocating capital to different productive activities. The means to that end is the economic policy of Structural Adjustment.

Structural Adjustment Policy consists of some very powerful economic policy tools. The most powerful one consists of opening the domestic market to the competition of foreign trade. Trade liberalization will get rid of the tariffs that begot the undesirable ISI. Letting the exchange find its own level removes the traditional overvaluation. The core element is thus almost-free trade with a cleanly floating exchange rate.

The second policy tool that backs up the core element is financial liberalization. Interest rates that have been negative in real terms have compounded the ISI problems. It is imperative to remove interest rate ceilings and other regulations and move to positive real interest rates, preferably market-determined ones. Furthermore, these two policy planks should be backed up by a third policy element consisting of the privatization of public enterprises. Public enterprise managers do not respond well to price signals; converting them to private enterprise will ensure that market prices will be able to do their job.

These policies should all be put in place as quickly as possible because rent seeking is ubiquitous and if the reforms proceed too slowly then the rent seekers will be able to subvert and stop the process. So structural adjustment should be undertaken quickly, cold turkey if possible, and be completed as soon as possible. This way it will be painful but short; afterward everything will be fine.

The purpose of the structural adjustment policy is to reallocate resources. However, on examination it becomes apparent that this purpose hides an asymmetry. Consider first the reallocation of labor and what this involves in physical terms. There are workers who, let us say, are producing airplanes and they will now stop producing airplanes and instead will produce shoes. This requires moving them from an airplane factory to a shoe factory. This move involves some human capital loss as well as some personal discomfort or even pain. However, given a reasonable period of time, both can be overcome and the reallocation can be accomplished.

Consider now the reallocation of land. Let us assume we are currently planting sugar. We now no longer want to do that, we wish to plant asparagus instead. We cut down the sugarcane and plant asparagus hills instead. There may be some loss of capital involved in cutting down the cane but we can clearly visualize how to accomplish the reassignment in the use of land.

Consider now the reallocation of capital. We wish to take those machines that were used to assemble airplanes and to machine airplane parts and use them to produce shoes. That is hard to visualize in quite the same way we can visualize moving workers from the airplane plant to the shoe factory. In fact, we are unable to accomplish the required feat. The capital stock is "clay," it is not "putty." And it refuses to become putty; once it congeals into clay, it can no longer be made pliable. And so what happens is that we do not really reallocate capital, we lost it—we write it off! That is the nub of the problem: structural adjustment involves the reallocation of labor and land, but requires new capital for the new activity. While that new requirement is becoming manifest, we junk capital in the old activities and thus make ourselves poorer; along the way we inevitably reduce the level of income and output.

So: our capacity to save falls, as a consequence of reducing current output and wealth as a result of junking "old" capital—even as requirements for new capital have increased. Structural Adjustment thus creates an imbalance between the supply and demand for savings.

Of course the place to turn to for a solution of this shortage of capital is the World Bank! It needs to come to the rescue and give or lend what is needed to bridge the gap. Unfortunately, the World Bank has limited resources and also faces other demands for funds. Thus it is unable to provide automatic cover for the increased capital requirement arising from structural adjustment. There just aren't enough free savings available through the World Bank or the other international financial institutions.

A nonpublic source for covering the capital requirement is the repatriation of each country's national capital from abroad. The Mexicans, for instance, are reputed to have more capital abroad than shows up on the official statistics. If some of this can be made available for use inside Mexico, that may not be additional wealth, but it is certainly relocating existing wealth to where it can help Mexico's structural adjustment. A similar effect can be obtained if capital outflow can be slowed down or stopped. That would also keep capital available inside the country, where it is needed to make the structural adjustment feasible. Thus there may be some options that will work for some countries. But one can hardly be optimistic about the supply of capital for all structural adjusters taken together. Lance Taylor has informed us that by his estimation we need to have a net swing of 80 billion dollars per year to achieve this objective.[1] The numbers are too big. It cannot be done.

AN ALTERNATIVE SCENARIO

A very different scenario would emerge if we were to change our tactic regarding the capital that we are writing off. If instead of junking the inappropriately placed capital in one fell swoop, i.e., shutting down the factories, we tried to extract from them whatever value we could, the future would look quite different. In that kind of scenario we would say: "We have these machines here that are the wrong machines, we should not have bought them to begin with but now they are paid for, let us get as much out of them as we can. Let us run them at full blast and run them into the ground." Now this capital stock would go into a period of high output and there would be a higher income base from which to save. A lot of employment would be generated. The whole economic environment would become one in which change could take place more easily because there would be an enormous economic expansion. In fact, it would be necessary to sell some of the new output abroad so vigorous export promotion would be a natural development. Foreign exchange receipts would increase substantially, based on the sale abroad of the new output from the factories being run into the ground.

The tax base would be broader and therefore the government would have substantially more revenue, which it could use to help the adjustment process along. The government could even use some of its revenue increase to hire better people and pay better salaries; the whole administrative system would become better. Government policies could be better designed and better run, there could even be better people to negotiate with the World Bank so they would be happier to give the country more money!

The whole nature of the policy environment would change: rather than a sudden shortage of capital and with a major recession under way, there would be an expansion designed to make liquid past investment in order to finance economic reconversion. Certainly a very different picture.

But doubt is bound to assail such a rosy view. If this were so easy it would have been done a long time ago! Besides, this scenario collides with some basic economic logic. The capital involved should not have been bought in the first place, its output is not competitive, and therefore these machines are not worth anything! Discarding this capital stock would result from a policy of almost-free trade, financial liberalization and so forth, precisely because its output is not competitive. This capital is inefficient in its productive processes, its social marginal product is zero. Therefore, operating that capital is wrong. It detracts from economic welfare rather than increasing it. So this beautiful scenario is not real. There is no alternative. The cost of having made mistakes in the past has to be paid.

MARKET PRICES AND TRUE SCARCITIES

The core argument in the rebuttal to the "embodied savings rescue" scenario is that there is nothing worth rescuing because the output at issue is not competitive at market prices, it has zero marginal social value. This is a very strong assertion indeed. It implies that market prices, especially those liberalized market prices that obtain just after the conventional structural adjustment policy has been put in place, in fact correctly reflect shadow prices, i.e., the real scarcities in the economy.

On this view, market prices have to reflect real scarcity not only after some time, but very quickly. Thus, for instance, if we put in the structural adjustment policy on January 1st and give it a month or two to settle in, by February 1 or at most by March 1st, we expect prices to be "right." In other words, one to two months into the new policy, market prices will be accurate indicators of social marginal cost and social marginal benefits, or at least they will be close enough so that it is not worth bothering with the difference. Consequently, after a few months, it is appropriate to take these new market prices, and competitiveness at these new market prices, as correctly measuring *social* marginal profit; and therefore it is also appropriate to accept the market's verdict on whether existing capital should be preserved or discarded.

One might be pardoned for being skeptical of the likelihood of things going that right that quickly. A number of reasons come to mind why market and shadow prices might not converge for quite a while.

First, in the long term even a good price system in a less developed country (LDC) would have some deficiencies. There is the well-established argument about externalities and market failure. As long as the externalities concerned are not more than the literature's bees and the honey and the pollination of trees and flowers, we have here a valid theoretical point but one that does not have much empirical importance. However, when it is recognized that reputation is important in export sales, an enormously important externality is at stake. Peruvian exports of shoes may be hampered because buyers have heard that there has been bad experience with Peruvian canned fish. U.S. manufacturers are worried about competition from Japanese goods because "all Japanese goods are good." Korean cars now sell well because Korean television sets are good. Reputation is central to exporting and each producer's reputation reflects on others from the same country. Reputation generates capacity to penetrate markets; it is an externality with major quantitative implications. Thus a classic and well-accepted reason for failure of the price system is of the first order of quantitative importance in less developed countries.

In addition to reputation effects, there are learning effects. More is continuously coming to light about how learning takes place at different speeds in different sectors and how synergy across the industrial sectors affects productivity and is much more pervasive and complicated than was previously thought. It is certainly much more complicated and diverse than described in the early articles about backward and forward linkages.

Furthermore, it is not uncommon to find coordination problems between firms in LDCs' typically oligopolistic markets, and firms in different markets or straddling markets—a market failure even in the long run.

All told, this means that one must envisage the occurrence of a long evolutionary process until markets in LDCs function as well as the markets in the United States do today. But if convergence of market to shadow prices is such a long-term process, one certainly has reason for pause when a policy requires market prices to reflect social marginal costs and shadow prices in the short run. Such is the long-run argument.

There is also a medium-run argument. This is based on markets in LDCs behaving in a noncompetitive fashion. A major part of LDC good markets are in the so-called "informal" sector. It is worth considering the process by which this informal sector grows.

A typical entrant into the informal sector is a person who has been looking for wage employment and did not get hired. After a search of varying length, he decides to leave the labor market and enter the goods market instead. To do so he buys a push cart and then some vegetables and goes from door to door ringing doorbells and peddling the vegetables. In the process the new vegetable vendor has increased the segmentation of the vegetable markets. An innovation has occurred generating product differentiation. The vegetable vendor is competing with the supermarket and the corner grocery store but the vegetables—the carrots and potatoes and the tomatoes he sells—are not the same items as those in the stores. First, they are very obviously differentiated by location. Second, as distinct from the supermarket where the vegetables come carefully packaged, the buying housewives may handle the merchandise. This allows testing for quality, ripeness, and so forth. A product you can touch is a different product from the one you may not touch. Third, pricing in the informal market is different. Within a range you have a bilateral monopoly between the vendor and the housewife. They know there is a top and a bottom and they bargain within that range. Finally, the service provided is quite different, for the buyer can tell the seller when to come back and with what kind of merchandise. No such instructions can be given to the store.

Any particular vendor will generate his own competition, as word spreads of his success at selling. Entry into vending is free in principle, even if at times established vendors forcibly protect their territory. Moreover, as profits drop in one line of sales, other products become informalized. It may start in vegetables, but quickly moves to clothes and shirts, tire repair and even to the fixing of automobile mufflers. Similarly, as one geographical territory loses profitability, others are invaded. It will typically begin in the wealthy districts of the capital, but will spread to the poorer districts and also the secondary cities.

The informal market has all the hallmarks of monopolistic competition. The similarity with the description of this market form provided by Edward H. Chamberlin in his classic work, *The Theory of Monopolistic Competition* (1934) is startling. Chamberlin showed that under monopolistic competition price will equal average cost, and that there will be excess capacity. In the informal markets of less developed countries, people are earning about enough to pay for the goods they sell plus a minimum of food per day. That is as close to average cost as you can come. There is also substantial excess capacity in the informal sector: underemployment is rampant, and informal sector vendors would be delighted to sell more at the going price.

It seems clear that monopolistic competition is the form of market organization in the informal market. However, this market is a very important part of the economy. It constitutes an important part of the goods market, but it is even more important for its interactions with the labor market, for individuals move between selling their labor for wages and "packaging" it with intermediate inputs in the informal goods market. This means that monopolistic competition operates in a major segment of the LDC economy, and, consequently, the Pareto conditions do not hold: marginal product in the wage labor market will be equated to average product in the informal sector. As a result, market wages even in the informal labor market will be greater than the marginal social cost of labor.[2]

Now, if one market in the economy does not operate competitively, that is enough to give you a general lack of equality between marginal and social cost and market prices. If this is an important market, then it will have a quantitatively important effect on all the other prices of the economy through the general equilibrium interactions. It follows that all the investment decisions taken on the basis of market prices turn out to be misallocating resources! This will be the result of the wedge in the labor market resulting from monopolistic competition in the informal sector. Moreover, that misallocation will continue as long as that wedge is there, and that wedge will be there as long as there is an informal sector . . . and, certainly, there is general agreement that the informal sector will take a long time to go away.

The short to medium run also contributes elements to market failure. One of the empirical regularities about the structural adjustment policies and external shocks is that they almost always induce recessions. This seems to be particularly so when the policy is fully conventional in putting together devaluation, liberalization and getting the interest rate "right." In these cases, a major fall of output is induced which, together with capital inflow, causes the free exchange rate to become overvalued. This undershooting in real devaluation causes even more loss of competitiveness and bankruptcy than would occur at the long-term equilibrium real exchange rate. Output thus falls well below its potential as a consequence of the contractionary impact of the structural adjustment policies and in addition because of the pressure from the overvalued exchange rate. The economy therefore operates in the short run inside its transformation curve. Consequently, the price system cannot correctly fulfill its function. Now, it should be noted that nobody ever claimed that when a country is off its transformation curve the price system works correctly. However, policy design typically proceeds as though it did.

In summary, then, we would expect that at the beginning of the structural adjustment program, prices would differ substantially from the corresponding shadow prices, perhaps more so than they would later on. In addition, we can see various reasons in the medium and long term which would cause us to expect the divergence between shadow prices and market prices to last. It follows therefrom that we are in grave error when we evaluate what ought to be operated and what ought to be shut down just on the basis of market prices, particularly on the market prices that rule immediately after the beginning of a structural adjustment policy.

But, unfortunately, matters are worse than that because as capital is junked, the divergences become greater. First, structural adjustment junks not only physical capital but also human capital. However, without the knowledge and expertise we call human capital no market can function well, and so, as our stock of knowledge decreases or becomes worthless, markets function on the basis of a greater proportion of ignorance, and hence, more poorly and imperfectly, particularly where intertemporal decisions such as investment are concerned.

Second, most of the physical capital which is junked comes from the modern sector. As a consequence, employment in the formal sector declines and more people are pushed into the informal sector. Adjustment in this sector takes the form of a reduction of average income and of innovations to informalize additional market segments in order to sustain income levels. As the informal sector spreads throughout the economy like an ink blot, an increasingly large part of the economy's markets function on the basis of monopolistic competition. Therefore there is less equality at the margin between market and shadow prices. Finally, the junking of capital is concentrated in the sectors producing traded goods, thus specifically increasing the true scarcity of foreign exchange, just as capital inflow makes it transitorily plentiful in the market.

The sum total is rather disconcerting. Structural adjustment policy is supposed to make things better. In fact it makes things worse, at least for a while. And rather than making allocation according to market prices more desirable, it makes it less desirable, as prices become even less correct indicators of where the economy ought to go.

Yet market prices can converge to shadow prices and it is useful to review what needs to happen for that to occur. First, exports have to rise so that there is no longer a foreign exchange constraint, and recessions no longer need to be induced to accommodate that lack of foreign exchange. Second, an increase in the capital stock is needed so that workers need not migrate to the informal sector to eke out income equal to average product at close to survival levels, and instead can become wage laborers in the modern sector, where wages equal marginal product. Third, an increase in productivity is needed so that the differences in response elasticities and costs between sectors get smaller and there is less segmentation. Fourth, there needs to be institutional development so that existing markets respond better, new markets appear where they are needed and market failures disappear as institutions work better.

All this amounts to saying that market prices will converge to shadow prices when countries become developed. So the development process by itself will get us to our goal. That is a gratifying conclusion but also a very frustrating one, because structural adjustment policy was devised in response to the conviction that development was not proceeding fast enough or smoothly enough and therefore policy to accelerate development was needed. Yet the policy devised involved discarding a portion of the economy's capital stock, ensuring further divergence between market and shadow prices and therefore misallocation of resources in response to wrong market prices, even poorer development, and a lengthening of the period it takes for market and shadow prices to converge. A veritable vicious circle seems indeed to be at work.

COMPETITIVENESS AND EFFICIENCY

Let us now formalize the distinction between competitiveness and efficiency in order to identify more precisely what causes the difference and also in order to be able to quantify it to see whether it is empirically important.

Competitiveness means the ability to compete in the world market; i.e., the domestic supply price is less than or equal to the world price. Naturally, we need to refer to individual processing activities and so competitiveness must be taken in relation to the value added in an activity rather than to the gross value of production. So, in order to find out if a particular activity is competitive, we take its value added in terms of domestic prices (VADP in Figure 12.1) and divide it by the market exchange rate (R) and then compare the result to that same value added, but valued at world prices. If the resulting ratio is less than one, it means that we can compete. If the cost of domestic value added, converted to foreign exchange at the market exchange rate, is above the world price of that value added, then we will not be able to compete.

To assess efficiency or, what is the same, national economic profitability, the same calculation is undertaken, but at shadow prices. Thus we take the domestic value added at shadow prices (VASP in Figure 12.1),

Competitiveness

$$C = \frac{VADP}{R} = \frac{L \cdot W + K \cdot \pi}{R} < VAWP$$

$$OR, \frac{L \cdot W + K \cdot \pi}{VAWP \cdot R} < 1$$

Efficiency

$$E = \frac{VASP}{P\$} = \frac{L \cdot P_L + K \cdot P_K}{P\$} < VAWP$$

$$OR, \frac{L \cdot P_L + K \cdot P_K}{VAWP \cdot P\$} < 1$$

Efficiency > Competitiveness

$$\frac{\dfrac{L \cdot P_L + K \cdot P_K}{VAWP \cdot P\$}}{\dfrac{L \cdot W + K \cdot \pi}{VAWP \cdot R}} < 1 \rightarrow \frac{L \cdot P_L + K \cdot P_K}{L \cdot W + K \cdot \pi} \cdot \frac{R}{P\$} < 1$$

Figure 12.1 Competitiveness and Efficiency

we divide it by the shadow price of foreign exchange (P$) and then we can compare the result to value added at world prices. If that ratio is less than one, we have efficient production, the sector has comparative advantage and national economic profitability. If the ratio is greater than one, the production is inefficient, the sector has comparative disadvantage and there is a national economic loss.

We can now compare the two indicators and ascertain the sources of any difference. In other words, we can compare efficiency to competitiveness. The resulting expression can be seen in Figure 12.1. The ratio of efficiency to competitiveness will be equal to the ratio of value added at shadow prices to the value added domestic market prices, multiplied by the ratio of the market exchange rate to the shadow price of foreign exchange.

Now if you have a situation where the shadow price of labor is far below the market price, the first one of those expressions is likely to be less than one. The second one is certainly going to be less than one, because in situations requiring structural adjustment, there is typically great scarcity of foreign exchange, hence its shadow price is above the market price. So the product of these two ratios typically results in a situation where efficiency is greater than competitiveness. This has a very important meaning and a very important policy implication. It means that if we open up the economy, if we adopt the structural adjustment policy as described in my introductory summary, we are going to wind up shutting down a number of activities that are in fact desirable. This will occur because the price system exhibits divergences between market and shadow prices that are substantial at the outset, actually become magnified at the beginning of the structural adjustment process, and take a long time to disappear.

A number of studies for Latin American countries have attempted to quantify what part of industrial production occurring behind import restrictions is efficient according to the definition discussed above. The results are presented in Table 12.1.

The first set of numbers refers to the short run, defined as the time frame for which it is not necessary to purchase additional fixed assets. In this time frame, fixed assets are a sunk cost and the calculations reflect marginal cost of raw materials, labor and working capital.

In the short run, about 80 percent of industrial production in the countries studied is efficient. A much smaller amount, 10–12 percent, is inefficient, and for some output there is doubt having to do with classification and aggregation issues.[3]

When the cost of fixed capital is added and the time frame is the medium run, the numbers in the "efficient" column go down. When the replacement cost of capital goods is taken into account, of course cost will be higher, and a smaller fraction of output will be efficient. This

Table 12.1 Industrial Efficiency in Latin America
(In percent)

Country	Year	Short Term			Medium Term			
		Efficient	In Doubt	Inefficient	Efficient	In Doubt	Inefficient	Excluded
Bolivia	1981	80.0	19.7	1.3	76.2	17.6	6.2	-
Ecuador	1983	85.4	3.7	0.4	47.4	22.4	19.7	10.5
Ecuador	1984	54.7	20.1	10.8	39.1	29.4	17.1	-
Honduras	1983	88.0	8.6	2.9	56.1	27.2	12.6	4.1
Guatemala	1983	88.7	4.8	1.0	82.5	10.8	1.1	5.6
Jamaica	1983	68.5	1.9	1.4	68.5	1.9	1.4	28.2
Peru	1986	76.6	23.4	-	53.3	33.6	13.1	-
Dominican Republic	1983	94.9	5.1	-	61.4	38.6	-	-
Venezuela	1985	74.1	12.7	11.2	69.9	17.1	11.2	2.0

Source: Schydlowsky (1989), p. 133.

fraction is still not very small because the divergences between market and shadow prices are still substantial.

The further you stretch the time frame, the more you are forced to take into account technological change, learning by doing, and so forth, and the harder it is to make these kinds of calculations. Therefore, the numbers that are available are all based on input coefficients and cost profiles actually in use in Latin American industrial establishments.

The figures shown in Table 12.1 are certainly at variance with "conventional wisdom." It is remarkable to find that in Latin America, where industry's high cost and inefficiency seem to be a well-established fact, 80 percent of the output is efficient. Indeed, one is tempted to suspect that the numbers must incorporate an overestimate of efficiency. Yet they come from very carefully done studies that incorporate the best microdata available. Hence, there is unlikely to be major error in them. But even if there were an overestimate of efficiency by, say, 20 percent, these numbers would still show that a very large fraction of output, while not competitive in market terms, is nonetheless efficient. The results are so robust that they resist almost any sensitivity analysis one may chose to subject them to.

Evidently one of the most important inputs into the efficiency calculation is the set of shadow prices underlying these calculations. These are shown in Table 12.2. P$/R is the ratio of the shadow price of foreign exchange to the market price and it can be seen that in the short run those numbers are quite large. In the medium term, they are somewhat smaller. One of the features of these shadow prices of foreign exchange is that they include and allow for the recession or depression that has been caused in the respective countries by the lack of foreign exchange. In Latin America, it is typical for countries to deflate in order to balance their external accounts; therefore, it is necessary to take into account the value of the final output realized through activation, when computing how much an additional dollar is worth.

In countries where the level of activity does not fluctuate directly with the availability of foreign exchange, where the balance of payments is adjusted by changes in relative prices with no contraction or expansion in output, smaller numbers for the ratio of the shadow to the market price of foreign exchange will be obtained. Such a calculation would result in numbers similar to those shown in Table 12.2 for the medium term, in which the macro effect in most cases is practically gone. It can be seen that the numbers are smaller but they are nowhere near one—they are still 1.45 or so. Thus there is a large and lasting differential between the shadow and the market prices of foreign exchange.

In the case of wages, which is the column PL/W, the calculations for Peru and Venezuela are particularly thorough. These calculations take

Table 12.2 Shadow Prices in Latin America

Country	Year	Short Term				Medium Term			
		P$/R	PL/W	Social Marginal Product of Capital	Private Profitability	P$/R	PL/W	Social Marginal Product of Capital	Private Profitability
Bolivia	1980	2.280	-	18.0%	-	1.600	-	12.0%	-
Ecuador	1983	2.153	0.500	6.0%	-	1.590	0.500	12.0%	-
Ecuador	1984	2.590	0.500	18.9%	12.0%	2.320	0.600	18.9%	-
Honduras	1983	1.485	0.566	6.0%	-	1.220	0.566	12.0%	-
Guatemala	1983	2.103	0.500	6.0%	-	1.424	0.500	12.0%	-
Jamaica	1983	2.026	0.500	6.0%	-	1.528	0.500	12.0%	-
Peru	1986	2.848	0.376 (1) 0.078 (2)	23.2%	17.1%	2.100	0.752 (1) 0.156 (2)	20.0%	14.7%
Dominican Republic	1983	1.805	0.440	6.0%	-	1.315	0.440	12.0%	-
Venezuela	1985	2.340	0.525 (3) 0.110 (4)	10.0%	12.0%	2.290	0.178 (3) 0.110 (4)	16.8%	14.0%

(1) White collar workers.
(2) Blue collar workers.
(3) Semi-skilled workers.
(4) Unskilled workers.

Source: Schydlowsky (1989), p. 135.

into account the extent of underemployment, the kind and extent of unemployment, and the order in which people get hired back into the modern sector as it expands. When these features of those economies are taken into account one obtains an enormous difference between the shadow and the market prices for labor. For unskilled workers the shadow wage is estimated to run between 8 percent and 15 percent of the market wage in these cases. Surely, there is a degree of error in these numbers, but even if, rather than 11 percent the correct number is 20 percent or 30 percent, the efficiency estimates will not show much qualitative change; i.e. efficiency will still be greater than competitiveness, although the gap between them might be smaller.

We thus confront a situation where if we simply apply a conventional structural adjustment policy, force the reallocation of resources by liberalizing trade, liberalizing the financial system and privatizing, and then sit back and let everybody go broke who cannot compete at market prices everything will be far from fine. We now have a presumption that we will incur a large amount of inappropriate discontinuation of production. If that is the best we can do, then that is surely most unfortunate. Economics and economic policy would be shown to have too limited a tool kit to deal with the policy problem it is faced with. But it is really not necessary to accept such an unsatisfactory outcome.

STRUCTURAL ADJUSTMENT POLICY IN THE NINETIES

In the nineties we should be able to do better. We should be able to assimilate the experiences of the eighties and go beyond them. At a minimum, this should mean that for the nineties we set ourselves the goal of extracting the socially valuable product from existing capital. As Milton Friedman would say, we should eat the lunch that we have already paid for. And having eaten that lunch, and being suitably strengthened by it, we must go on and learn to cook new meals, i.e. produce goods more suited to our long term comparative advantage. Structural Adjustment Policy in the nineties should not only draw lessons from the mistakes of the past, it should also draw resources out of the investment of the past, to build a better future.

A number of elements are required to achieve this end.

First, an active government is needed. Government should have a strategy for development and a strategy for allocation of resources. Its policy has to be purposive. Moreover, it must start from the assumption that we know quite a bit about the process of development and about what kind of policy intervention is helpful. Starting from the notion that we know nothing only leads to policy paralysis. So we must start from the notion that we have a substantial stock of useful policy knowledge, and that data are at hand to find out more. In addition, a mindset is required that admits that we are capable of compensating for some of the major distortions that we have inherited from the past. An attitude of prudence is needed, of careful balance, of cautious common sense and of firm determination to improve our policy management.

Such an activist policy does not mean that we start from the assumption that all capital was put in the right place. There should be no denial of past errors. These must be recognized and become the starting conditions for progress beyond them. Hence it becomes necessary to differentiate between activating existing capital in order to extract as much benefit from it as possible, and investing in new capital. Those two activities have to be clearly distinguished. It is only if we thought that we had made no mistakes in the past that we would want to simply replicate the existing deployment of capital. It is abundantly clear that this should not be the objective. But it is equally clear that simply junking the old capital should not be the objective either. Hence, differentiation in treatment between existing and new capital is essential.

Two distinct policies are thus needed: an activation policy for the existing capital stock and an investment policy for new acquisitions of capital stock. They will differ in their use of price policy and may also incorporate the use of some nonprice instruments. Such a combination of price and nonprice instruments can achieve a much higher response elasticity than price measures alone.

Second, a new policy for the nineties means that the lessons from ISI need to be learned and incorporated, in particular as regards the development of exports. The activation of the existing capital stock will produce output that has to be sold somewhere. Yet the sectoral distribution of that capital stock makes it impossible to sell its output only on the domestic market. A very important part of that output will have to be exported. On the other hand, activating that capital stock will require the availability of imported inputs. However, these can only be paid for if additional foreign exchange is available. Hence, from this vantage point also, additional exports are desirable. Therefore, activating the existing capital stock has to involve a proactive export policy. However, a policy based only on devaluation will not do: it will not accommodate the required differentiation.

Because the capital stock is not evenly distributed across the economy, there are some sectors that have substantial excess capacity and others that do not. This provides a first dimension of required differentiation. In addition, sectors differ in the extent to which they lack competitiveness. Unless we are prepared to provide significant windfall profits, this provides a second dimension of required differentiation. And, third, the export policy needs to confront the consequences of a production structure inherited from the ISI period, in which the bulk of exports are produced in primary sectors generating substantial amounts of Ricardian rents on land and mineral resources.

The importance of this dual production structure, and the generation of the consequent Ricardian rents, cannot be overemphasized. Such a production structure signifies that a country is endowed with very strong comparative advantage in certain kinds of natural resource-intensive production and that there is a gap in productivity between such "strong comparative advantage" production and the next "medium comparative advantage" sectors. It follows that the social supply curve of foreign exchange will not be smooth, but will have steps in it. On the other hand, such a structure of production means that the exchange rate will be a price with especially large income distribution consequences. A devaluation will raise the rents accruing to owners of land and mines at the expense of consumers and perhaps others in the economy; a revaluation would go the other way. An export policy that causes a deterioration in the income distribution may not be desirable on its own terms, but if it causes massive income redistribution, it may simply not be sustainable in economic or political terms. Therefore, devaluation is a very blunt tool for export promotion, particularly if the purpose is to promote exports from particular sectors. Rather than making export production more profitable and setting the country on an export-led growth path, a devaluation may trigger income distribution effects that overwhelm its allocation effects, leading to a stagflationary spiral.

Third, the new policy should be very conscious of the factor price distortions existing in the economy. Typically, capital will be underpriced compared to its shadow cost and labor will be overpriced compared to its shadow wage. This is precisely one of the reasons that drives recommendations for higher interest rates. However, the economic reasoning underlying such a policy recommendation disregards the different roles played by fixed assets and working capital. That is partly because economic theory generally tends to neglect treating working capital.[4] By contrast, businessmen are very conscious of the importance of working capital as an essential element in the process of production. Now, in a context in which we wish to activate existing capital stock, but not necessarily to expand capital stock in those same sectors, the distinction between working capital, which is a complement to existing capacity, and new fixed assets, which are a substitute to existing capacity, is of crucial importance. It follows that making working capital cheap will be an incentive to capacity utilization, while making new fixed assets expensive will be a disincentive to capacity expansion.

Working capital consists essentially of two elements: embodied raw materials in goods in process, and embodied labor in goods in process. Making working capital cheap is one way of making it cheaper to hire labor, hence compensating for a market wage above the shadow price of labor. On the other hand, making it expensive to buy new machines makes it relatively more attractive to use the machines that are already installed. The interest rate is not capable of easily producing a simultaneous reduction in the cost of working capital and increase in the cost of fixed capital. It is possible to produce twists between long-term rates and short-term rates and there is some room for administrative differentiation between lending for the purchase of new machines and lending for the accumulation of inventory; but the limitations on such differentiation are very tight: money is just too fungible! It is necessary to look to instruments other than the interest rate to accomplish this objective.

For instance, a tariff or tax on machines will affect purchases of new capital goods while it will not affect the cost of working capital. A decrease in payroll taxes will lower the cost of labor to the firm, hence lower the cost of goods in process and therefore reduce the amount of working capital required. The same will happen if the supply price of labor falls. Hence, a greater supply of social services which result in a reduction in the supply price of labor will also contribute to an increase in capacity utilization. It follows that an appropriate policy to deal with factor market distortions requires the careful combination of several policy instruments.

Finally, a policy element that has to be part of this package is adequate monitoring of coordination failures. A situation where everybody is waiting for someone else to do something and therefore nobody does anything is not a prescription for economic success. One difficulty about relying entirely on the invisible hand is that sometimes that hand is neither visible nor active. Because everyone is waiting for someone else to take the first step nothing at all happens. Unfortunately, there seem to be quite a few cases in which everybody is waiting for somebody else to invest first and therefore nobody invests.

Activist policy has its limits, and a cautionary note needs to be introduced. What has been said so far does imply a substantial amount of government intervention and therefore it is necessary to be fully cognizant of the lessons of experience regarding the capability of government. There are severe limitations on the effectiveness of government. Hence, it is necessary to target intervention efforts very carefully. One cannot pretend to do everything; one cannot attempt to do everything; selectivity has to be the rule.

There is a lot of experience now about the failure of government intervention. A lot has also been learned about market failures and how they are persistent. We have learned something, although not very much, about the dynamic stagnation trap which occurs when we rely entirely on the invisible hand. And we have not yet learned enough about successful government intervention.

There is little doubt that there are major administrative constraints on government intervention in the economy and that these constraints vary by country. In some countries it is plausible to despair of anything working other than the unfettered market. In other countries the civil service is remarkably capable. Whatever the situation, it has to be factored in. As a result, there seems to be no choice but to make structural adjustment policies in the nineties fully country-specific.

Thus, moving forward in the nineties appears to have two facets. One facet involves expanding the tool kit. Moving to greater reliance on the market is surely desirable, but getting the prices really right involves bringing in much more centrally the causes of market as well as government failure and the time profile on which both can be overcome. The second facet involves making use of the heritage of the past, particularly a large capital stock that should have been of a different shape but from which it behooves us to rescue as much as we can. In the nineties it is important to be careful and cautious but nonetheless quite inventive and determined about the kind of government intervention that we want.

I am convinced that if we move ahead in this direction, we can only do better. The notion that we should just stand back and resign ourselves to watching the market either work or fail, with the full conviction that this is the best we can do, seems to me to be throwing in the towel. We still need a sensible, cautious and well-designed mix of market function and public policy. Human beings and institutions are never perfect and certainly at the beginning of the nineties our economies are working far from perfectly. We should be able to make them better. And it seems to me that we have some experience and some knowledge about how to make them better, certainly more than we had ten years ago. It is worth putting that experience and knowledge to work.

I conclude with the conviction that capacity utilizing structural adjustment policy for the nineties is something worth taking a hard look at. Countries should eat the lunch that has been paid for, feel strengthened by it and go on to build a better future!

REFERENCES

Betancourt, Roger R. and Christopher K. Clague. *Capital Utilization* (New York: Cambridge University Press, 1981).

Schydlowsky, Daniel. "La Eficiencia Industrial en América Latina: Mito y Realidad," *Pensamiento Iberoamericano* 16: 131-166, p. 1989.

NOTES

1. See chapter 3 in this book.

2. Market wages in the formal sector may be higher still as a result of labor legislation establishing minimum wages and other labor standards. In turn, the cost of labor to employers may exceed market wages by legislated fringe benefits.

3. For detailed description see Schydlowsky, "La eficiencia industrial en América Latina: Mito y realidad," in *Pensamiento Iberoamericano* 16: 131-66, 1989, or any one of the original studies given in the bibliography cited therein.

4. An exception is the economic theory of capacity utilization. Cf. Betancourt, Roger R. *Working Capital and Shift-Work in Imperfect Capital Markets.* Unpublished mimeograph, University of Maryland, 1976. See also Schydlowsky, "Influencia del mercado financiero sobre la utilización de capacidad instalada," in *Desarrollo Economico* 14: 269–88, 1974.

Name Index

Subject Index

About the Contributors

GEORGE B. N. AYITTEY contributed to this conference as Visiting Associate Professor of Economics at The American University in Washington, DC, a position he continues to hold at present.

ELLIOT BERG contributed as Vice-President for Research of Development Alternatives, Inc., a position he continues to hold at present.

FERNANDO FAJNZYLBER contributed as Director of the Joint Program on Industrialization, United Nations Industrial Development Organization/United Nations Economic Commission for Latin America and the Caribbean. He is now deceased.

STANLEY FISCHER contributed as Professor of Economics at the Massachusetts institute of Technology. He is now First Deputy Managing Director of the International Monetary Fund, on leave from MIT.

NORBERTO GARCÍA and JAIME MEZZERA contributed as officials of PREALC, the regional employment program of the International Labor Office for Latin America and the Caribbean. They continue to be officials of the ILO.

STEPHAN HAGGARD Contributed as Associate Professor of Political Science at Harvard University's Kennedy School of Government. He is now Professor of Political Science at the Graduate School of International Relations and Pacific Studies of the University of California at San Diego.

RICHARD J. MOORE contributed as Assistant Professor of International Development at The American University in Washington, DC. He is now an official at the World Bank.

DANIEL M. SCHYDLOWSKY contributed as Professor of Economics at The American University in Washington, DC, a position he continues to hold.

PAUL STREETEN contributed as Professor of Economics at Boston University and as the editor of *World Development*. He is now Professor Emeritus of Boston University and continues to edit *World Development*.

LANCE TAYLOR contributed as Professor of Economics at the Massachusetts institute of Technology. He is now Arnhold Professor of International Cooperation and Development in the Department of Economics at the Graduate Faculty of Political and Social Sciences in the New School for Social Research in New York City.

JAMES H. WEAVER contributed as Professor of Economics at The American University in Washington, DC. He is now Professor Emeritus.

JOHN WILLIAMSON contributed as Senior Fellow at the Institute for International Economics in Washington, DC, a position he continues to hold.